Conflict, Discourse and Cognition

Bloomsbury Advances in Critical Discourse Studies

Series Editors: David Machin, John Richardson and Michal Krzyzanowski

Bloomsbury Advances in Critical Discourse Studies is a series that looks at exciting, cutting edge work in critical discourse studies, in terms of its multidisciplinarity of method, theory, and topic of analysis. The series explores how critical discourse studies engages with the social, political and ideological landscape of the modern world, and how these contexts are reflected, (re) produced and mediated through language and other modes of communication.

Titles published in the series:

Critical Discourse Studies and Technology, Ian Roderick
Constructing the Welfare State in the British Press, Malgorzata Paprota
Constructions of Migrant Integration in British Public Discourse, Sam Bennett
Discourses of Men's Suicide Notes, Dariusz Galasinski
The Discursive Construction of Migrant Identities, edited by Charlotte Taylor, Simon Goodman and Stuart Dunmore
European Identities in Discourse, Franco Zappettini
The Politics and Rhetoric of Commemoration, Michael Billig and Cristina Marinho
Popular Music and Multimodal Critical Discourse Studies, Lyndon C. S. Way

Conflict, Discourse and Cognition

Political Discourse in Northern Ireland

Laura Filardo-Llamas

BLOOMSBURY ACADEMIC
LONDON • NEW YORK • OXFORD • NEW DELHI • SYDNEY

BLOOMSBURY ACADEMIC
Bloomsbury Publishing Plc, 50 Bedford Square, London, WC1B 3DP, UK
Bloomsbury Publishing Inc, 1359 Broadway, New York, NY 10018, USA
Bloomsbury Publishing Ireland, 29 Earlsfort Terrace, Dublin 2, D02 AY28, Ireland

BLOOMSBURY, BLOOMSBURY ACADEMIC and the Diana logo are trademarks of Bloomsbury Publishing Plc

First published in Great Britain 2026

Cover design: Jade Barnett
Cover image © Maria Stavreva/iStock

A catalogue record for this book is available from the British Library.

A catalog record for this book is available from the Library of Congress.

ISBN: HB: 978-1-3503–7376-1
ePDF: 978-1-3503-7377-8
eBook: 978-1-3503-7378-5

Series: Bloomsbury Advances in Critical Discourse Studies

Typeset by Newgen KnowledgeWorks Pvt. Ltd., Chennai, India

To Nacho, Gadea and Neila.

Contents

Figures

Tables

Acknowledgements

This book is the final destination of a long academic journey researching the relation between language and conflict. As in any journey, I have been lucky enough to be accompanied by different people since I started working on this theme in 2004. As in life, all the experiences I have gone through since then have shaped and influenced my work. Still, several people have made this writing journey easier, and I would like to express my heartfelt gratitude to them.

Special thanks are due to John Richardson, without whose patience, support and constant encouragement this book would certainly not exist. I would have never started writing if John had not reached out and if he had not believed so deeply in my work. It's been always helpful to know he had confidence in me finally arriving at 'submission line', even when I didn't think I would make it. Thank you also to the editors and assistant editors at Bloomsbury: Morwenna Scott (in the very early stages of this project), Sarah MacDonald and Laura Gallon. It has been a real pleasure to work with them all, and they have really made the process much easier with their patience and constant assistance.

Finding the time to write was eased by the scholarship awarded by the Universidad de Valladolid under the Requalification programme (Grant no 2021-REC-TEY12). This gave me time for focusing on research while also enjoying the company of friends and colleagues at the Vrije Universiteit of Amsterdam, where I spent the academic year 2023–4. I am particularly indebted to Alan Cienki for hosting me there and for discussing academic (and personal) problems with me at times when work became difficult. Thank you also to Bertie Kaal for always listening to me, for giving me feedback when I struggled and for finding time for leisure activities. Space reasons prevent me from mentioning everyone else I met and talked to while in Amsterdam, but the conversations with Tina Krenmayr, Hernán Labbé Grunberg and Natalia Rivera-Vera were often helpful.

All journeys need nurturing, and this has been also my case. The premises in this book have massively benefited from conversations in the academic field. I cannot stress enough the help provided by Northern Irish scholars in the early stages of this research: Arthur Aughey, Henry Patterson and Carmel Roulston discussed many of the ideas in this book with me and they really helped all the times I went to the University of Ulster. My friend Berneice Carey was the best company, and she took me to the many (conflictual) places I wanted to visit. That helped a lot in grasping the complexity of Northern Ireland. I have also profited from talking with colleagues working on Critical Discourse Analysis and/or Cognitive Linguistics. It is virtually impossible to name everyone as I have been lucky to meet and talk with many people, but for different reasons I am particularly indebted to Isabel Alonso Belmonte, Michael Boyd, Christopher Hart, Veronika Koller, Marlene Miglbauer, Esperanza Morales, Lorena Pérez Hernández, Dolores Porto and David Pujante. To all my other academic friends, your role is also acknowledged. I am extremely sorry for not including a long list of names, but it would take up all my space! I am also really grateful to my friends and colleagues at the English Department at the Universidad de Valladolid. I share the space with wonderful colleagues, but special thanks are due to Sara Medina, Elena González-Cascos and Marta Mª Gutiérrez for endlessly listening to me any time I knocked at their door, even if they were busy with doing something else. My deepmost gratitude also to Marta for revising the whole manuscript looking for typos and mistakes, in spite of having to read about linguistics.

And last, but certainly not least, any journey needs a shelter space. I would have never finished writing this book without my family. My parents have provided a much-needed refuge at times when I could barely keep up with work. Massive thanks to Nacho, my husband, for navigating this long academic (and writing) travel with me and for steering our family to good port all the times I've been physically or mentally absent. I am really grateful to him and my daughters, Gadea and Neila, for coping with all the turmoil that being part of this trip (both literally and metaphorically) has meant. Succeeding in writing this book would not have happened without our family success.

***

I am grateful to the following publishers for granting me permission to reproduce the following content:

Table 4.1 and Figures 5.2 and 5.5 in this book are reproduced with permission by John Benjamins. These are based on table 12.3 and figures 7.2 and 6.2 as initially published in the following book: Radden, Günter & René Dirven. 2007. *Cognitive English Grammar*. Amsterdam: John Benjamins.

Figures 5.1 and 6.1 in this book are reproduced with permission by Oxford Publishing Limited. These are based on figures 4.13 and 2.8 as initially published in the following book: Langacker, Ronald. 2008. *Cognitive Grammar. A Basic Introduction.* Oxford: Oxford Publishing.

***

Funding acknowledgementPart of this research has been carried out under the grant PID2023-146434NB-I00 funded by MICIU/AEI/10.13039/501100011033 and by the European Regional Development Fund, EU.

Abbreviations

CDA	Critical Discourse Analysis
CDS	Critical Discourse Studies
CL	Cognitive Linguistics
CL-CDS	Cognitive Linguistics Critical Discourse Studies
DST	Discourse Space Theory/Deictic Space Theory
DUP	Democratic Unionist Party
EU	European Union
ICM	Idealized Cognitive Model
IDC	Inside the Deictic Centre
IICD	Independent International Commission on Decommissioning
IRA	Irish Republican Army
MEPs	Members of the European Parliament
NI	Northern Ireland
NP	Noun Phrase
ODC	Outside the Deictic Centre
PSNI	Police Service of Northern Ireland
PUP	Progressive Unionist Party
RUC	Royal Ulster Constabulary
SDLP	Social Democratic and Labour Party
SF	Sinn Féin
SNP	Scottish National Party
STA	Space, Time, Axiology
TWT	Text World Theory
UDA	Ulster Defence Association
UDP	Ulster Democratic Party
UK	United Kingdom
UUP	Ulster Unionist Party
UVF	Ulster Volunteer Force

1

Introduction

'All stories are love stories' writes Robert McLiam Wilson (1996) as the introductory words to his novel *Eureka Street*. I would argue that this is a question of how we perceive the world as all stories could also be conflict stories. This is exemplified very well in McLiam Wilson's book, which is not only a story about love but also a story about the Northern Irish (NI) conflict and how that can be explained as narratively constructed by different communities. Through the story of friendship between two Belfast men, one Protestant and one Catholic, we do not only read about the efforts of those two friends to find love, money and fame, but we can also find an attempt at critically and morally evaluating a political situation which was sometimes perceived as a stalemate but in which political participants also sought to find a means of ending the period of overt violence known as 'The Troubles'. The initial quote of this novel is not only a means of acknowledging its main theme as dissociated from The Troubles, it can also be understood as a means of compelling the readers of the novel to react in a particular way (Farquharson, 2005). Such is certainly my case when writing this book. I do not only intend to provide a linguistically informed exploration of the complexities that underlie the NI political conflict but also reflect on the role of language in creating, spreading and solving such conflict with the aim of providing further evidence and understanding of human communication in conflictual situations. Likewise, this book is not only about NI but also seeks to explore the role that discourse and cognition play in conflictual situations, regardless of whether they are ethnonationalist (as is the case of NI), social, cultural or of any other kind.

This personal stance is what motivates the main claim underlying this book: there is an inextricable link between discourse, conflict and cognition which cannot be neglected when studying political conflicts, such as the NI one. It is thus the aim of this book to explore how conflict may result from two different relations between discourse and cognition. One is related to misunderstandings and misinterpretation of linguistic choices which are the consequence of a lack of shared knowledge between participants in the discourse event (Janicki, 2015). The other is the existence of alternative representations to one sociopolitical reality and how these result from using different linguistic forms (Filardo-Llamas, 2010). Being aware of the relationship between knowledge (cognition), language (discourse) and representation (conflict) is not only useful for explaining the potential harmful effect of many linguistic choices but can also be useful for adopting new and different approaches for conflict resolution (Ramsbotham, 2010).

Recent studies on the relation between language and conflict (Filardo-Llamas and Morales-Lopez, 2021; Janicki, 2015; Jeffries and O'Driscoll, 2019) emphasize the need to explicitly refer to how conflict is defined and understood, as this may vary depending on the author (Janicki, 2015). How *conflict* is understood is also particularly important in NI, where the meaning of words is frequently contested. This can be seen, for example, in the first use of the word 'peace' by Sinn Féin (SF) in 1987. They believed that by appropriating themselves of 'the language of peace', a strategic change could be enacted, and the meaning of the NI conflict could be redefined. This strategy did not only open a new communicative dimension for SF in the political process, but it also helped them gain political legitimacy and a new role in the peace process (Shirlow, 2004, pp. 61, 67). I thus follow Janicki's (2017) non-essentialist proposal, where he claims that authors should provide their working definition of the concept under analysis. In this book, the word 'conflict' is not understood as necessarily involving physical violence or being overt, but as an explicit or implicit dispute between two or more participants who are understood to be opponents in a (symbolic) communicative situation. This understanding of conflict does not only align with Jeffries and O'Driscoll's (2019, p. 2) definition and their explanation of opposition as being instrumental, intellectual or emotional, but it also emphasizes the cognitive component of conflict in the explicit references to disputes being conceptually conceived as such by the discourse participants.

A number of ideas stem from the previous definition of conflict. First, the importance of language both in the construction and resolution of conflict cannot be neglected (also in Dédaic and Nelson, 2003; Evans, Jeffreis and O'Driscoll, 2019; Filardo-Llamas et al., 2021; Janicki, 2015; Schäffner and Wenden, 1995, among others). Language is not only the means through which conflict is conducted; linguistic choices can also result in conflictual constructions of reality via discourse. Second, in order to understand how conflict may result from discursive choices, we shall consider the role of knowledge and beliefs in our interpretation of discourse (Janicki, 2015, pp. 52, 153). Although with variation in terminology,[1] different authors have tried to explain the role of such previous beliefs in the interpretation of discourse and the effect that this could have in generating conflicting views. Finally, implicit in the understanding of conflict mentioned above is the idea that 'binary oppositions' (Janicki, 2015, p. 41) underlie communication in the public sphere, particularly in political discourse. This is frequently presented in terms of the opposition between an ingroup (the self) and an outgroup (the others) (Van Dijk, 1997, 1998), and it is referred to in discourse studies as 'the ideological square'. It implies a foregrounding of the positive attributes and actions of the self and the negative ones of the other while silencing the negative features of the self and the positive ones of the other. Previous studies have proved how linguistic choices can contribute to a process of 'otherization' (Dédaic and Nelson, 2003, p. 454) which could result in a promotion of conflict. Likewise, psychologists have proved that through language we can influence how people behave. If public discourses contribute to the presentation of the other as an enemy, this may result in a psychological construction of a 'hostile imagination' (Zimbardo, 2007).

Language and conflict

As shown above, the importance of language for the study of conflict cannot be neglected. There are two possible explanations for how conflict stems from linguistic choices. One of them would involve looking at the interactional dimension of communication, that is, how we express disagreement; the other is related to the representational dimension of language and seeks to explain how we create discursively a view of the world. These two types of conflict are related to the two types of 'meaning' which may stem from the two broad roles of language: 'interacting with other individuals in social groups and representing states of affairs' (Chilton, 2004, p. 29).[2]

This understanding of the functions of language also underlies the classification of the different approaches to the linguistic study of conflict which can be followed, and which are summarized in Evans, Jeffreis and O'Driscoll (2019). First, the focus could lie on the analysis of textual cues, and this would involve looking at the way in which we express ourselves to build up a world view that texts present to the audience (Jeffries and O'Driscoll, 2019, p. 13). Underlying this approach to the study of conflict is the idea that the meaning of a text is not only the result of the basic meaning of its linguistic components but also of the 'propositional meaning' (Jeffries and O'Driscoll, 2019, p. 14) that results from the choices made between different alternatives. As will be explained below, linguistic choices may result in alternative construals of reality (Langacker, 2008; Hart, 2014). This is the approach which characterizes much of the work on Discourse Analysis (DA), where analysts seek to 'explain how language usage makes meaning over and above the basic propositional content but stopping short in many cases of characterising the full interpersonal and situational context' (Jeffries, 2019, p. 15). It is also this descriptive approach to explaining textual choices that has characterized much of the work in Critical Discourse Analysis (CDA), where text-driven analyses are related to the actual context (both of production and interpretation) in an attempt to explain how ideologies are transmitted. While the objective of most CDA studies is shared, there is not a systematic framework to be applied, and this varies depending on the school followed by scholars (see Wodak and Meyer, 2016; Flowerdew and Richardson, 2017, for an overview). However, relevant for this work are the approaches followed within Critical Stylistics (Jeffries, 2010), Cognitive Linguistics (Chilton, 2004; Hart, 2014; Filardo-Llamas et al., 2016) and (Systemic) Functional Linguistics (Bloor and Bloor, 2007; Van Leeuwen, 2008). Among the latter, those which incorporate a multimodal dimension to the study of discourse (Machin and Mayr, 2012) are of particular interest. In my view, all these conflate with what can be considered a conceptual approach to the study of the relation between language and conflict, whose main objective is the identification of the mental representations that are activated through linguistic choices.

Second, some approaches to the study of the relation between language and conflict have focused on the interpersonal function of communication, that is, on how people 'do' conflict when they interact with each other (O'Driscoll, 2019a, p. 167). Underlying this is the idea that conflict is not only caused by what we communicate but also by how we communicate. Hence, they pay attention to what has been called 'conflict talk' (Grimshaw, 1990) and they explain how the action of communication between the two parties unfolds. While most of the studies within this group do not look at 'large-scale conflict' (O'Driscoll, 2019a, p. 168), findings are still important for understanding human communication. Given that this interpersonal dimension is not the main objective of this book, only a brief overview of the strategies which are analysed by scholars working in the interactional dimension is given. Many of the studies within this group follow Conversation Analysis (Schegloff, 2007) and apply this theory – or specific aspects of it – to explain how conflict unfolds in concrete moments (Hutchby,

1996; Mateo and Yus, 2013; Tagg et al., 2017). Many studies (such as O'Driscoll, 2007, 2013) also rely on Brown and Levinson's (1987) Politeness theory and subsequent developments of this framework (Culpeper, 2011; Watts, 2003). Finally, the interpersonal dimension also lies at the core of research exploring how the context determines textual choices, that is, the importance of genre and appropriateness in communication. As such, they tend to explain how lack of adaptation to the context may result in conflictual interactions (see Sifianou, 2019, for an overview).

Finally, some approaches to the study of language and conflict acknowledge what could be considered a variational dimension, that is, they stress the conflictual effects of choosing different varieties of language as these function as an index of oppositional stance and may be the object of contention (O'Driscoll, 2019b, p. 332). While slightly different from the other conceptual and interactional approaches – as here the focus is not on what the words denote but on how meanings are inferred from the actual form of words –, we cannot forget that the variety we consciously or unconsciously choose when we communicate also transmits meaning about our identity as utterers (Mac Coinnigh, Ervine and Deeds, 2019). Variational approaches to the study of conflict rely on a double relation between language and identity: how some varieties (including accents, dialects or different languages) are associated with particular groups and how others perceive the identity of such groups (O'Driscoll, 2019b, p. 334; Pavlenko and Blackledge, 2004). It is such associations that may result in conflict erupting over the use of particular varieties. Some studies within this approach have adopted an ethnonationalist perspective and have focused on explaining the role of linguistic varieties in multiple places, including NI (e.g. Crowley, 2005; O'Reilly, 1999, among others). The impact on linguistic policies of such linguistic choices – and the potential creation of conflict stemming from them – cannot be negated. It should also be noted that some studies within this variational approach reflect on the role of varieties in the public sphere, and notably in linguistic landscapes (e.g. Ben-Rafael et al., 2006).

While the three dimensions to the study of conflict could be found in the NI context, it is the conceptual and variational dimensions that will feature mostly in this book. On the one hand, it is the aim of this book to look at the influence of cognition in the discursive configuration of conflict. Hence, I will focus on how linguistic choices may result in alternative meanings, or construals, and hence in the discursive creation of different world views. This is consistent with the representational approach to meaning (see Saeed, 2015, for an explanation) and with previous studies on political discourse (notably Chilton, 2004). On the other hand, murals and commemorative plaques are important for understanding the configuration of the public space in NI (Filardo-Llamas, 2012; Filardo-Llamas and González-Cascos Jiménez, 2014). This will be particularly significant in the last case study included in Chapter 6, and it tightly connects to variational approaches to the study of conflict as explained above.

Language and conflict in Northern Ireland

The importance of looking at language in the NI conflict cannot be denied, and it can be ascribed to two types of choices: (1) a language variety for communication (i.e. Irish vs English), and (2) textual and semiotic cues within a single variety (i.e. how to name things in English).

In relation to the linguistic variety chosen, under the auspices of the 1998 Peace Agreement, a new body, called Foras na Gaeilge, is established with the aim of promoting the use of the Irish language throughout the island. Despite not being explicitly associated to any community in the agreement, the use of Irish proved to be a divisive element as it was understood to be a key tenet of Republican and Nationalist politics, and hence a mark of their identity (Mac Coinnigh, Ervine and Deeds, 2019, p. 558; Mac Giolla Chríost, 2003, 2005). Even if the Irish language is to be actively promoted throughout the island, the lack of progress on related legislation has been a common source of conflict and political division, and its importance was raised in talks over devolution leading to the St. Andrews Agreement (2006). Although calls for an Irish Language Act have been constantly made by Republican and Nationalist political parties (Mac Coinnigh, Ervine and Deeds, 2019, p. 559), it was not until 2022, with the enactment of The Identity and Language (Northern Ireland) Bill in the month of December, that the official status of Irish is recognized in NI. Even if linguistic conflicts have developed mostly around the role of Irish, public debates on the role of Ulster Scots shall also be mentioned, including those which question whether it is a (British) dialect or a language (Nic Craith, 2001, p. 24). Ulster Scots is often presented as a response by the Protestant/Unionist community to the growing consciousness of Irish nationalism and the changing concept of 'Britishness' (Stapleton and Wilson, 2004). While Ulster Scots did appear in the Multiparty negotiation leading to the 1998 Peace Agreement, debates around it have not featured as prominently. Still, its role cannot be neglected in a context where political conflict is also reflected on a linguistic one.

The studies mentioned above all belong to the variational dimension in the study of language and conflict. While significant for understanding the linguistic conflict in NI, their prominence is less relevant for this book, which is mostly concerned with the conceptual dimension, that is, how through the analysis of linguistic choices we can explain the emergence of conflictual views about reality. Still, being aware of variational approaches to the study of conflict informs the inextricable link that can be established between the conceptual and variational dimensions in geopolitical conflicts. As noted by Storey (2001, p. 103), language divisions may be a cause of instability in geopolitical contestations of space. Besides the choice of a language variety, such contestation can also be seen in the names given to particular aspects of reality, such as locations, which do not only construct a given view of reality but also function as markers of belonging to a particular community of practice. This is also the case in NI, where there is an intrinsic relation between language and identity: 'Language, its definition and use, creates chains of equivalence which enclose subjects within not only a sectarian but at times entirely self-referential and self-sustained notion of identity and communal dedication' (Shirlow and McGovern, 1998, p. 173). Linguistic choices in NI thus perform an indexical function as words do not only have denotational – dictionary – meaning but also have a social value which may be associated with a given community. These are often equated to the distinction between Republicans/Nationalists and Unionists/Loyalists or between Catholics and Protestants.

The notion of community of practice as 'aggregates of people' who develop and share similar ways of talking and beliefs (Eckert, 2000, p. 35) is particularly important in NI as choosing one term over another may single out a speaker as belonging to a given community, and can be a source of conflict in locations where communities are already split (see Kelleher, 2003, for an example). Some of these uses have had both a local impact in the community and a bearing on political life, where naming disputes have, for example, erupted over how to refer to Londonderry or the City of Derry (with a council vote being held in 2015 over this name and new legislation being passed in 2016).[3]

The importance of choosing names in NI has been acknowledged by political scientists, who talk about the existence of a 'war of words' where 'definitions of words are strongly contested' (Dixon, 2001, p. 37). As mentioned above, this is mostly the case with proper names. Apparently, names are merely 'labels for people, places, etc., and often seem to have little other meaning' (Saeed, 2015, p. 27). Nevertheless, it should be stressed that sometimes names perform a role in perpetuating and transmitting social knowledge, and it is the case that language used to describe the conflict in NI is understood to be 'politically loaded' (Edwards and McGrattan, 2010). While the importance of lexical selection will be studied in detail later in this book (see Chapters 5 and 6), I still want to emphasize how important this is in the NI context. The following quote, taken from *Divorcing Jack*, a novel about The Troubles, serves as an example. In it one of the characters explains the magnitude of proper name selection in NI as follows:

> 'And stick to calling it Northern Ireland, although you'll hear variations. If you're a Loyalist, you'll call it Ulster, if you're a Nationalist you call it the North of Ireland or the Six Counties, if you're the British Government you call it the Province.'
>
> 'And what do you call it, Mr Starkey?'
>
> 'Home.' (Bateman, 1995, p. 46)

Research paradigm and book overview

This book seeks to explain the role of language in the discursive construction of the NI conflict. While it mostly relies on NI as a case study, I hope that theoretical claims about the relation between discourse and cognition can also be extrapolated to the study of other social and political conflicts. The case studies included in the analytic chapters reflect historical events which are characterized by the absence of overt violence. This aligns with this broad objective and with the definition of conflict provided above, as opposition in these cases is not necessarily only manifested via violence but also relates to communication misunderstandings and construals of other communities beyond the self (see Janicki, 2006 and Evans, Jeffreis and O'Driscoll, 2019). As shown by Mac Ginty, Muldoon and Ferguson (2007, p. 7), there is still an intrinsic division in NI society which is manifested in identity preference and in political and social attitudes. While not necessarily physical or overt, it can be argued that a hostile imagination (Zimbardo, 2007) still exists and characterizes the relationship between the two NI (imagined) communities, and that this hostility becomes more or less prevalent in the public sphere when different controversial policies are to be implemented. Underlying the notion of hostile imagination (Zimbardo, 2007) and imagined communities (Anderson, 1991, p. 7) is the idea that cognition and beliefs are shared between members of those groups. Thus, it is the aim of this book to contribute to discourse-based approaches to conflict studies (Ramsbotham, 2010, 2021), as understanding how different views are linguistically created 'can give hints on how to avoid violence' (Smith, 1997, p. 190).

As will be further explained in Chapter 3, this book aligns with the contemporary constructivist emphasis on the social sciences, which stresses the integral role of language in the creation of realities (Jeffries and O'Driscoll, 2019). Two main aspects shall be mentioned for understanding this. On the one hand, the role of cognitive conditioning in public discourse cannot be neglected (Zimbardo, 2007, p. 312) as it is through language that images of the other as an 'enemy' can be created. Likewise, the notion of 'radical disagreement' (Ramsbotham, 2010) is equally important as it emphasizes the existence of a cognitive basis of conflict, which may result from the *perceived* situation of incompatibility between two sociopolitical groups.

NI has been chosen as a case study in this book for two reasons: first, it allows consistency and unity throughout the book. Second, violence in NI allegedly comes to an end with the signing of a Peace Agreement in 1998. Still, this document contributed to creating a paradoxical, discursive, reality. The language of the Agreement was so vague that it could be interpreted in different ways by both NI communities. The concept of 'paradoxical reality' (Aughey, 2002, p. 2) has been used by political scientists to explain how politicians discursively portray one specific event or various political issues in different ways, depending on the aspects which are highlighted by the uttering source. As will be explained in Chapter 2, a parallelism can be established between such concept and Langacker's (2008, p. 4) notion of construal. When choosing a linguistic expression, this imposes a particular construal, 'reflecting just one of the countless ways of conceiving and portraying the situation in question'. It is thus argued that in NI, linguistic choices made by politicians do not only result in different representations of reality, which may align or misalign with their own perception of reality, but also that these linguistic choices may result in conflict maintenance, or they may help in solving it. This ability to tweak language in such a way that it may lead to multiple (conflictual) interpretations is of particular importance in NI, where misunderstandings are part of a culture in which both NI communities know each other so well that they certainly are aware of how to use language in a way that it can be interpreted differently and that finally results in conflict (Stewart, 1989; Edwards and McGrattan 2010). Likewise, the conflict in NI is (originally) a territorial conflict, but contestations of space are discursively intertwined with other non-physical and symbolic elements. As such, it allows for multiple layers of meanings to be explored, thus stressing the inextricable link between spatial cognition and political discourse (see Levinson, 2003 and Filardo-Llamas, Hart and Kaal, 2016).

It is because of this parallelism between the creation of a paradoxical reality and the notion of construal in cognitive linguistics that this book is organized as follows. In Chapter 2, I explain the main theoretical tenets of this book, including spatial cognition (Levinson, 2003), cognitive linguistics (Croft and Cruse, 2004), and applications of both to the study of political discourse, mostly based on Discourse Space Theory (DST) and Text World Theory (TWT) (Chilton, 2004; Hart, 2014, 2025; Filardo-Llamas, Hart and Kaal, 2016). The notion of construal will be the guiding parameter in this book, and hence previous explorations of language and ideology from a cognitive linguistics perspective will be explained as being related to one construal operation. This decision has been taken for explanation purposes, although it is necessary to emphasize that all of them have a bearing on the construction of discourse worlds, that is, textually triggered representations of reality which are contextually meaningful (Chilton, 2004). Given the importance of context and shared knowledge in (successful) communication, I provide an overview of the NI conflict in Chapter 3. This is necessary for understanding the peculiarities of this particular political context and it will help in explaining the nuanced meanings of some lexical choices that will appear in the analysis.

The analysis section covers Chapters 4 to 7. In each of these chapters, one of the four construal operations established by Croft and Cruse (2004) and Hart (2014) is studied. As such, each analytic chapter connects explicitly to the operations explained in Chapter 2 by providing a more detailed theoretical description of the dimension under analysis together with an analytic parameter. In each of the chapters, two or three examples are provided as case studies. In these, the conflictual-consensual interpretation of the linguistic choices covered in the theoretical section of the chapter is explained. The book finishes with a conclusion where I do not only summarize the main ideas covered throughout the book but also reflect on how the theoretical premises guiding this work can be extrapolated to other contexts.

A final comment shall be made about how the book is organized. In spite of the main case study being post-agreement NI, the specific events covered in Chapters 4 to 7 do not follow a chronological order. This book was not intended as a diachronic study of the evolution of political discourse in NI, but rather as an exploration of the relation between discourse, conflict and cognition. Thus, the analytic chapters are sequenced following previous accounts of construal operations in cognitive linguistics and thus go from more schematic to more complex operations. This is done in such a way that readers can see how multiple layers of meaning are added to the discursive construction of world views. However, a brief chronological organization of events is given in the Appendix so as to provide a different structure which might be of interest to readers whose emphasis is not so much on the linguistic-discursive elements but on the discursive-political findings.

2

What can cognitive linguistics offer for conflict studies?

This book is grounded on the growing impact of constructivism in the social sciences and the humanities (Piaget, 1959; Vytgotsky, 1986; Chilton, 1996, p. 27; Jeffries and O'Driscoll, 2019, p. 7). This mostly implies that how we communicate shapes both our way of looking at the world and how we think, speak, act and evaluate such world (Shotter, 1993, p. 129). Constructivist approaches to the study of discourse, thus, argue that the social and cultural reality in which we participate is discursively signified and that discourses shall be understood as 'constructions that interpret and seek to understand the various situations and social actions that these discourses respond to' (Pujante, 2016, p. 37). While often not explicitly acknowledged, the integral role of language for political discourse studies cannot be neglected as it is through linguistic choices that meaning is transmitted and world views are spread (Chilton, 1996). Thus, a common stance is found between constructivism and cognitive linguistics (CL) as they both view language as being an integral constituent of the world which presents, at least partly, the users' experience of the world (Cienki and Yanow, 2013).

This social constructivist view aligns with the one held by other studies on discourse and conflict. Since discourse is a meaning-making activity, understanding how it works can help us explain how conflicts are ignited, hence providing new tools for resolving them (Chiluwa, 2021). The language we use does not reflect the world but rather plays an active role in how we construct our views of such world. Language is situated and hence meanings of concepts are totally inseparable from the contexts in which they are used (Chilton, 1996, p. 25). Given the socio-cognitive focus of this book, context is not only understood as the situation in which communication takes place but also as the common ground shared (or not) by participants in a communicative event (Werth, 1999; Gavins, 2007; Van Dijk, 2005, 2008). The fact that meaning is socially (co-)constructed is important for understanding how conflict works as the struggle between different views of the world, ideologies or beliefs that underlie any conflictual relation can not only be reflected in linguistic choices but also determined by different understandings of a single discursive interaction. The contest between various knowledge claims about the world is thus a struggle between discourses which represent those different understandings of the world and the construction of different identities (Chiluwa, 2021, p. 3).

This view of conflict as incompatible world views which are reflected and constructed via discourse has also guided previous studies on conflict and conflict resolution. Among them, two are of particular interest. First, Oliver Ramsbotham (2010, 2017) proposes the concept of 'radical disagreement' to explain how intractable conflicts work because such disagreement is 'the chief verbal manifestation of intense political conflict' (Ramsbotham, 2010, p. 6). This is reflected in a clash of discourses in the public sphere where each political participant tries to impose their own language and their own lens for viewing the conflict. This is why 'discursive battles' – or radical disagreements – lie at the heart of many political conflicts such as the ones in NI, Sri Lanka or Palestine (Ramsbotham, 2010, p. 19). The notion of 'radical disagreement' proves the cognitive basis for conflict as the incompatibility between one group's beliefs (or intentions, actions or goals) and those of another group is just perceived and managed via discourse.

The notion of perceived incompatibility also underlies Aughey's (2002) description of the political situation in NI as reflecting a 'paradoxical reality'. The term was originally coined by political scientists to refer to the portrayal of one specific event or political issue in different ways, depending on the highlighted aspects. In NI, this is a way of managing conflict. A clear example is seen in the apparent incompatibility of discourses surrounding the 1998 Agreement, a document which was crafted with vague language, hence allowing it to be interpreted differently by opposed communities. Relying on ambiguous and vague language was, at that time, a mechanism for solving the conflict and seeking consensus between politicians around a single document which apparently reflected the point of view of both NI communities, even if diverse realities seemed to stem from it.

The two studies above have been influential in showing the relation between discourse and conflict, and they have clearly stressed the importance of language in analysing political relations (see also Chilton, 1996, 1998; Cienki, 2013; Cienki and Yanow, 2013). However, in this book I go beyond showing the relation between discourse and conflict by reflecting on the mediating role of cognition. Previous studies have explained the influence of public discourse on people's behaviour by relying on four cognitive mechanisms: (i) creating a moral justification for a given action, (ii) diffusing or dissolving our personal responsibility over a potential harmful action, (iii) ignoring or minimizing the negative consequences of a reproachable action and (iv) constructing the self as victims by dehumanizing others (Zimbardo, 2007, pp. 310–11). Such cognitive mechanism can be discursively created.

However, it is not only the language of the elites that affects social behaviour, as for any individual to be understood, 'they have to assume the concepts and values of their constituencies' (Chilton, 1996, p. 28). That is, there is a collective base to any individual (or political) utterance and interpretations of these are influenced by 'cultural cognition' (Kahan and Braman, 2006). Cultural cognition is defined as 'the psychological disposition of persons to their factual beliefs about the instrumental efficacy (or perversity) of law to their cultural evaluations of the activities subject to regulation' (Kahan and Braman, 2006, pp. 149–50). This implies that citizens' views about particular policies are going to be interpreted on the basis of their own previous cultural beliefs. As such, public discourses are likely to be interpreted by citizens in a way which reflects and reinforces the actual world view they adhere to. This is also likely to be influenced by people's perception of the uttering politician, with them adhering better to the politician's world view when the utterance is produced by someone sharing the same cultural values, that is, belonging to the same community.[1] It is thus predictable that if cultural cognition is not shared, interpretations of public discourses are likely to differ, hence resulting in what could be seen as incompatible views about a political reality.

Discourse and conflict

The last years of the twentieth century have seen an upsurge of discourse analysis studies focused on political speech (see Filardo-Llamas and Boyd, 2017). Among them, several authors have tried to establish a relation between language and conflict – and/or language and peace (Schäffner and Wenden, 1995; Wright, 1998; Dédaic and Nelson, 2003; Cohen, 2010; Janicki, 2015; Evans, Jeffreis and O'Driscoll, 2019; Chiluwa, 2021).[2] While it is not the aim of this section to provide an overview of all such studies (some of which have already been discussed in the introduction), it is necessary to emphasize here the inextricable link between discourse and conflict. Human conflict begins and ends with text and talk (Billig, 2003, p. xviii), and it is via language that 'we generate, shape, implement, remember and forget violent behaviour between individuals, communities and states through a specific discourse. It is discourse that prepares for sacrifice, justifies inhumanity, absolves from guilt, and demonizes the enemy' (Nelson, 2003, p. 449). While conflict is not necessarily only linked to language, the key role of discourse in constructing (opposed) sociopolitical identities cannot be neglected (Chiluwa, 2021, p. 5). Likewise, experimental studies on political and public communication have proved how words can frame, mobilize and motivate political action and thought (Zimbardo, 2007; Flusberg, Matlock and Thibodeau, 2018; Brugman, Burgers and Vis, 2019). As argued by Suurmond (2005, p. 7), discourse analysis has become an increasingly important tool in conflict research (see also O'Donnnell and Hayward, 2010) because it can help in 'studying the realities and the meaning attributions of actors in a conflict' (Suurmond, 2005, pp. 7–8).

Two ideas need to be stressed when looking at the relation between discourse and conflict. First, conflict is not to be understood only as the opposition or misunderstanding between two participants in everyday conversations. Early linguistic studies on interactional sociolinguistics looked at this dimension and showed the role that interactional breakdowns had in managing social relations (Filardo-Llamas and Morales-López, 2021; Gumperz, 1982). Conflict is rather understood as a discursive construction which shows opposed and antagonistic views. Thus, conflict may not only appear linguistically on the surface but can also reflect a 'deeper' opposition between core values and beliefs held by different communities (Filardo-Llamas and Morales-López, 2021).

Second, studies on discourse and conflict should acknowledge not only a cognitive dimension (see Brugman et al., 2019, for example, on the importance of considering the conceptual dimension in the analysis of political discourse) but also an interactional one (Chilton, 1996, pp. 30–1). While the cognitive dimension can help us uncover the relation between belief systems and utterances, it is also via language that those systems are negotiated and changed.[3] Hence it is important to anchor discourse-based analyses of conflict to particular situations as meanings are contextual and may be 'implied and inferred in the process of communication in particular settings' (Chilton, 1996, p. 31). Thus, not only can discourse convey different versions of reality – as implicit in the notions of radical disagreement or paradoxical reality mentioned above – but such views of reality are situated and shall be treated as such.

Conflict, thus, may arise when words are taken as symbols whose meaning is attached to objective, unchanging, realities (Chilton, 1996, pp. 65–6; Janicki, 2015, pp. 10–14). Meaning, however, is not objectively conveyed. Rather, words activate concepts in our minds, and such concepts are experientially grounded (Lakoff, 1987). Hence, if people have experienced different things, conflict may arise in interaction as there is not a shared understanding of the same word. This means that lack of shared knowledge – understood as an individual's physical, social, cultural and political cognition – may cause conflict. Some examples can be found not only in Janicki (2015, pp. 10–15) but also in the political arena at the time of writing this book, with ongoing debates over the definition of the term 'woman', for example, and the debate caused by the definition of 'lesbian' as 'non-man attracted to non-men' in the dictionary of LGBTQ terms published by Johns Hopkins University.[4] In the case of this sociopolitical conflict, attitudes and beliefs of speakers influence not only how they frame their definition of what a woman is but also how they understand and react to definitions different from their own. While it could be argued that 'woman' is just a word which may be objectively defined, its use in discourse may activate different cognitive-affective experiences on the minds of users, some of which may even clash with each other. Examples like this show that conflict may not only be discursively created but that it also results from the activation of different kinds of knowledge, which could not only be personal but also interpersonal, related to community beliefs or to institutional patterns (Van Dijk, 2005).

The example above aligns with previous claims in the literature that there is a cognitive basis for the creation of conflict, which is understood as a perceived situation of 'incompatibility' between one group's beliefs (including intentions, actions or goals) and those of another group. As explained above, this is discursively manifested as a 'radical disagreement' between groups and may contribute to some societies apparently living in what could be considered paradoxical realities.

Why cognitive linguistics?

Awareness about the cognitive basis of conflict (as shown, for example, in Zimbardo, 2007) justifies the need of relying on linguistic theories which account for the cognitive dimension in language use and which align with the socio-constructivist turn in the social sciences and the humanities. CL, in its broadest understanding, seems to provide the necessary tools to do so. While it is difficult to find a unifying definition of all the theories included under the CL approach (Geeraerts and Cuyckens, 2007), they all seek to explain how our linguistic interactions are intermediated by the structuring nature of our mind.

CL shows how structures in language reflect their users' 'general conceptual organization, categorization principles, processing mechanisms, and experiential and environmental influences' (Geeraerts and Cuyckens, 2007, p. 5).

Three main tenets characterize CL and have justified previous applications of this approach for explaining the relation between language and ideology (Geeraerts and Cuyckens, 2007; Hart, 2014, 2018).[5] First, CL believes in the primacy of meaning, which is justified by the emphasis on understanding the users' conceptual organization. This 'symbolic thesis' (Hart, 2017, p. 78) claims that words and grammatical structures are paired with abstract knowledge structures that are conceptual in nature. Linguistic expressions evoke background knowledge which is shared across speakers and addressees and which could adopt multiple conceptual forms (Cienki, 2013, p. 295). Because they depend on background knowledge, interpretation of linguistic expressions could vary, particularly when dealing with abstract words such as 'democracy', for example (see Chilton, 1996 for changes in the conceptualization of 'security' throughout time). The second thesis in CL claims that meaning is encyclopaedic, that is, it is associated with knowledge about the world, and hence it is open-ended as users may experience the world in multiple ways. Third, the 'experientialist thesis' (Geeraerts and Cuyckens, 2007, p. 5; Hart, 2017, p. 78) is related to the perspectival nature of linguistic meaning, as language does not reflect the world objectively but rather the needs, interests and experiences of individuals and cultures (Geeraerts and Cuyckens, 2007, pp. 5–6). As shown by studies on spatial cognition (Levinson, 2003), knowledge structures, and eventually human reason, are derived from our universal organic embodiment and from our individual and collective experiences as members of a particular culture or society. We can thus talk about embodied cognition – that is, how language reflects our relation with the physical world – and extended embodied cognition, in which the human conditions of other people are also part of a person's experience (Stockwell, 2020).

The three theses mentioned above are related to spatial cognition (Levinson, 2003) and justify the need to consider political discourse as showing a 'particular, socially embedded vantage point on an event as expressed in language by the speaker' (Cienki, 2013, p. 296). Meaning is situated (Hart, 2017, p. 79), and hence it is bound to one's position in the cultural and physical context of production and interpretation. When the two contexts differ – either on a situational or abstract dimension – conflict may appear. Thus, we should not only study what leaders as individual speakers say; rather, awareness about the situatedness trait of discourse justifies the need to explore political discourse as a collective process which reflects conceptual differences across several political cultures (Chilton, 1996, pp. 28–31). This is the first reason why CL is of use for the study of conflict: awareness about the different elements in the background knowledge shared by discourse participants can help us explain radical disagreement. Conflictual interpretations arise from a given linguistic expression when the mediating structures in the mind are not shared. The open-ended encyclopaedic nature of meaning is thus of use for explaining conflict.

The second reason justifying the usefulness of CL is related to the experientialist thesis. Language does not reflect an objective view of the world, but rather the position and embeddedness of the utterer (Cienki, 2013; Levinson, 2003). Language uses may reflect alternative positions – or world views – about an event, and these positions may seem, at times, to be paradoxical and contradictory. The notion of construal, as used in CL, is of interest for explaining this. Construal is defined by Langacker (2019) as our ability to conceive and portray the same situation in alternative ways. As such, it serves to explain how meaning is related not only to the concept evoked by a linguistic expression but also to how that content is presented by a speaker. As argued throughout this chapter, different linguistic choices contribute to portraying – and therefore legitimizing – alternative views of the same reality in the political realm.

Construal and political discourse

Following a meaning-based approach to the study of political discourse and conflict advocates for focusing on the notion of construal, whose prominence in CL has been widely justified (Croft and Cruse, 2004, p. 3; Hart, 2014; Langacker, 2019, among others). This concept can help us explain two of the main ideas underlying CL: first, that conceptualization is ubiquitous in language use. No matter what we say, it is deemed to activate a particular representation in our mind. Regardless of individual, social or cultural differences, any word or sentence triggers a particular conceptualization of the world. It suffices to show what would happen if we heard a word as simple as 'tree'. Each of us may picture a different image of a plant, but still the word triggers a conceptual representation. Second, that 'all aspects of conceptual structure are subject to construal' (Croft and Cruse, 2004, p. 3). Grammatical inflections, syntactic constructions, or lexical choices play a role in how experience is communicated in specific ways. At the time of writing this book, the 300-year-old sycamore tree on Hadrian's Wall in Northumberland (UK) was cut. While this is a single event, looking at some news headings accounting for this story (examples 1 to 5 below) can show how choices of words (e.g. 'cut down' vs 'deliberately felled'), phrases ('The Sycamore Gap tree' vs 'famous "Robin Hood" tree' vs 'a much-loved tree') or syntactic structures (passive voices with or without agent) present a (slightly) different view. For instance, in these representations, diverse agents are highlighted or silenced, and contextual knowledge about the importance of the sycamore tree is assumed on the part of the reader or provided explicitly. These headings exemplify the cognitive capacity of 'conceptual alternativity' (Talmy, 2000b, p. 14), which states that 'the same ideational complex can be represented in terms of alternative conceptualizations'. This means that from all the possible conceptualizations for an ideational complex – that is, the sycamore tree being cut – writers chose a particular one which conveyed the representations they wanted to communicate. Relying on the conceptual approach to CL, we can identify 'the patterns in which and the processes by which conceptual content is organized in language' (Talmy, 2000b, p. 2).

[1] Famous Sycamore Gap tree at Hadrian's Wall found cut down. (*The Guardian*, 28/09/2023)

[2] Sycamore Gap: Teenager arrested in England over 'deliberate' felling of famous tree. (*Euronews*, 29/09/2023)

[3] Sycamore Gap: 16-year-old boy and man in his 60s arrested after famous tree 'deliberately felled'. (*CNN*, 30/09/2023)

[4] A second man is arrested over the felling in England of a much-loved tree near Hadrian's Wall. (*AP News*, 29/09/2023)

[5] UK teen arrested after famous 'Robin Hood Tree' cut down at Hadrian's Wall. (*South China Morning Post*, 29/09/2023)

As examples [1] to [5] show, conceptual alternativity is what allows speakers to choose from the multiple existing options in discourse, depending on what they want to communicate. The resulting alternative conceptualizations are thus explained through the notion of construal. The examples above also help explain meaning-making in discourse as textual elements invoke the conceptual structures and processes they conventionally index (e.g. a/the tree, or the action of cutting down). The explicit explanation in some of the examples above of the importance of the tree and the place where it can be found (e.g. 'much-loved', 'near Hadrian's Wall') also show how meaning is intersubjectively constructed and how this representation is necessarily related to a given referential situation (Hart, 2017, p. 79).

The need of incorporating a cognitive dimension to the study of political discourse has been already discussed in previous studies (Chilton, 2004; Cienki, 2013; Cienki and Yanow, 2013; Hart, 2014, pp. 107–12). Acknowledging the cognitive dimension, and the importance of conceptualization, allows scholars to answer questions about how meaning is made, and hence tries to solve some of the problems encountered in the early years of Critical Discourse Analysis (CDA)[6] which were mainly stemming from the lack of attention paid by CDA scholars to the human mind (Chilton, 2005a, p. 23). This has led to what could be called the cognitive turn in CDS, exemplified by CL-CDS. In it, the notion of construal is paramount (Hart, 2014, pp. 108–12, 2017, 2025). Looking at construal – and alternative conceptualizations – can help us explain the causal relation between language use – that is, discourse found in the public space – and social actions – including casting votes, accepting policies, respecting other groups and so on. The cognitive dimension, thus, allows us not only to explain the constitutive elements of political discourse (and the dimensions adopted in the analysis) but also how each of those becomes a constituting factor in the creation of conflict (see Figure 2.1; Filardo-Llamas and Morales-López, 2021, pp. 5–8; Wodak and Meyer, 2016, chapter 1).

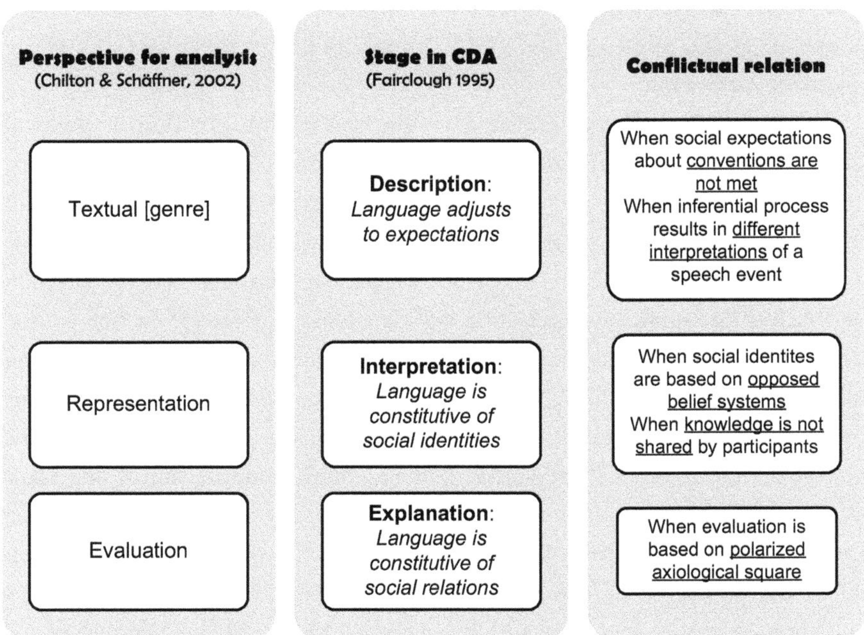

Figure 2.1 Political discourse, CDA and conflict.

Figure 2.1 shows the link between the stages in the analysis, as proposed in CDA (Fairclough, 1989), and the perspectives which have been usually advocated in the analysis. These suggest focusing on the textual dimension of what constitute genres traditionally associated with political discourse, on the representational dimension (i.e. which view of the world is discursively presented) and on the evaluative dimension (or the stance adopted by the speaker in relation to a given event) (Chilton and Schäffner, 2002). The figure also shows how the focus on these dimensions can help us explain different approaches to the study of conflict. As such, conflict may arise from different expectations about what constitute political discourse genres and how these are to be used in given contexts, from the different understandings of particular utterances (which may stem from opposed beliefs and/or from different inferential processes being followed, as explained for the notion of 'tree' above) and from a diverse array of moral values being indexed via discourse. As mentioned above, conflictual relations can be explained by the lack of intersubjective agreement between utterer and audience on the mental representations activated by each of the analytic dimensions. In line with Chilton's (2005a, pp. 23–4) claims in favour of the cognitive dimension in CDA, this book does not only seek to explain how conflict is produced, but it also claims that being aware of the principle of conceptual alternativity can help us explain why conflict is produced: either as a consequence of alternative conceptualizations being proposed for a single event (as in examples [1] to [5] above) or as the result of different (often opposed) interpretations of a single linguistic expression.

The explanation above is related to the legitimizing function of political discourse (Van Leeuwen and Wodak, 1999; Chilton, 2004; Cap, 2010; Hart, 2011b; Reyes, 2011).The process of legitimization is particularly important in areas of conflict as it involves justifying a behaviour, and doing so by argumentation (Reyes, 2011). Previous studies on the legitimating function of political discourse have identified different types of strategies which can be deployed, such as relying on emotions, (moral) authority or narrative (among others) (Van Leeuwen, 2007; Reyes, 2011). However, these studies mostly focus on types of strategies but do not relate them to the cognitive representations activated via discourse. Incorporating such a cognitive dimension is necessary as discursive legitimization is just one of the social actions performed via (public) discourse, and for legitimization to be effective the cognitive dimension is necessarily involved: 'Discourse can only be constitutive of social identities and social relations if it is first and foremost constitutive of "knowledge", which ultimately of course resides in human minds' (Hart, 2014, p. 108).

As explained throughout this section (and argued in most CL-based studies of political discourse) (Chilton, 2004; Dunmire, 2012; Hart, 2014; Filardo-Llamas, Hart and Kaal, 2016; Cap, 2017), explaining alternative construals for a single event could be of use for discourse-based proposals for the resolution of conflicts (Ramsbotham, Miall and Woodhouse, 2011). Empirical studies in psychology support this claim because they have found that behaviour changes depending on the level of construal that is discursively activated. For example, psychological distance, which is paired with schematic, abstract representation, seems to have an effect in the process of consumer decision-making (Trope, Liberman and Wakslak, 2007).[7]

Three main approaches can be found in CL-informed studies on political discourse: (1) those explaining the role of metaphor in legitimizing particular world views (Charteris-Black, 2005, 2014; Goatly, 2007; Hart, 2008, 2020; Koller, 2004; Musolff, 2012, 2017, among others), (2) those adopting other analytic categories in Cognitive Semantics, mostly relying on the analysis of image schemas (Chilton, 1996, 2017; Núñez-Perucha, 2011; Hampl, 2021) and force dynamics (Oakley, 2005; Hart, 2011a), and (3) those relying on Deictic/Discourse Space Theory (Chilton, 2004, 2005b, 2014; Filardo-Llamas, Hart and Kaal, 2016; Kaal, 2024) and proximization (Cap, 2010, 2013, 2017; Kopytowska, 2015). Following claims in CL-CDS, all these studies share the common objective of explaining how meaning is conceptualized in political discourse and how this relates to its legitimizing function. The two sections below will be organized in relation to those three approaches and focus on what I believe are the two main elements which characterize construals: categorizing entities (i.e. actors, locations, policies, etc.) and presenting discourse from a particular perspective. In my view, both elements contribute to constructing a perspectivized world view in which different elements of a given event are made salient.

Construal and categorization

Different authors in CDA have advocated in favour of analysing what could be called referential or nomination strategies, that is, exploring which linguistic cues are used to construct social actors, phenomena, events, processes and actions (Reisgil and Wodak, 2002). Some authors also establish a connection between nomination and categorization (Van Leeuwen, 1996). The notion of categorization will be developed in more detail in Chapter 6, but it is necessary to mention here some of the devices which are considered to be categorizing by some CDA scholars: verbs and nouns or tropes including metaphors (Resigil and Wodak, 2002). Such attribution of categorizing properties to nouns or metaphors can be explained through CL.

Metaphor studies are among the best known and most prolific examples of cognitive tools applied to the study of political discourse. While reviewing them all lies outside the scope of this book, it shall be noted that metaphors allow political speakers to 'characterize entities, relations, and processes, bringing abstract concepts to a concrete level of reasoning' (Cienki, 2013, p. 296). Metaphors thus arguably have a double function as they are both pedagogical – allowing complex (abstract) concepts to be understood – and persuasive – as they do not only reflect the speaker's choice but also allow for the world to be understood semantically on the basis of analogy while at the same time pragmatically providing evaluations (Charteris-Black, 2004, pp. 23–4).

A clear link can be established between metaphors and other analytic categories in cognitive semantics, such as image schemas. Image schemas are also cognitive mechanisms for conceptualizing our experience. These are less detailed than metaphors, and they are mostly 'distillers' of our spatial and temporal experience, which is mapped onto conceptual structures (Oakley, 2007). As noted by Cienki (2007, pp. 178–9), both image schemas and metaphors have a structuring role in Idealized Cognitive Models (ICMs), which are ways in which we organize knowledge according to certain cognitive structures. These models are not necessarily objective, but they reflect our experiential understanding of the world. In his study of metaphorical conceptualizations of the word 'security', Paul Chilton (1996) does not only provide a very clear explanation of how the CONTAINER image schema underpins many of the conceptualizations of 'security' found in international relations, but he also makes a major claim about the importance of looking at image schemas (and metaphors) as the pre-conceptual basis of conceptual and linguistic organization both in everyday life and in the political and public domain. These ideas will be further developed in Chapters 4 and 6 of this book.

A connection can be established between metaphors and image schemas, with the latter lying at the core of many metaphorical conceptualizations, which can be understood as extended instantiations of basic image schemas. Examples include force dynamics being related to water metaphors when talking about immigration (Porto, 2022), or CONTAINER schemas featuring prominently when talking, for example, about the European Union as a house (Chilton and Ilyin, 1993). Metaphors are more culturally specific and richer in detail, while image schemas are more schematic, that is, they include less specificity relative to one or more parameters. The relation between image schemas and metaphors is best explained by Kövecses (2017) and Dancygier and Sweetser (2014), who propose looking at them as conceptual structures which occupy different levels in schematicity hierarchies. This consideration of hierarchies is important for understanding how conflictual interpretations of a given metaphor/schematic construction arise as 'a variety of inferences can be derived depending on the level of schematic structure and the framing chosen' when processing discourse (Dancygier and Sweetser, 2014, p. 215).[8] The discursive function of image schemas and metaphors differs because they perform different cognitive operations. As such, they will feature prominently in separate chapters: image schemas as constructing a particular structure of the world, in Chapter 4, and metaphors as part of the framing strategies, in Chapter 6.

The link between image schemas and metaphor is also related to the understanding of both as cognitive models which trigger a particular construction of the world.[9] The degree of schematicity pairs the level of categorization provided by the linguistic choices, which may be richer or lower in detail. Because they are richer in detail, metaphors have frequently been studied as part of the framing strategies in CL-CDS (Hart, 2014, p. 111), as affective qualities and evaluations are attributed to entities and processes depending on the metaphor chosen. This attribution of qualities is related to the priming effect of linguistic choices (Janicki, 2015, p. 46). Priming means that the words chosen to refer to an entity may influence the way people think and behave, and this results from the activation of particular concepts and associations in the minds of people via discourse. A clear example can be seen in communicative events at the time of writing, particularly in relation to the rise of violence in the Gaza Strip. On the opening of the Winter Assembly of the twenty-fifth Knesset session, Israeli Prime Minister Benjamin Netanyahu uttered the following words: 'This is a struggle between the children of light and the children of darkness, between humanity and the law of the jungle.'[10] Those words were later posted by Netanyahu's office on X (formerly known as Twitter). However, one day later, the post was deleted in the aftermath of reports on an explosion on a hospital in Gaza.[11] Controversy arises by comparing the more metaphorical and less metaphorical understandings of the quote by Netanyahu, which implies a categorization of children based on a moral evaluation stemming from the binary opposition between light and darkness metaphors, where the former – children of light – is understood as being positive, moral and engaged in positive behaviour in contrast with the latter (Yu, 2022, p. 119). A similar evaluation is conveyed by the opposition between the dehumanizing view encompassed in 'jungle', where social actors in that group are implicitly evaluated as not only being wild but also dangerous. Both features convey a negative moral evaluation of these actors (Zinken, 2003), and hence delegitimize their sociopolitical actions while legitimizing those associated to the self.[12] While explicit reference to the sociopolitical actors is not found in the quote, who they are can be inferred from the context in which the utterance is found: the Israeli government versus Hamas (which is explicitly mentioned by Netanyahu in the same statement).

Controversy over the interpretation of the quote above arises in the aftermath of the explosion at the hospital in Gaza. The quote allowed for a metaphorical construal of children as descendants of the moral evaluations triggered by light or darkness, and also for a non-metaphorical interpretation, as some of the civilians who died in the explosion were actually children. This example does not only show the categorizing and framing potential of metaphors but also how the interpretation of the linguistic choices has both a conceptual and an interactive dimension.

While several studies have been conducted on metaphors in political discourse, these are not the only example of categorizing language (Cienki, 2013; Cienki and Yanow, 2013). Other figurative (e.g. metonymy) and non-figurative uses of language shall also be considered. As will be developed in Chapters 5 and 6, the linguistic choices we make to refer to particular entities do not only have an indexical function – that is, referring to a particular entity – but they also provide a particular representation of the said entity via the foregrounding of particular features. References to actors can indicate how those actors are posited in the speaker's discourse world, that is, the mental space entertained by a speaker as 'real' (Chilton, 2004, p. 53). Regardless of whether these references are figurative or not, this necessarily involves some kind of categorization. The ability to categorize is part of our communicative process, and understanding how we perform categorization discursively can help us understand which conceptual structures count as categories (Lakoff, 1987) in given political contexts. This has important implications in political discourse as the discursive creation of categories contributes to public perceptions about social actors (Van Leeuwen, 1996). The inferences drawn from linguistic choices result in a construal where particular features of entities, processes or events are foregrounded. As explained above, in the Discourse-Historical Approach of CDA (Reisigl and Wodak, 2002, pp. 95, 113), this process has also been considered as part of nomination and predication strategies, which result in the discursive characterization of the said entities and processes.[13] Our sociopolitical and cultural understanding of the profiled features results in the (de)legitimization of political actors, actions or policies, and is closely related to the discursive construction of an ideological square and the opposition between us and them (Van Dijk, 1998; Zimbardo, 2007).

Construal and perspectivization

Several studies on political discourse have focused on metaphor and figurative language. However, other studies have tried to explain how utterers position themselves when sending a given message. Two main but closely related theories have been used to approach this. Inspired by the concept of mental spaces (Fauconnier, 1994; Fauconnier and Turner, 2002), Chilton (2004) proposes the analysis of discourse worlds as a key tool in political discourse analysis.[14] Discourse worlds are explained as the mental space discursively entertained by the utterer as real. What is relevant is not only that he proposes to see how social actors and entities are discursively represented but also that he incorporates the notion of positioning. This means that when analysing discourse worlds, we shall acknowledge how meaning is generated in relation to a particular situation, that is, a physical location and a point in time (usually related to the utterance time) relative to which events are given meaning (Chilton, 2004, p. 56). Following the DST model,[15] we shall understand how a conceptual space is discursively activated. This conceptual space is constructed on the basis of a number of coordinate systems, which in theory are associated with three axes: space, time and modality. These can help us explain how the speakers – or cognizers – situate themselves and their world views. The conceptual space, which Chilton (2014) labels deictic space, allows us to explain how abstract concepts are modelled and related to the experience of the speaker from whose perspective the world is conceptualized. As shown in the simplified version included in Figure 2.2, the model is based on a proximal-distant relationship being established between the utterer (S) and the entities present in the discourse world.

The geometrical representation in Figure 2.2 is arguably also a way of representing the conceptualization of (epistemological) stance, as it assumes that the closer entities, actors or processes are in space, time and modality with the speakers, the more aligned they are with them.[16] This representation of the conceptual space as showing the speaker's position is an attempt to acknowledge the situatedness of political discourse. This visual depiction thus reflects the speaker's cognitive position in space. As noted by Chilton (2005b, p. 111), this shows how the self is established in space, time and in relation to possibilities

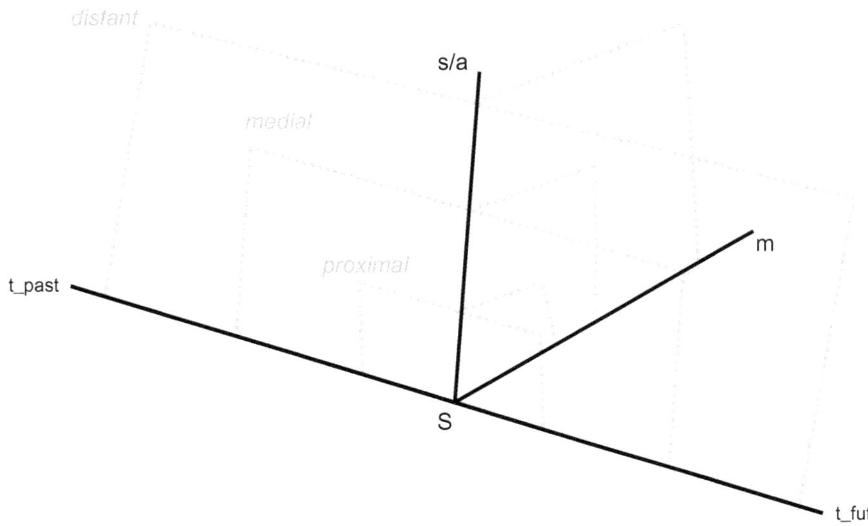

Figure 2.2 DST model, Simplified representation (based on Chilton 2004).

and counterfactuals. In the original theory, positioning just relates to the self, and the others are discursively presented as being close or distant from such self. Because meaning is not only representational but also interactive, it can be argued that the audience's lack of alignment with the speaker's position may be a source of disagreement and conflict.

The possibilities that DST offers for the study of conflict and political discourse can be better seen in subsequent developments of the theory, and mostly those related to Proximization Theory (Cap, 2010, 2013, 2017). Departing from the three-axis DST model, Cap (2013) proposes that an utterer's representation of the world distinguishes between IDCs – that is, concepts which are familiar to the deictic centre – and ODCs – or concepts which are outside the deictic centre. The deictic centre is defined along the three dimensions mentioned before: space, time and modality, which in Cap's model is called axiology (Cap, 2010).[17] Proximization theory has been mostly used to explain how outgroups – ODCs – are discursively delegitimized because they are a threat to the deictic centre. Eventually, this legitimizes policies such as intervention in war or anti-immigration measures (Cap, 2013, 2018b, 2018a). While this already shows how proximization contributes to a speaker conceptualizing a conflictual relationship between social actors which are located in different mental spaces, other studies have shown that proximization can in fact also be constructed dialogically and that the strategies used are purpose, content and context dependent. In a study done by Kowalski (2022), variation in proximization strategies depended on who was using them – journalists versus readers –, on the genre – the actual news versus the comments to them –, or the content and context covered in the news (Poland and Romania in Kowalski's case study). This shows that points of view are not only discursively constructed but also negotiated, and it is this interactive dimension that may result in different conceptualizations of the IDCs and the ODCs, whose discursive position relative to the speaker and hearer may change in interaction.

Both DST and Proximization Theory clearly relate to one of the dimensions of construal: the notion of perspective (Talmy, 2000b; Croft and Cruse, 2004; Langacker, 2008). Perspective involves establishing a relationship between the object of conceptualization and the subject of conceptualization (Verhagen, 2007). The relationship can be physical, as when from a particular location we see something, or metaphorical. This metaphorical 'seeing' – or conceptualizing – of an event may result in a profiling of particular aspects of that event while silencing other aspects, as it would happen depending on the position from which we see a scene.[18] The profiling or silencing of particular aspects of sociopolitical events has consequences in how we perceive reality, and it may result in conflictual – and even paradoxical – representations of the same reality. Thus, 'language is perspectival in that various options on the lexical, grammatical, contextual, and conversational level allow for conceptualizing the same extra-linguistic situation in different manners so that every utterance is based on a set of choices by the speaker' (Zeman, 2017, p. 1). As will be explained in Chapter 7, different linguistic choices have been suggested for the analysis of perspectivization through language (see, for example, Dancygier, 2017). However, Proximization Theory and DST have mostly focused on the analysis of deixis. How the adoption of different perspectives can help us explain the discursive construction of a single political event can be seen in the following two headlines about the siege of Gaza City in November 2024 (examples [6] and [7]).

[6] Israeli army 'encircles' Gaza City as US calls for pause in fighting (*Financial Times*, 2 Nov 2023)

[7] Israel's army meets fierce resistance 'at the gates of Gaza City' (*Al Jazeera*, 2 November 2023)

The linguistic choice of two different verbs indicating spatial anchorage – 'encircle' and 'meets' – in the two examples above results in two world views being presented. In example [6], the Israeli army is presented as surrounding a space (Gaza City) whose inhabitants are silenced. However, in example [7] the lexical choice of the verb 'meet' implies the existence of two participants which happen to be in the same place – 'at the gates of Gaza City'. The 'resistance' feature of actors in the city is also emphasized. In spite of both examples apparently being an objective representation of a given event, they adopt different perspectives resulting from a different spatial conceptual configuration. This also suggests different possible outcomes for the situation.

Construal operations

Conceptualization is ubiquitous in linguistic expressions, and any kind of utterance implies a given conceptual structure of the experience conveyed (Croft and Cruse, 2004, p. 40). CL-informed studies on political discourse have mostly focused on the role of figurative and non-figurative categorization and perspectivization, both of which are closely related to the conceptual operations which can help us understand our experience of phenomena in the world (Hart, 2014, pp. 110–12). Researchers on CL have made different attempts at explaining how conceptualization processes are linguistically realized. These conceptualization processes are called 'construal operations' (Croft and Cruse, 2004), and there have been different attempts at grouping construal operations, most notably by Talmy (2000a, pp. 40–96) and Langacker (2019).[19]

Particularly interesting is Christopher Hart's (2014, pp. 108–12, 2025) exploration of the relationship between construal operations and the discursive strategies which they potentially realize. Three terms are of importance here: (1) cognitive systems, which are the general abilities that we all have and upon which conceptualization lies; (2) construal operations, as the processes which take place in interactions; and (3) discursive strategies, or the more or less intentional and/or institutionalized 'plan of discourse practices whose deployment results in a particular, systematically structured and internationally coherent, representation of reality which ultimately leads to the legitimation and/or mobilization of social actions' (Hart, 2014, p. 110). The relationship between the three cannot be negated: We all possess cognitive abilities which are related to different construal processes. Including the idea of discourse strategies – which had not featured prominently in theoretical descriptions of the notion of construal – allows us to acknowledge the perlocutionary effect of using particular linguistic choices and to explain the (de)legitimizing effect of political discourse as being related to different – even opposed – construals stemming from a variety of linguistic choices.

Following the classification of construal operations provided by Hart (2014, 2025) and by Croft and Cruse (2004, p. 46), in this book I explore how the

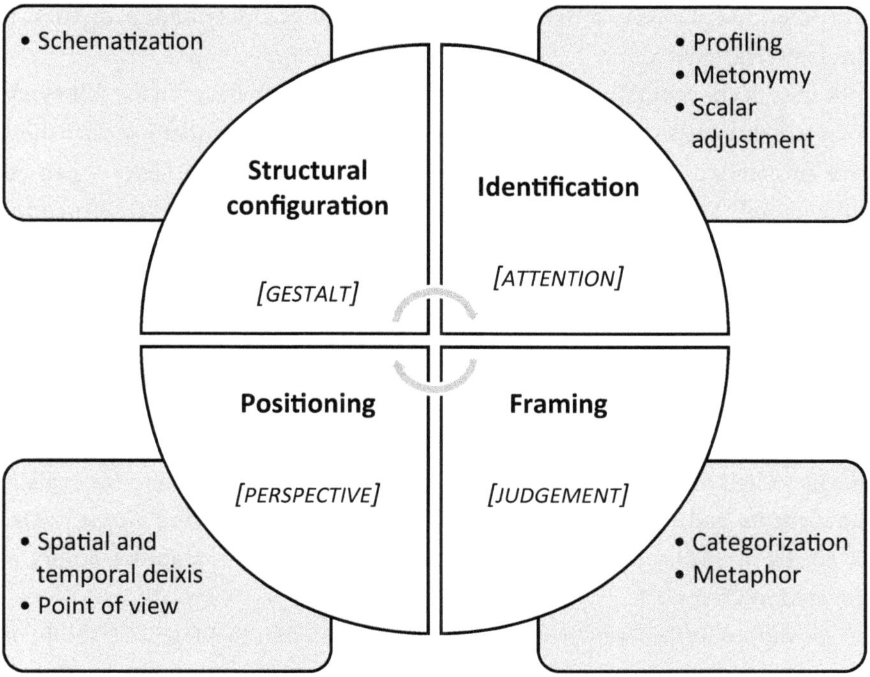

Figure 2.3 Construal operations and linguistic strategies.

linguistic realizations associated with four discursive strategies – which are, in turn, related to four cognitive abilities – contribute to the creation of opposed representations of the world. In Figure 2.3, a relation is established between the discursive strategies (in the centre, in bold type), the cognitive ability (in the centre, in small capital letters) and some of its possible linguistic realizations (as subordinated to each of them). A basic description of each strategy is provided below although this will be further explored in the four chapters devoted to the analysis. Likewise definitions of each cognitive ability – gestalt, attention, judgement and perspective – will be included at the beginning of each chapter. Two further things shall be noted at this point: First, the linguistic realizations explained in this book have been selected on the basis of their potential to increase or decrease conflictual world views. Hence the linguistic construal operations included here cannot be understood as an exhaustive list, rather it is a reflection on the role of language in creating or solving disagreement between political parties and the communities for which they stand. Second, linguistic operations have been grouped as prominently being related to a discursive strategy and a cognitive ability for the sake of simplicity and organizational purposes. This has been done following previous studies, but it shall be noted that one linguistic operation may be related to more than one cognitive ability and/or discursive strategy (Hart, 2025).

While each conceptualization process will be explored in detail in the following chapters, it is necessary to provide a description of each of them so that their role in creating mental representations of reality – or world views – can be understood. Following Croft and Cruse (2004) and Hart (2014), *structural configuration strategies* are those which contribute to the conceptualization of the structure of the entities in a scene. This operation is related to the most basic level of conceptualization. The combination of multiple, and seemingly fragmental, basic schemas allows users to conceptualize complex scenes as gestalts, that is, an organized structure of experience which results from the combination of features from its multiple components. Previous studies have mostly relied on the analysis of image schemas and force dynamics to explain how events and entities are discursively configured (Croft and Cruse, 2004, p. 63; Hart, 2014, pp. 110–11). The analysis of the gestalt cognitive ability is covered in Chapter 4.

Identification strategies are those which are related to the cognitive ability of attention, and they involve the activation of conceptual structures which enhance a particular phenomenon's salience. While attention is a complex cognitive ability which involves different subprocesses, it can be argued that through identification strategies we are not only selecting particular aspects of a given scene but we are also providing them with different degrees of salience in our mental representation. It is thus via linguistic choice that we highlight different facets of a single scene. Such linguistic strategies are mostly related to referential expressions – as they do help in indexing different elements of the scene while profiling different aspects of such reality – metonymy and scalar adjustment. Further detail on attention and salience will be provided in Chapter 5.

Framing strategies are mostly related to the cognitive ability of judgement or comparison. This involves two conceptual members being included: that about which something is affirmed (i.e. the entity or event in the scene) and that which is affirmed (i.e. the prior knowledge or experience which is used to qualify the scene). Through comparison we attribute qualities to entities and actions, both figuratively and non-figuratively. While framing strategies have been frequently associated with metaphor, the analysis of non-figurative language is equally important because it may activate knowledge which functions as a frame of reference. Two main conceptual operations are thus to be considered here: categorization and metaphor. The need to incorporate an intertextual dimension to the study of framing strategies is also justified in Chapter 6.

Finally, perspective is the cognitive ability associated with *positioning strategies*. Given that any instance of discourse is situated, an utterer's conceptualization of a scene is always relative to their position in the world. The analysis of perspective as a conceptual process requires looking at the situation of an entity/action relative to a particular spatial, temporal, cultural or axiological location. While most analyses of perspective have relied on deixis (Croft and Cruse, 2004, p. 58), it can be argued that other related construal operations are objectivization and subjectivization, and point of view (Hart, 2025), as will be explained in Chapter 7.

Much of the work on CL looking at alternative ways of presenting a scene – that is, a construal – has focused on the study of single sentences whose conceptual representations are compared (Croft and Cruse, 2004; Verhagen, 2007; Langacker, 2008, 2019). When applied to the analysis of political discourse, I believe that such alternative construals contribute to the configuration of different discourse worlds. Such discourse worlds are the mental spaces entertained by a speaker, and they stem from coherent chains of propositions which, combined, establish a view of reality. Discourse worlds, thus, have several meaning components, most notably 'who does what to whom, when and where' (Chilton, 2004, p. 54). Chilton's proposal for the analysis of discourse worlds is based on an adaptation, among other theories, of Paul Werth's Text World Theory (Werth, 1999). Mental representations of reality necessarily require the presence of entities and actions for a text to be coherent. Entities – understood as participants and their qualities – are part of the world-building elements, within which also places and times are to be included. It shall be noted that construal operations feature prominently in how alternative views about such (political) entities are conceptualized. Alternative views result from entities being situated in a particular place and time, that is shown from a particular *perspective*. Some of them may feature more prominently in discourse – hence attracting further *attention* – and they are also ascribed different qualities – via figurative and non-figurative *judgement*. Sociopolitical participants also perform different actions or are involved in different kinds of relationships. These are part of the function-advancing propositions of a text-world. Such relationships can be conceptualized via basic schematic processes which together constitute a *gestalt*. All together political discourse worlds are complex configurations which represent what utterers present as an objective depiction of society. Still, what may be discursively construed as objective is just the point of view of particular speakers (and usually also one of the communities they stand for). It is via linguistic choices that such alternative mental representations of reality are constructed.[20]

It is the aim of this book to explore the relationship between cognition, discourse and conflict. Throughout this chapter, I have argued that exploring how different discursive choices result in different construals can help us explain the (de)legitimizing function of political discourse. In conflict situations, such (de)legitimating function is closely related to representations of the self and the other, and to negotiations of those representations via discourse. In the following chapters I reflect on the role of construal operations in negotiating conflictual relations. As explained in the Introduction, the conflict in NI has been selected as the case study, though it is hoped that findings from this specific context can be extrapolated and applied to the study of other (ethnonationalist) conflicts. Since the aim of the book is to reflect on the role of language, different historical moments after the signing of the 1998 Agreement will illustrate each chapter. Still, a historical account of political life in NI is provided in Chapter 3 with the aim of aiding to understand social, cultural and historical references in the analysis. Different data has also been gathered for each political event, including mostly institutional statements by the political actors involved. The analysis is qualitative and it relies on introspection as a research method, which is common in CL (Hart, 2025).

3

The choreography of Northern Ireland: Historical and political background

An overview of the characteristics of the NI political situation and how this has been shaped by years of history and sectarian feelings is included in this chapter, whose title 'The Choreography of Northern Ireland' is aimed at showing the complexity of the NI conflict. This paraphrases a type of language which was frequently used in the news to describe the political process after the 1998 Agreement.[1] Throughout these years, dance became 'a metaphor for action, indicating that movement may focus political concerns and route them in a new direction' (Morrison, 2004, p. 109) by articulating intricate political manoeuvres. The complexity of the NI political situation cannot only be seen in those complicated political moves but also in the impact of history in shaping those movements, as many historical events are still remembered – and recalled – by the two NI communities. In NI, history is not merely something that is remembered, but it also has an impact on the present (Alonso, 2001, p. 77). So much so that history is an important component in the building of national identities, which, in turn, endows historical events with a symbolic and mythological trait that is sometimes recalled in contemporary NI political discourse.

For that reason, this chapter includes a short recollection of the history of NI from its foundation to the negotiations on the border following the withdrawal of the UK from the European Union (EU). This chapter is not intended as a comprehensive description of NI history, for which other sources can be consulted,[2] but it rather focuses on explaining those aspects which can be symbolically evoked by politicians in order to justify specific perceptions. The first sections of the chapter include the historical description, and an overview of ideologies, NI political parties and controversial issues is provided in the final section of the chapter.

The origin of the Northern Irish conflict

There are different theoretical explanations for the origin of the modern NI conflict. Legally, Northern Ireland, as we know it today, began its existence with the Government of Ireland Act, 1920. This established the jurisdictions of Northern Ireland and the Irish Free State, which would become the Republic of Ireland in 1949 (Dunn and Dawson, 2000, p. 109). Also important for the origin of NI is the Anglo-Irish Treaty signed in 1921, in which Westminster gave 'dominion status to the Irish Free State and Home Rule to the six north-eastern counties' (Bardon, 1993, p. 467). This was the outcome of several years of civil war – known as the Anglo-Irish War, or the 'War of Independence' in the South – which lasted from 1919 to 1921 (McKittrick and McVea, 2000, p. 4). This division of the island into two parts has become known as 'partition', and it is frequently used by paramilitary groups as part of their narrative to 'justify' the origin of NI (Feldman, 1991, pp. 17–18).

The immediate origins of NI lay in the upheavals of the Home Rule Crisis of 1912–14 and the First World War (Hennessey, 1997). In 1912, the British government passed a Home Rule Bill aimed at giving Ireland the possibility of governing itself. This was opposed by the unionist community, and as a consequence two different and opposed forces were created in 1913, the Ulster Volunteer Force (UVF) and the 'Irish Volunteers'. Both forces are frequently alluded to by paramilitary groups in order to justify their origin. At Easter 1916, radical nationalists took advantage of the war in Europe to rise against the British, announcing the creation of a government for the Republic of Ireland, which from that moment was considered an independent state (Alonso, 2001, p. 103). The subsequent execution of the leaders of The Rising by the British government helped to increase the feeling of sympathy towards the Nationalist/Republican cause (McKittrick and McVea, 2000, p. 4). When the First World War ended in 1918, Irish Nationalists did not want Home Rule anymore, and they demanded an independent Irish Republic. Thus, there was a combination of an armed campaign and political moves, among which the creation of an Irish Republic in 1919 and Eamon de Valera's election as president of that new Republic can be highlighted. In the armed campaign, 'the republican forces, efficiently organized by Michael Collins who took command of what came to be known as the Irish Republican Army (IRA), waged guerrilla warfare against the British government' (Buckland, 1992, p. 18), and this led to the Anglo-Irish War mentioned above. It can thus be argued that 'the new state was created in the midst of the troubles and divisions which were to characterize its history' (Darby,

1976, p. 9). These events – and in particular the Easter Rising of 1916 – have served to enact the notion of sacrifice and martyrdom inherent to the republican movement (Alonso, 2001, pp. 104–5). Furthermore, the origin of some of the current NI political parties, such as Sinn Féin (SF) – founded in 1907 – and the Ulster Unionist Party (UUP) – which emerged from the Ulster Unionist Council organized in 1905 (Darby, 1976, p. 8) – can also be established in this period.

While partition is frequently presented as the origin of the NI conflict, some authors (Darby, 1995, p. 16; Dunn and Dawson, 2000, p. 218) trace it back to the Ulster Plantation of 1603, when the British crown seized the land from the native Irish Catholics and gave it to English and Scottish settlers in order to counteract the opposition of the natives to the British. This period was characterized by the occupation of one single territory by two hostile groups. Besides, it is in this period when cultural and religious differences between the two groups started to be outlined, as they identified with different values as well as with different territorial sections. The Plantation of the seventeenth century had an important effect, and it resembles some of the feelings still experienced by both contemporary NI communities.[3] By looking at the nature of the settlement in the Plantation – one single territory containing two groups differing in political allegiance, religious practice and cultural values – we may understand the broad outlines of the conflict, as one group thought its land had been stolen while the other had a constant feeling of apprehension (Darby, 2003).

Attempts by the Catholics to get back their lands and the crowning of Protestant William of Orange in 1688 also had an impact on the contemporary imaginary. The first event relates to what is known as 'the siege of Derry', that is, the 105 days during which the gates of this city were closed for fear of an attack from the Catholic forces of James II. The second ties back to the 'Battle of the Boyne' in 1690, which resulted in the victory of William of Orange and a subsequent Protestant majority in the Irish Parliament. This victory is often represented in murals and banners as 'the victory of the "Prods" over the "Mikes"' (Darby, 1983, p. 15), and it is commemorated every 12th of July with parades by the Protestant community.

The second half of the eighteenth century is characterized by the creation of secret organizations, including 'the United Irishmen' – which asked for Catholic emancipation, the reform of Parliament and the independence of Ireland (Stewart, 1989, p. 101). The increasing number of rebellions at this time made the British aware of the problems in Ireland, and in 1800 they approved the amalgamation of the British and Irish Parliaments. In 1801, the Act of Union was passed, and from then on Ireland became part of the UK. No more upheavals took place in Ireland until the 'Irish Republican Brotherhood' stated that independence from Britain could only be achieved by means of violence. This resulted in another aborted rebellion in 1867, and in some other different movements which would end in the Home Rule Crisis of 1912–14.

Most of these historical events are recalled by both NI communities in their contemporary discourse, and they show that sectarianism is nothing new in the modern conflict, but it has been a constant feature in the history of (Northern) Ireland throughout the years. Besides, these events have also contributed to the creation of symbols and myths such as the Catholic rebellion of 1641, the Battle of the Boyne of 1690, the unionist resistance to Home Rule between 1912 and 1914, or the Easter Rising of 1916. Such mythology has also influenced the different perceptions that both Catholics and Protestants have about the conflict: perceptions which sometimes seem to underlie their own ideological beliefs. In particular, these events have contributed to the building of a siege mentality in the Protestant community, whose members perceive themselves to be always under threat; a threat which is mostly related to the rights and liberties they believe can be stolen from them because of their minority status in the whole of the island. Likewise, the Catholic community links their lived experiences to a ghetto culture which is bound to their role as a minority, something which is frequently alluded to by means of a victimization process (Alonso, 2001, pp. 128–9). This also ties in with the importance of martyrdom and sacrifice for republicans. In any case, both communities perceive themselves as victims of the other community, who seems to be always attacking them (Alonso, 2001).

The birth of Northern Ireland: The Stormont years

The new state created through the Act of Ireland, 1920 was born in the midst of troubles and divisions, which were manifested in a number of riots resulting from the competition between both communities for jobs and houses (Darby, 1983, p. 17). The proposal of two parliaments in the island was ratified by the Anglo-Irish Treaty signed in 1921 by Michael Collins – leader of the IRA – and Arthur Griffith – representing the British government. This treaty established a partitioned twenty-six-county Irish Free State, and it allowed NI[4] to decide whether it wanted to belong to the Free State or to the UK. The establishment of these two entities within Ireland was differently understood by each of the communities. On the one hand, it meant a partial triumph for Irish Nationalists, although there was division within them, with SF rejecting the 'Partition Act' and continuing with their struggle to make the Dáil the Parliament for the thirty-two counties of Ireland (Bardon, 1993, p. 479). On the other, it increased the feeling of abandonment and betrayal of the Unionist community, which wanted to remain governed by Westminster (Buckland, 1992, p. 19).

Since NI had decided to remain part of the UK, it was endowed with the possibility of having its own Parliament although Westminster was still responsible for defence, foreign policy and concerns within the UK (Darby, 2003). In 1921, three parties contested the elections for the first Parliament in NI: the Ulster Unionists, led by James Craig; the Nationalists, led by Joseph Devlin; and SF, with Eamonn de Valera as candidate for county Down (Bardon, 1993, p. 479). The NI Parliament was officially opened on 22 June 1921, with James Craig as prime minister. It was ruled by a Unionist majority, mainly as a consequence of Catholic unwillingness to participate in a state whose existence they did not recognize (Darby, 1983, p. 21). The Nationalist community did not trust this Parliament, which began introducing measures to ensure a 'Protestant Parliament for a Protestant state' (Alonso, 2001, p. 133), thus becoming a symbol of Protestant dominance. This contributed to increasing the alienation feeling of the Catholic community, which claimed that the Stormont Parliament was carrying out discriminatory practices, particularly in relation to six areas: the electoral system, public employment, private employment, public housing, regional politics and policing. Some of these areas have remained controversial in present days.

One of the most controversial events in this period was the enactment of the Special Powers Act in 1922, which gave the minister of home affairs the authority to arrest suspects of terrorism and to set up special courts to judge them. This law could be applied both to the Protestant and the Catholic community, but, taking into account the mostly Protestant nature of the RUC,[5] it was mainly applied against the nationalist community. Consequently, Catholics often complained that policing had a military character and an intimidating effect. This helped to fortify the alienation feeling of the Catholic community and the siege one of Protestants.

The following twenty years in NI were characterized by relative peace, which overlapped with a time of economic expansion of the Province (Darby, 1983, p. 23). Nevertheless, this was also a phase of political stagnation, as a distinctive trait of the Stormont system was the lack of opposition in the elections. 'The 1960s started as the decade of hope' (Darby, 1983, p. 24), but it is also the time when important contemporary figures and institutions appear. Among them, Ian Paisley can be highlighted because he used an incendiary rhetoric which articulated and amplified the fears of many Protestants. As he did not want to join any of the unionist teams, he formed the Protestant Unionist Party, which would later become the Democratic Unionist Party (DUP) (McKittrick and McVea, 2000, pp. 32–5). This time is also characterized by an upsurge of loyalist violence, and the demonstrations and protests organized by the Northern Irish Civil Rights Association (NICRA), a Catholic organization modelled following the idea of the Black Liberation Movement led by Martin Luther King in the United States (Alonso, 2001).

The beginning of the twentieth century in NI served to heighten the perceptions each of the communities had about the other. Unionists felt they were under threat, as also observed in the siege mentality they had inherited from the Plantation times. That developed a defensive attitude which became 'evident in the later unionist slogans of "No Surrender", "What we have we hold", and "Not an inch"' (McKittrick and McVea, 2000, p. 7). The alienation feeling of the Catholic community can be likewise tracked back to events in the past; to them, Stormont, as the NI Parliament, was only a symbol.

The Troubles

The NI conflict is frequently associated with the time which is euphemistically known as 'The Troubles'. Many chronologies and history books have already been written about this time (Bew and Gillespie, 1999; Eliott and Flackes, 1999; McKittrick and McVea, 2000; Feeney, 2004; see also the chronologies included in Melaugh, 2023). For the sake of space and simplicity, I will only focus on those events which have had an impact either on the perpetuation of the siege and alienation mentalities of each of the NI communities or on the development of political progress.

The violent conflict that erupted in the late 1960s shows a pattern of violence which is characterized by inter-communal rioting (Darby, 2003), a pattern which would gradually change throughout the years of conflict until it reached a triangular conflict in which the protagonists were the British state, the republican paramilitaries and the loyalist paramilitaries. This understanding of multiple actors is important in contemporary interpretations of the NI conflict, and it also lies at the core of attempts to reach a peaceful solution to the conflict, among which the 1998 Agreement can be included.

The lack of reform of the NI institutions in the early 1960s gave rise to a series of organizations, among them the secular NICRA, as mentioned in the previous section. In a context where the Catholic community perceived to be discriminated, it can be argued that some of the protests and demonstrations organized by NICRA were, at least partly, the origin of civil strife. The brutal response of the RUC against the marchers in (London)Derry in October 1968, and the loyalist attack on marchers at Burntollet Bridge, near (London)Derry, resulted in a different perception of the conflict. Disturbances were no longer related to the demand of civil rights, but they merely reflected the historical conflict between national and religious identities (Alonso, 2001, p. 142). As Bryan (2003) explains, the Civil Rights Movement and the political tension arising from it represented another shift in the understanding of conflict, which was understood on ethnic terms from this time on: the issue of civil rights had become secondary to that of nationality. Because of the peak of violence in 1969, the British troops were deployed in the streets of Belfast and (London)Derry in mid-August 1969. At the beginning, the nationalist community welcomed the arrival of troops. Nevertheless, the lack of reaction of the British Army when the Orange Order[6] tried to go through the Ardoyne area in Belfast changed that perception: Unionists believed that the British Army allowed Republicans to operate with impunity while Catholics thought they had to look to their organizations for defence.

Nationalist distrust of the British troops was exacerbated by the discriminatory practices carried out under the auspices of the introduction of internment without trial, with the army arresting hundreds of suspects of terrorism under the Special Powers Act (Bew and Gillespie, 1999, p. 36). This increased the feeling of Catholic alienation (Hennessey, 1997, p. 193) because most of those arrested belonged to the nationalist community. This measure was propagandistically employed by the republican movement to justify its violence: something they would do again when the dramatic events of January 1972 – known as 'Bloody Sunday' – took place.[7] That became another myth for the republican movement, and it was soon introduced in their discourse to symbolize everything that this community perceived as unfair because of its connection with Great Britain (Alonso 2001: 166). On the contrary, unionists believed that it was merely an event that should be regretted but which did not need any more explanation. As a consequence of these events and the raising of violence, the Stormont Parliament was suspended on 24 March 1972, starting a long period of 'direct rule'. This measure was originally devised as a temporal one.

Two concepts characterize the shift in British security policy: 'criminalization' and 'Ulsterization'. The first term refers to the denial of the political motivation of terrorist acts and the treatment of these crimes as if they had been perpetrated by 'ordinary decent criminals' (McKittrick and McVea, 2000, p. 123). The second term – 'Ulsterization' – consigned the replacement of the primacy of the British Army by a leading role of the RUC and the Ulster Defence Regiment (UDR). In that way, the British government could present itself as a neutral actor and promote an internal interpretation of the conflict as one between both NI communities, thus weakening the perception of the Irish being oppressed by the British (Alonso, 2001, p. 206).

A similar internal view results from the outbreak of the Civil Rights movement, which eventually emphasized the essence of the problem in NI resulting from the antagonism between those who lived and still live there. Each of the communities perceived (and still do) the problem in a different way. Protestants usually see the conflict in constitutional and security terms, and they are primarily concerned with preserving the Union with Britain and resisting the perceived threat of a United Ireland. Two broad categories can be identified within Catholic views. The first one perceives the issue as a nationalist struggle for self-determination, while the other one – also subscribed by some Protestants – believes it is a problem of corruption or unfair practices by successive unionist governments between the 1920s and the 1970s, which, if removed, would create a society in which both Catholics and Protestants could live peacefully (Darby, 1997, p. 65).

The struggle that took place in NI after 1972 is characterized by the demand of different things by each of the groups involved in the conflict and the perception that accepting the other's demands would result in a weakening of the position of the self. This caused objections from either one group or the other at every attempt to rearrange the NI political framework. This is also followed by different attempts to find common ground between the political parties in NI, including a white paper and elections for the new Assembly (Bew and Gillespie, 1999, p. 61). Showing a common pattern with other political moments, a new Executive is announced in November 1973, and a new deal – known as the Sunningdale Agreement – is reached on 9 December 1973 (McKittrick and McVea, 2000, p. 95). Sunningdale was a 'masterpiece of balance and ambiguity' (Buckland, 1992, p. 169) where the really controversial issues were not overtly dealt with. This meant that it could be justified differently by each of the communities. Nevertheless, it ran against a lot of opposition coming both from the IRA and the Protestant community (McKittrick and McVea, 2000, pp. 98–9). In the end, the unionist community managed to bring it down, and different moves were made by the British government to resolve the situation.

Following some talks between the British government and the IRA, the latter called a ceasefire in 1975. The republican community perceived the IRA ceasefire as a disaster, and they interpreted the new legislation as a repressive measure. Therefore, a new strategy, known as 'the long war', was developed: 'IRA activity would be refined and take the form of "armed propaganda" aimed at eroding the British will to remain in the North' (Patterson, 2002, p. 250). This meant that Republicans perceived Unionists as mere 'puppets of British imperialism', who was the real enemy (Patterson, 2002, p. 128). Besides, this strategy acknowledged two angles, involving a combination of political negotiations and military action (Alonso, 2001, p. 245). This became clearer after the hunger strikes of 1981.

On the fifth anniversary of the ending of political status, Bobby Sands, leader of the IRA prisoners at The Maze prison – which Republicans called 'Long Kesh' – started a hunger strike aimed at regaining the previously denied political status (Hennessey, 1997, p. 260). Several protests had taken place before, but this one resulted in the death of ten men, who became symbols of the idea of martyrdom which was so deeply embedded in Catholic thinking. In republican minds, they resembled the martyrs of the 1916 Easter Rising. The hunger strikes also represented a turnover in the politicization of SF as Bobby Sands managed to get elected as MP at Westminster. This success in gaining political status made the leaders of the republican movement aware of the advantages of this new and dual strategy, which consisted of contesting elections while at the same time continuing with their military campaign.

The hunger strikes transformed the political situation in NI. Republicans had won the propaganda war – and they had also created another myth for their tradition – both nationally and internationally. They now appeared as prepared to suffer for their cause instead of inflicting pain on others. Besides, the British and Irish governments had become aware of – and were frightened by – the possibilities of SF taking over the SDLP as the main representative of the Catholic population. Consequently, the hunger strikes became a turning point which eventually led to the two governments signing the Anglo-Irish Agreement (AIA) in 1985 (Bew and Gillespie, 1999, pp. 158–9).

The AIA consisted of twelve clauses, and the most striking innovation was the creation of an Intergovernmental Conference which would meet regularly to promote cross-border cooperation on security, legal and political matters (Bardon, 1993, p. 756). This implicitly meant the recognition of the role of the Irish government in any possible solution to the conflict. Another significant aspect was the reinforcement of the principle of consent if the status of NI was to be changed. As on previous occasions, this agreement was a masterpiece of ambiguity, which suggests that it was written with the idea of balancing the aspirations of each of the communities.

Unionists rejected this agreement, or 'Diktat' as they had named it (Patterson, 2002, p. 257), because they saw it as a victory for constitutional nationalism, something with which the SDLP also agreed. Therefore, they organized boycotts, protests, mass rallies and demonstrations, and there was also an increase in the level of loyalist violence. The AIA accentuated the fears of British betrayal in the unionist community, and they engaged in a campaign aimed at destroying it. Republicans were not happy either with the Agreement because the Irish government had conceded that sovereignty over NI would only change if desired by a majority in the North (Morrow, 1996, pp. 26–7). Nevertheless, the Agreement survived, and 'for many this implied the eventual evolution of a formalized system of joint authority' (Bew and Gillespie, 1999, p. 191).

Growing disenchantment among Unionists resulted in an increased level of violence, and reactions to the AIA stressed the already-existing polarization. Therefore, new inter-party talks were started. At the same time, secret channels of communication had been established between the British government and the republican movement, between the Dublin government and John Hume, leader of the SDLP, and between the latter and Gerry Adams. All these talks and consultations resulted in John Major – British prime minister – and Albert Reynolds – Taoiseach of the Republic of Ireland – issuing a joint declaration on NI on 15 December 1993. This came to be known as the 'Downing Street Declaration' (Bew and Gillespie, 1999, p. 282), and its main feature was once again ambiguity because it was intended as a frame for a peaceful solution to the antagonisms present in NI society. In this declaration, which was dominated by the republican claim of 'self-determination', the British were facilitators for an agreed Ireland – as opposed to a united one, although that had to be based on the consent of the majority of the people in the North. This declaration, together with the negotiations leading towards it, marks the beginning of the so-called peace process, that is, the search for a definite end of violence in NI.

The peace process

Fitzzduff and O'Hagan (2009) suggest a series of factors that helped the peace process develop. First of all, both the IRA and the British Army realized that the war could not be won militarily, which resulted in the politicization of SF. The social and economic context that gave birth to The Troubles had also changed, and some of the issues of discrimination against Catholics had already been addressed. Likewise, the political landscape had been altered through the development of some new – although small – political parties. Finally, the international perception of the NI problem had also changed because of US involvement and some assistance from the developing peace process in South Africa.

It was in this context that the Downing Street Declaration was signed, and the ambiguity of its wording became a useful measure of balance which acknowledged the complexity of the situation in NI, where a one-sided process would never be accepted by the other side because it would be perceived as a defeat (Alonso, 2001, p. 304). It was due to this ambiguity that neither of the communities reacted to it in a negative way, although it was received with suspicion. Following growing pressure, the IRA called a ceasefire on 31 August 1994.[8]

While perceived as a new era, the time known as the peace process – usually dated between 1993 and 1998 – is characterized by a multiplicity of talks in which parties were gradually allowed to enter, suspicions by the two communities on the measures and policies implemented, and announcements of cessation of violence by paramilitary groups belonging to both NI communities. These announcements were sometimes presented as dependent on the actions of groups belonging to the opposed community. This time is also characterized by a clear move from violence to more political solutions (McKittrick and McVea, 2000, p. 201).

There were several moments when the peace process seemed about to collapse. Fear of this happening during President Clinton's visit to NI in November 1995 made the British and Irish governments reveal a 'twin-track strategy', based on new inter-party talks and on the creation of an international body to look at arms decommissioning. US Senator George Mitchell, as chair of this body, issued a report in which he proposed that negotiations ran in parallel to decommissioning, thus trying to encompass the view of both the republican community (or SF) and the British government. It shall be noted that he identified the lack of trust between the two traditions as the element behind the stalemate in the process, and he perceived the question of weapons to be at the core of the problem. This is why he suggested the creation of the previously mentioned independent commission to verify the disarmament of paramilitary organizations.

The talks were suspended after the IRA detonated a bomb at Canary Wharf in London in February 1996. This moment is of significance as Gerry Adams – then leader of SF – rejected to condemn the bomb. Such rejection shows a new approach in the republican movement, which intends to separate the IRA from SF, presenting Republicans as a disunited movement (Bew and Gillespie, 1999, p. 323). This strategy still seems to be followed by SF, which ambiguously distances itself from the IRA when addressing a non-republican audience, while trying to retain the (at least symbolic) links between the political party and the paramilitary organization in the eyes of the republican community (see also Filardo-Llamas, 2013).

Although several attempts were made for restarting the talks, the main change was brought about by the Labour Party's victory in the General Election of March 1997. Tony Blair reopened the contacts with SF, raising the hopes for a renewed IRA ceasefire, which was eventually announced on 19 July 1997, a month after the multi-party talks had been resumed at Stormont. This renewed ceasefire enabled SF to enter the multi-party talks two days later although it meant the boycott of the DUP and the United Kingdom Unionist Party (UKUP) amid allegations of treachery towards the unionist cause. David Trimble became the most prominent unionist leader involved in the negotiations. Even if he agreed to talk to SF, the question of weapons still had a leading role (Alonso, 2001, p. 356). Eventually, after several months of intense negotiations, on 10 April 1998, following a whole night of talks, an agreement was signed. This agreement became known as the 'Belfast Agreement' or the 'Good Friday Agreement'.[9]

Throughout the peace process, some of the features that have characterized the problems for the implementation of the 1998 Agreement can be already observed. First of all, the unionist community followed a pattern of fearful pessimism, always fearing retreat and decline, and constantly accusing the British government of betrayal. This is characterized by Protestant alienation, which seems to be the consequence of their siege mentality and their fear of becoming a minority in a United Ireland. The republican movement has not rejected its primary objective – expelling the British out of Ireland – although the means through which they intend to achieve it have changed. Such patterns and feelings, which have motivated the behaviour of the two NI communities all throughout their history and even more during the peace process, will feature prominently in the analysis section of this book.

The 1998 Agreement

The Agreement signed in 1998 represents an effort to bring peace and political stability to NI, and it has put an end to over thirty years of violent conflict in which more than 3,600 people have been killed and over 30,000 injured

(Fitzzduff and O'Hagan, 2009). The Agreement was endorsed by the main NI nationalist parties and by most of the unionist ones, with the exception of the DUP and the UKUP (Eliott and Flackes, 1999, p. 267). This accord emphasized the commitment of all participants in the negotiations to solve their political differences only through peaceful means, and it outlined several constitutional issues, which included the right of the people of Ireland to 'self-determination' – although subordinated to the principle of consent – and the birthright of all the people of NI to identify themselves either as 'Irish' or as 'British', or both. This involved changes in British and Irish legislation, the most significant being the changes to be made to the Irish constitution in order to end its territorial claim. The Agreement includes an organization around three strands which point to different sets of relations: strand one regulates democratic institutions in NI, and it provides for a 'democratically elected Assembly' which would operate on a cross-community basis in order to ensure key decisions. Strand two and strand three rule the relations outside NI. The former acknowledged the need of the Irish dimension for the resolution of the conflict, and it established the creation of a North/South Ministerial Council. In order to safeguard Unionist approval of this point and to avoid this body becoming a step towards a united Ireland, the interdependency between the Council and the NI Assembly was stated (NIO, 1998). The latter ruled the relationship between the British Isles, for which two institutions were established: a British-Irish Council and a British-Irish Intergovernmental Conference.

Apart from those aspects, the Agreement also contained issues related to rights, safeguards and equality of opportunity, by which the participants in the multi-party talks declared their 'commitment to the mutual respect, the civil rights and the religious liberties of everyone in the community' (NIO, 1998). Likewise, more controversial aspects were also covered, including the question of decommissioning. Participants reaffirmed their commitment to the total disarmament of paramilitary organizations within two years and to be monitored by an Independent Commission. In the same way, the British government noted the need for a normalization of security arrangements and practices in NI, which involved, among other things, a reduction in the number and role of the Armed Forces, and the removal of security installations and emergency powers in a way that was consistent with the level of threat existing in NI. The Agreement recognized that the question of policing and justice had been an emotive one in NI, and it therefore provided for the opportunity of a new beginning to policing which would be monitored by an Independent Commission. The criminal justice system in NI was also to be revised, and an accelerated programme for the liberation of prisoners was to be enforced, except for those belonging to organizations which had not declared a complete ceasefire.

There were different reactions to the Agreement, which were partly encouraged by the ambiguity of the language employed in it (Bew and Gillespie, 1999, p. 359; Alonso, 2001, pp. 434–6; Hayes and McAllister, 2001, pp. 75–8, 86–7). This use of language was motivated by the need to respect the rights of both communities equally and to accommodate their different needs and goals. It was soon clear that most Republicans and Nationalists, except dissident groups, supported the Agreement because it represented an advance in meeting their aspirations and demands, even if it failed to deliver a united Ireland. Unionists, on the contrary, were split, with David Trimble (leader of the UUP) as the main pro-Agreement representative claiming that the Union was stronger under the terms of the Agreement. Still, this was not the perception by the whole unionist community, and major disputes among them were based on decommissioning, the early release of prisoners, human rights legislation and safeguards, commissions on policing and criminal justice, and a British commitment to demilitarization.

Regardless of what it might seem, the Agreement did not reduce polarization between the two communities, and a high level of sectarian violence could still be found in NI society[10] (Bryan, 2003, p. 11). This is a consequence of mistrust between the two communities, which arises particularly from issues related to areas such as policing, prisoners and decommissioning. This distrust has determined the process of implementation, with politicians constantly blaming the other for the lack of advance, mainly in those areas of the Agreement characterized by its ambiguity. Therefore, even if NI was no longer involved in a violent overt conflict, it was immersed in a word-dominated one, which mainly relied – both in the social and political arena – on the antagonistic and paradoxical understandings of NI society held by different actors. This makes this geographical location a very interesting area for exploring the relation between discourse and the transmission of conflict.

Post-Agreement Northern Ireland

Clear and highly detailed explanations of post-Agreement NI can be found in Edwards and McGrattan (2010) and Cochrane (2021). Still, it is necessary to present an overview of how the implementation of the Agreement unfolds, with a particular focus on those areas which have been problematic and/or which may be significant for understanding the discursive paradoxical reality that was created in NI at the time.

The Agreement was ratified through a referendum held on 22 May 1998 both in NI and in the Republic of Ireland, after a campaign in which NI was not so much focused on the constitutional issues arising from the Agreement, but on its elements for peace, involving the release of prisoners, decommissioning and the reform of the RUC (Bew and Gillespie, 1999, p. 360). All of these were understood in a different way by each of the four main NI parties. Although the Agreement represented a new beginning for peace, implementing the structures proposed in it has not been easy and several crises have taken place. Decommissioning became an unresolved issue that presented a problem for the implementation of the Agreement, due to the centrality it played on unionist policies, and David Trimble refused to form an administration that included SF until this issue was seriously addressed (Patterson, 2002, p. 338). New multi-party talks were called, and powers were eventually devolved to NI on 2 December 1999. In the meantime, Chris Patten, chair of the Independent Commission on Policing, had released its report, which recommended the disbanding of the police force and its restructuring in order to increase Catholic representation. Other controversial issues in the report included the change of the name from the RUC to the Police Service of Northern Ireland (PSNI), suggestions on the use of symbols and redesigning the uniform (Feeney, 2004, p. 118). The new PSNI came into effect on November 2002.

The issue of weapons was also complicated and triggered negotiations between the International Independent Commission on Decommissioning (IICD) and the IRA in 2000 and 2001. This process was also accompanied by suspensions and restorations of the NI Assembly. Each period of twenty-four-hour suspension in 2001 allowed for a further period of six weeks of talks. This time of dysfunctional devolution (Cochrane, 2021, p. 206) lasted between 1999 and 2002, and it was accompanied by growing (political) distrust and lack of public support to former important political leaders, such as David Trimble. New elections for the Assembly were called in 2003. The outcome was the two parties on the extremes – the DUP and SF – becoming the most voted ones within each community (see Cochrane, 2021 for a more detailed account of events). While at first this looked disastrous for the peace process, SF and the DUP eventually agreed on a way forward which they were determined to maintain and which resulted in a renegotiation of the Agreement in meetings held by the parties in 2006 in St Andrews. The outcome of these talks was a new document – known as the St. Andrews Agreement – which eventually helped restore devolution to NI after new elections to the Assembly were held in March 2007. May 8 was the date established as 'Devolution Day', and it was the first time SF and the DUP did not present political events as the victory of their own community, but rather as a 'joint enterprise for the benefit of all the people in Northern Ireland' (Cochrane, 2021, p. 235). This change in the public unfolding of political events is probably best exemplified by the iconic photograph of Ian Paisley and Martin McGuinness involved in jovial conversation while sitting in a red sofa. This, which would have been unthinkable of in the past, took place in their first official engagement as first and deputy first ministers of NI: the opening of a new IKEA superstore near Belfast. This photograph is arguably a representation of the end of political conflict, which is marked by the existence of devolved institutions.

Devolution could be understood as an indication of the success in the constructive interpretation of the ambiguities of the 1998 Agreement, which have been adapted to fit different meanings by the political elites (Cochrane, 2021, p. 220). However, it did not mean the end of animosity and hatred between the two communities, but rather a different kind of sectarianism (Edwards and McGrattan, 2010, p. 146; Cochrane, 2021, p. 212). Examples of this can be seen in the increasing number of 'peace walls' in NI – that is, walls whose purpose was to separate communities within a city –, problems during the summer marching season or sporadic outbreaks of intercommunal rioting (Burke, 2020).

From devolution to Brexit

Two periods of devolved government can be mentioned in post-Agreement NI: between 2007 and 2011 and between 2011 and 2016. Both meant a period of stability though this went little beyond that as the new Executive failed to 'deliver effective governance that made a positive difference to people's lives' (Cochrane, 2021, p. 237). The lack of effective policies being implemented does not only show a gap between the challenges of governance and traditional political attitudes in NI, but it also reflects the dysfunctional nature of a system which was dominated by the DUP and SF, whose mutual distrust also grew in the second period of devolution, with a marginal involvement from other political parties. The inability of devolved institutions to deliver a clearly set policy agenda can be explained as a consequence of 'the evolution of a political system based on what people would not accept, rather than on what they could unit around' (Cochrane, 2021, p. 243).

The incompatibility in the relationship between the DUP and SF resulted in a new collapse of the NI Assembly after the 2016 election. This shows that even if power sharing has been traditionally implemented to avoid a winner-loser perception in conflictual societies where violence has come to an end, this can only work if political parties are not influenced by their ethnonationalist demands. This new collapse of the Assembly was marked by Martin McGuinness's resignation as deputy first minister in January 2017 and by a subsequent suspension of NI's institutions between 2017 and 2020, as these were dependent on power-sharing agreements.

It shall be noted that the situation in NI cannot only be explained as a consequence of internal political events but also as related to the other developments in the UK, including their decision to leave the EU in June 2016 and the British government's negotiation of the terms of their withdrawal from the EU (i.e. the process known as 'Brexit'). Narratives on how Brexit has affected the 1998 Agreement differ, particularly along some of the main terms of the document, including 'North–South cooperation, choice of identity, cross-border equivalence of rights and the principle of consent' (De Mars et al., 2018, p. 16). Perceptions of Brexit in NI communities mirror their votes, with 85 per cent of the nationalist community voting to remain and a majority of the unionist community wanting to leave. Nationalist political parties saw Brexit as destabilizing the institutions established under the terms of the 1998 Agreement while the majority of Unionists considered it to be just a bump in the peace process (Moltmann, 2017; Cochrane, 2021, pp. 296–305). Besides the effect of Brexit on the deterioration of Anglo-Irish relations, there are two aspects whose (symbolic) importance has to be discussed when looking at the effects of Brexit negotiation: identity and borders (Colfer and Diamond, 2022).

On the one hand, the question of identity shall be mentioned. Under the terms of the 1998 Agreement, people born in NI had the right to dual citizenship, that is, to being British, Irish or both. Legislation following the UK's withdrawal from the EU and changes in the UK's immigration law have not conformed to the terms of the Agreement, as they would require people born in NI, who are British by birth, to renounce their British identity so that they could claim their Irish one (Cochrane, 2021, p. 302). This does not only have consequences on the rights that people could have (De Mars et al., 2018), but it also has a bearing on how people self-identify themselves in relation to their own experience of the conflict (Canavan and Turkoglu, 2023).

On the other hand, the role of borders in the negotiation of what came to be known as a 'hard' or a 'soft' Brexit shall also be accounted for.[11] Borders were particularly important in the case of NI as they did not only refer to the economic measures that would regulate the relation between the EU and the UK, but they also had implications on free movement across the invisible border between the North and the South of the island, which had been demilitarized and removed after the 1998 Agreement (De Mars et al., 2018). Sociopolitical perceptions about Brexit in NI did not only reflect preferences about where to locate the (invisible) border – with Nationalists preferring it in the Irish sea and Unionists advocating for the border to be placed between NI and the Republic of Ireland – but also perceptions about the likely effect that Brexit could have on the maintenance of the constitutional status of NI: a gradual/soft Brexit would less likely affect the political status quo, while a harder Brexit would make it necessary to rethink 'the viability of Northern Ireland's current political geography' (Cochrane, 2021, p. 307). Different possibilities related to the border between NI and the Republic of Ireland were explored (Gadd, 2019, pp. 6–7) and eventually the Northern Ireland Protocol was signed in which a 'backstop' was operationalized. This would guarantee the maintenance of the terms of the 1998 Agreement and of the open border between the Republic of Ireland and NI (Gadd, 2019, p. 8). This perceived threat of a 'new' border lay at the core of a small rise in loyalist intercommunal violence. Likewise, the British government's attempts to renegotiate the NI protocol in spite of the EU offering just some amount of flexibility increased the instability and uncertainty of the future of NI politics (Spisak, 2022).

Northern Ireland after the 1998 Agreement and the impact of Brexit

Groups of people reacted and experienced differently the effects of the 1998 Agreement. As explained above, the political elites successfully exploited the ambiguities of the document so that they managed to go from several political deadlocks to successful power sharing. Changes in the public perception of the role of the SDLP and the UUP – traditionally with a more middle ground political stance – and their position being gradually occupied by the more extreme SF and the DUP helped in this. Political advances in two of the main controversial topics – decommissioning by the paramilitary groups and the policing reform – also played an important part. This political success has been explained by some authors as the exploitation by local NI political elites of the chances that the new political structures in NI offered to 'pursue their long-term goals through political channels' (Edwards and McGrattan, 2010, p. 148).

However, this political success has not been paired by similar moderation and accommodation in society, where sectarian attitudes do not only exist but they are also perpetuated by 'a political culture based on division and confrontation' (Edwards and McGrattan, 2010, p. 148). Examples of this are not only the existence of peace walls, as explained above, but also the public symbols – such as flags, banners or murals – showing support for paramilitary organizations and/or remembering past events. How to deal with commemoration has not only been controversial but also difficult in NI (Cochrane, 2021, pp. 327–32). Questions related to the definition and identification of innocent victims and guilty perpetrators lie at the core of it, though they are combined with lack of consensus on narratives about the past. An example of the complexity of such an issue can be seen in the difficulties for selecting a date on which to commemorate the centenary of NI in 2021, with different possibilities being discussed and justified depending on which historical aspect was to be highlighted. Eventually, centenary commemorations were marked by historical talks, debates and webinars, but an absence of symbolically significant shared events could be observed (Simpson, 2021).

Republican and loyalist paramilitary groups have also gone through different processes after the 1998 Agreement, mainly also because they have been subjected to different demands, among which calls for decommissioning play a key role. While the handing of weapons was to be done by both loyalist and republican groups, it was the IRA[12] that was presented as one of the main actors whose (lack of) action was to influence the political evolution of events (Cochrane, 2021, pp. 206–8). The IRA has also been the object of much media attention, particularly because their actions, including those of dissident groups within Republicanism, have been presented as politically motivated.[13] This is not the case of loyalist paramilitary groups, whose political presence has been lower (as the political parties associated with such groups were not able to capitalize their actions, unlike SF) and whose dissidence has not been necessarily always motivated by political demands. This is, in fact, one of the characteristics of current dissident loyalist groups, whose violence is directed inwards to other members of the community, and whose internal tensions have been understood as presenting a clear degree of incoherence, as some former militants turned to democratic, community-based activism while others 'determined to use the remaining paramilitary infrastructure to criminal ends' (Cochrane, 2021, p. 277).[14] While the end of political violence in NI is frequently associated with the ceasefires and decommissioning, the reality is that there is still violence, as can be seen in the number of attacks or punishments that are reported in the media (Cochrane, 2021, pp. 278–9).

Rioting, particularly within the loyalist community, has increased as a consequence of Brexit. This has also been accompanied by some clashes between communities, and it is at least partly explained by the threat of a border being imposed on the Irish sea between Great Britain and NI as a consequence of the UK's withdrawal from the EU. The loyalist/unionist community perceives some insecurity about the Union, which they feel is being undermined. In spite of a long negotiation of peace, this just shows the fragility of peace in NI and how discourses and political positionings are often adapted to changing circumstances. The fear felt by loyalist paramilitary groups can also be seen in political parties, with the DUP adopting tight politics which prevented the formation of government as a response to SF's electoral majority in 2022. While institutions seemed to work for a while, the sectarian attitudes which were prevalent in society have re-emerged as a consequence of Brexit, with institutions embedding sectarianism in a way which had not been formerly intended (Barry, 2023).

Northern Irish communities and political stance

The historical description of sociopolitical events in this chapter shows a number of patterns that are worth emphasizing. Among them is the contradiction between peace arriving in NI and it being based on 'an uneasy acceptance of the importance of the constitutional and communal divide' (Edwards and McGrattan, 2010, p. 149). As such, political life in NI is still affected by people's perceptions of the past, political mistrust and a 'struggle for ethnic supremacy' (Patterson, 2002, p. 343). The NI conflict is thus characterized by the 'apartheid-style separation of the Catholic and Protestant communities' (Cochrane, 2021, p. 213), with people sometimes living apart (in different areas of the cities) and communities being physically bound to different locations.

The reference to two communities aligns with the most common explanation of the conflict as involving two 'opposing sides', which are usually designated to be 'Protestant-Catholic', 'Unionist-Nationalist', 'Loyalist-Republican' or 'British-Irish' (Edwards and McGrattan, 2010, p. 124). These paired labels show the complexity of the NI conflict and its frequent understanding as being related to '(a) religious differences, (b) inter-communal or ideological divisions, (c) nationalist antagonism, or (d) some combination' of those things (Edwards and McGrattan, 2010, p. 124). These labels also reflect an ethno-nationalist understanding of the conflict[15] which led to violence due to various historical conditions. As such, the paired labels mentioned above show that the conflict in NI is the consequence of a complex set of interlocked and confused problems (Dunn, 1995, p. 7). It could be argued that the main reason for the conflict is a question of national allegiance, but that is intermingled with other aspects such as religion, economy, politics or the above-explained historical events. Therefore, the NI conflict is not a religious war – as it has frequently been portrayed in the international media – but the consequence of the difference in the perceptions of two communities.

In order to understand the importance of history of NI, in this chapter I have tried to focus on those events that have promoted specific feelings and allegiances in both of the NI communities. Besides, some of the historical events mentioned have become myths which frequently intermingle with political and religious backgrounds in a way that helps in shaping 'imagined communities'. These communities are limited by perceived boundaries and are based on a comradeship relationship between its members (Anderson, 1991, p. 7) which is frequently antagonistic to the connection with members of other communities. Although many features can be employed to describe the two NI communities, in this book I will focus on their political allegiances, as this may help in understanding the ideological position of the uttering politicians in the analysis chapters. Likewise, it allows me to select a terminology to refer to members of those communities, which will be from here on Nationalists or Republicans and Unionists or Loyalist.

A broad definition of Unionism is based on its constitutional aspiration of NI remaining as part of the Union with Great Britain, 'constituting the United Kingdom of Great Britain and Northern Ireland' (Dunn and Dawson, 2000, p. 288). Aughey (1996, p. 31) places the origin of this movement at the Home Rule crisis, with the majority of Irish Protestants trying to defend the Union of Great Britain and Ireland. This defence was more acute in the nine counties of Ulster, which were perceived as a distinct entity because of their economic prosperity. Over time, some tensions have been found in the unionist community, reflecting two main types of Unionism: first, Ulster loyalism, based on the connection between politics and religion and loyalty to the Crown. The term Loyalism has also been frequently used to refer to the most extremist position within Unionism, and it is often associated with paramilitary actions. Some of its features can be observed in the DUP, although at times they may also be strategically employed by the UUP. On the other hand, 'Ulster British' believe that the broad community to which they belong is Great Britain, with NI being merely a region of it. The most important aspects of the Union are based on the economic and liberal values it may promote, and not so much on the religious loyalty to the Crown. Such beliefs are mostly exemplified by the UUP.

Two basic ideas can be found at the heart of Unionism (Aughey, 1996, pp. 34–7): the Britishness of the NI population, which should be durable, and their fear of losing this status, which has motivated their constant perception of being under threat to the nationalist community. This is related to the unionist siege mentality. Many unionist parties can be found – namely the UUP, the DUP, the UKUP and the Northern Ireland Unionist Party (NIUP). However, references in the analysis chapters will be made mostly to two of them – the DUP and the UUP – as they are not only the most prominent ones in NI politics but also the ones that show better changes in their discourses and political actions.

The broad aspiration of Nationalism relies on their goal of a united Ireland with the right to self-determination, something which can be traced back to the Home Rule crisis. Nevertheless, a differentiation can be established between Northern nationalists, who were worried by the strength of Ulster unionism and the question of partition, and Irish nationalists in the South of the island. The goal of achieving a united Ireland determines some of the characteristics of the nationalist community, among which their sense of Irishness needs to be emphasized. Besides, the historical and political features that have characterized the existence of Northern nationalists have contributed to the creation of an alienation mentality, that is, they felt discriminated by the NI government and sometimes they still allude to that. That can be linked to the 'grievance mentality' (O'Connor, 1993, p. 93) of the Catholic community, which can be, in turn, connected to the myth of martyrdom and the subsequent portrayal of this community as victims of the other. Unlike in Unionism, religious affiliation is not as important in the building of the nationalist identity (Morrow, 1995, pp. 162–3), mainly because they are not as divided and they do not need an 'external' aspect to define their identity, and because there is no specific figure representing the Catholic Church together with the idea of Irishness – as it is the case of the British monarchy for Unionism.

There is less division within the nationalist parties than within the unionist ones, with one main party representing each of the trends within Nationalism. Constitutional nationalism – or the political philosophy that 'aims at the creation of a united Ireland by non-violent constitutional methods' (Dunn and Dawson, 2000, p. 58) – is typified by the Social Democratic and Labour Party (SDLP), while (Provisional) Sinn Féin (SF) is the major voice of Republicanism – or the political philosophy which also has the objective of a united Ireland although it is 'more likely to accept the need for violence' (Dunn and Dawson, 2000, p. 233).

Republicanism is also often associated with paramilitary groups, among which the IRA has to be highlighted.

Many of the elements that characterize each of these communities will be alluded to in the analysis of the different construal operations. When necessary, references will be made to this chapter for clarification purposes. A short chronology of events in post-agreement NI has been included in the appendix so as to help in identifying political events and the relation with the involved communities.

4

Gestalt and structural configuration

What do we mean by gestalt?

Text analysis for the cognitive ability of gestalt implies exploring how entities in a scene are conceptualized at the most basic level of structural configuration (Croft and Cruse, 2004, p. 63). As noted by Hart (2025, p. 42), the structural configuration of an event 'define[s] its basic organisational properties taking in such matters as topology, sequence and causation'. The analysis of gestalt properties is based on gestalt psychology, which argues that the human mind construes a unitary 'complex object from fragmented perceptual sensations' (Croft and Cruse, 2004, p. 63). The importance of gestalt psychology cannot be overlooked when exploring how CL can inform political discourse analysis, as many of its principles have guided the development of this theoretical framework. The following gestalt principles thus provide a structure that constrains our experience, and they certainly influence how we (discursively) perceive reality (Evans and Green, 2006, pp. 65–8):

- *Human perception segregates a scene into a figure and a ground.* The figure refers to the entity that is dominant against a background, which would be the ground. This clearly relates to the cognitive ability of attention, as will be explained in Chapter 5.
- *Human perception is dominated by a principle of proximity.* Elements in a scene that are closer will be seen as belonging together in a group (Evans and Green, 2006, p. 66). Linguistically this can be realized, for example, via the use of collective nouns or individual nouns, with each of these types rendering a different configuration of a scene. This can be seen when comparing the effect of using 'jury' or 'juror', both referring to the entity involved in a court of law. Because it is also prominently related to the cognitive ability of attention, linguistic choices related to this configurational property are discussed in Chapter 5.

- *Human perception is dominated by a principle of similarity.* Entities which share defining characteristics are perceived as belonging together in one group. This principle of similarity is what underlies processes of categorization (see Chapter 6) and the classification of social actors via shared traits (Van Leeuwen, 1996; Koller, 2012). Examples of linguistic choices would be referring to different groups of individuals as 'the immigrants' or 'women'. The structural configuration of such entities depends on the features which are profiled, that is, their foreign or female traits in these examples.
- *Human perception is dominated by a closure and continuity principle.* The human mind prefers to see complete and continuous images and, thus, it would fill any kind of missing information via inferential processes. These are determined by the experiential knowledge of both utterer and audience. As will be shown below, closure and continuity determine how particular structures are processed because missing information is inferentially filled by participants in a communicative situation so as to comply with the internal structure of gestalts (Johnson, 1987, p. 44). For example, when perceiving a container, we will complete information related to the inside, outside and boundaries, regardless of whether these are explicitly conveyed in discourse. Likewise, a path is perceived as a continuous entity regardless of whether it is blocked by other entities and/or whether it is, in fact, made of multiple components. These aspects will feature prominently in the remainder of this chapter.
- *Human minds tend to perceive small entities more readily.* Because of our experiential understanding of figure and ground, we tend to perceive small entities more easily as the figure against the larger (back)ground upon which they are profiled. In my view, this explains why in spite of gestalts being unitary and coherent meaning structures (Johnson, 1987, p. 41), certain elements of the gestalt are to be profiled. As will be shown below, what is foregrounded can be linguistically indicated.

Linguistic gestalts can be defined as the operational structures that are applied when cognitively processing language. Like categories (in Chapters 5 and 6), these basic structures are unitary and based on a distinction between prototypical and non-prototypical properties. The components of a gestalt have internal relations with other components which also influence how they are to be interpreted. Such interpretation can also be shaped via external relations to other gestalts, which may be found in multiple semiotic modalities (Lakoff and Johnson,

1980; Cienki, 2007). Because they are basic conceptual structures, gestalts are also inextricably linked to concepts and cues covered in the three other analysis chapters of this book. While in this chapter the basic configuration of entities and processes is covered, the three remaining chapters can be understood as anchoring these structures to spatial and temporal frames of reference or as more detailed (and often specific) elaborations of these basic structures.

The notion of gestalt is useful for understanding the abstract relationship between linguistic meaning and human cognition. As mentioned in Chapter 3, meaning is organized around multiple levels of cognition which are determined by different factors that can be placed along a knowledge and experiential continuum. As such, when used in context, linguistic meaning presupposes the existence of a basic conceptual structure, part of which depends on very basic schemas derived from our bodily experience, which also form more developed, often figurative extensions or elaborations of meaning (Johnson, 1987, p. 4; Langacker, 2008, p. 4). Such basic structural configuration is embodied and lies at the core of more developed, frequently figurative, extensions and elaborations of meaning. Still, such basic structural configuration is not objective: it is a mental representation that is constructed by our cognitive apparatus when processing a number of linguistic cues, among other modes (Johnson, 1987; Evans and Green, 2006, pp. 67–8). As noted by Johnson (1987, p. 5), the conceptual and propositional meaning of an utterance 'is possible only by virtue of a complex web of nonpropositional schematic structures that emerge from our bodily experience'.

This chapter thus seeks to shed light on how the selection of a particular schema defines the basic organizational properties of discursive representations of an event. These structural configuration strategies can be related to three main aspects, as will be explained below: topology (i.e. the defining properties of configuration), sequence and causation (Hart, 2025). All these aspects are inextricably linked to schematization.

Gestalts and image schemas

As mentioned above, the basic categorization – and resulting structural configuration – that characterizes gestalts reflects experiential and embodied cognition. It is defined via schemas, that is, 'the kinds of imaginative structures required for the definition of concepts' (Lakoff, 1987a, p. 135) and the conceptual configuration of events. Image schemas, unlike more elaborated structures such as categorization or metaphor (in Chapters 5 and 6), 'are not rich, concrete images or mental pictures' (Johnson, 1987, p. 23).[1] Rather, they are general, abstract preconceptual structures. They can be of use for identifying patterns of basic elements which can help us organize and understand our experience and thus they are instrumental for the construction of meaning (Johnson, 1987, p. 28; Chilton, 1996, p. 48). Image schemas mostly result from our interaction with the physical environment, and they are predominantly spatial. For example, an image schema can be vertical, indicating a range of movement UP and DOWN but it might also indicate static CONTAINMENT.

Multiple attempts have been made at classifying image schemas (Johnson, 1987; Lakoff and Johnson, 1980; Talmy, 2000b; see Cienki, 1997 and Hampe, 2008 for more detailed descriptions). A close look at those studies shows that image schemas can be broadly described as being related to one of the following spatial constructions: (1) orientation (e.g. UP-DOWN; CENTRE-PERIPHERY), (2) containment (e.g. IN-OUT, SURFACE), (3) locomotion (e.g. SOURCE-PATH-GOAL) or (4) force (e.g. BLOCKAGE, COMPULSION). These types of construction are not exhaustive, nor do they function in isolation. For example, the idea of CONTAINMENT can also be related to the conceptual structuring of a position within that container as being in the centre or the periphery.

Understanding how image schemas are embedded in language is of particular importance for the explanation of ethnonationalist conflict. As noted by Storey (2001), territoriality, nationhood and ethnicity can be explained via the relation between people and a territory, understood as an area of bounded space. These concepts are of particular importance in NI (as shown in Chapter 3), where disputes originate from a claiming of space. This establishes a relation between the NI area and its surrounding national spaces (i.e. the Republic of Ireland and the UK). Such claiming of space is linked to other elements such as religion or cultural values. Still, it is the structural configuration of space that determines how relations between inhabitants in these three areas unfold. It can be argued that political discourse (in NI) is, by definition, spatial, just like an image schema and that any instance of discourse uttered in this land evokes a basic spatial configuration which is specified, extended and perspectivized via other construal operations, as will be also shown in the following chapters.

Given the spatial nature of image schemas, two properties are of importance when exploring how uncovering the basic structural configuration that permeates discourse can help in explaining the discursive construction of conflictual relations. First, 'image schemas can be construed as dynamic or static scenes, i.e. as processes or states' (Oakley, 2007, p. 261). This is important if we consider, for example, construals related to the CONTAINMENT image schema, in which we can profile either the static existence of a container or the dynamic action of moving in or out. While the structural configuration is the same, a semantic distinction is inferentially made. These differences in how the world is viewed (and what is foregrounded or silenced) lie, for example, at the core of nominalization, as explained in Chapter 5. While the word 'dynamic' mostly implies the possibility of construing events as actions or static situations, it shall be noted that it also means that image schemas can take on multiple instantiations in different contexts (Hart, 2025). As such, dissonance in the construal of an image schema may result in conflictual representations.

Second, image schemas exhibit a bipolar property 'of conferring positive or negative associations' (Oakley, 2007, p. 261). This bipolar property is related to axiological values, which are not explicit but embodied. For example, we tend to understand BALANCE as positive/plus and IMBALANCE as negative/minus. Similar associations can be observed in orientational schemas, including the symbiosis of UP or CENTRE with positive/plus and DOWN or PERIPHERY with negative/minus. Such associations of image schemas with positive or negative traits can shed light on how axiological concepts such as 'good' or 'true' are prototypically construed. However, as mentioned above, the activation of axiological entailments is contextual and may vary depending on which values are shared by a community. This can be seen if we compare, for example, binary and non-binary understandings of gender and how they relate to the idea of being inside a container, as discussed in Filardo-Llamas and Roldán-García (2024). The relation between image schemas and axiological values is also closely linked to the cognitive ability of perspective and to DST (Chilton, 2004, 2014) and proximization (Cap, 2013a), as applied in political discourse analysis (see Chapter 7).

Previous studies applying image schema to the analysis of political discourse have focused on three different types of schemas (see Chilton, 1996, pp. 50–5 for a description of their basic conceptualizing features): (1) the CONTAINER image schema – which foregrounds the existence of an interior, a boundary and an exterior – has been the focus of studies on international relations and political discourse (Chilton, 1996, 2017; Hampl, 2021) and discourses related to immigration (Hart, 2010, 2011c); (2) the PATH image schema – which foregrounds the experience of motion and frequently appears in combination with CONTAINER ones (Chilton, 2017) – is also frequent in political discourse, mostly with the aim of justifying political policies or dealing with counterterrorism (Chilton, 1996; Hampl, 2021); and (3) the FORCE image schema (or force dynamics) – which implies the physical experience of pressures and resistances, that is, forces which may be exerted and/or received – has been studied both in relation to discourses related to defence and war justification or prevention (Chilton, 1996; Oakley, 2005) and in relation to immigration (Hart, 2011a; Romano, 2019; Romano and Porto, 2021). Other image schemas have also been identified and have featured, with less prominence, in political discourse studies, such as LINK schemas – stemming from the experience of attachment between entities, UP-DOWN schemas – mostly when dealing with supremacy, sovereignty and control, and CENTRE-PERIPHERY schemas – which are of use to refer to the role of states and groupings of states. A close connection can be observed between the three main image schemas and Hart's (2025) explanation of the relation between structural configuration strategies and topology, sequence and causation.

The topological construction of space: CONTAINMENT

Exploring the topological construction of a scene requires acknowledging that our conceptual structure is governed by image schemas. Likewise, identifying the topological nature of how space is discursively constructed means exploring its inherent conceptual structure (Evans and Green, 2006, p. 302). As such, I believe that the topological construction of a scene implicitly requires it being perceived as an entity involved in a process, and that its structure is experientially construed. This idea of entity correlates, in my view, with attempts at describing some stative basic conceptual structures such as the OBJECT schema (Santibañez, 2002) or the CONTAINER image schema (Johnson, 1987; Lakoff, 1987b; Cienki, 1997; Talmy, 2000a, 2000b). The experiential and embodied construction of image schemas, for example, CONTAINMENT, shapes our acts of understanding and knowing, and such structural configuration can help participants in a communicative act to make sense of different aspects of the (political) experience. Even if the analysis of image schemas has been mostly grounded on the identification of patterns of structure, it can be argued that a qualitative dimension should also be included when exploring image schemas. The meaning of a basic structure, such as the CONTAINER one, can also be determined by how each individual experiences it. As explained by Johnson (2008, p. 28), different feelings may emerge from being held tightly in someone's arms or from being constrained inside a small room. Likewise, I believe that contextual parameters related to perceived relations between social actors might also influence such an experience and its associated meaning (it would be different for a child, for example, to be held tightly in their parents' arms or in an unknown person's arms). The basic structure of the CONTAINER image schema will be explained below although further co(n) textual parameters will be significant when exploring how such image schemas structure thinking in political discourse.

The CONTAINER image schema implies the existence of three key elements, which may also interact with other image schemas (Lakoff, 1987b, p. 272; Chilton, 1996, pp. 50–1). These three elements determine the basic structural elements of a container: an INTERIOR, a BOUNDARY surface and an EXTERIOR. This basic configuration interacts with other schemas, as entities can be static or move IN or OUT of the container (thus establishing a relation with the PATH schema), they can be located at the CENTRE or PERIPHERY when being inside (or outside), and the BOUNDARY may be open or closed (thus relating to the closure principle explained above). Interactions with other image schemas could also determine, for example, the actual or perceived size of the container and/or whether these are presented as uniplex (single) or multiplex (fragmented) entities, that is, as being a whole or composed of other containers, for example. All these combined possibilities are linked to how we structure events and show a complex picture emerging from very basic conceptual possibilities, as explained above. Likewise, the spatial CONTAINER image schema is necessary for understanding more elaborated instantiations of it via categorization, or metaphorical extensions based on spatial configurations (as explained in Chapters 5 and 6) or proximal-distant relations established via proximization (as explained in Chapter 7). The structural configuration of CONTAINER schemas can be seen in Figure 4.1.

The analysis of the CONTAINER schema can be related to a number of linguistic cues (see Oakley, 2007 for a brief overview). However, given its pervasiveness, it is complicated to provide an exhaustive list of lexico-grammatical realizations. Following Oakley (2007, p. 249), any linguistic cue can trigger conceptual structures (Kövecses, 2020), which can be placed in a continuum ranging from schematicity to specificity (as shown, for example, in the organization of the analytic chapters in this book). Still, some linguistic instantiations of the CONTAINER schema can be mentioned, including, for example, the use of some transitive verbs (such as 'give') or verbs of movement ('enter' or 'put'). Of particular interest for the analysis of how containers are construed are prepositions, as they can index not only physical spaces but also metaphorical projections of them (as shown when referring to time) or even abstract relations such as emotions (see Radden and Dirven, 2007, and Table 4.1). Sentences [1] to [3] exemplify uses of the CONTAINER schema to talk about space, time and emotions.

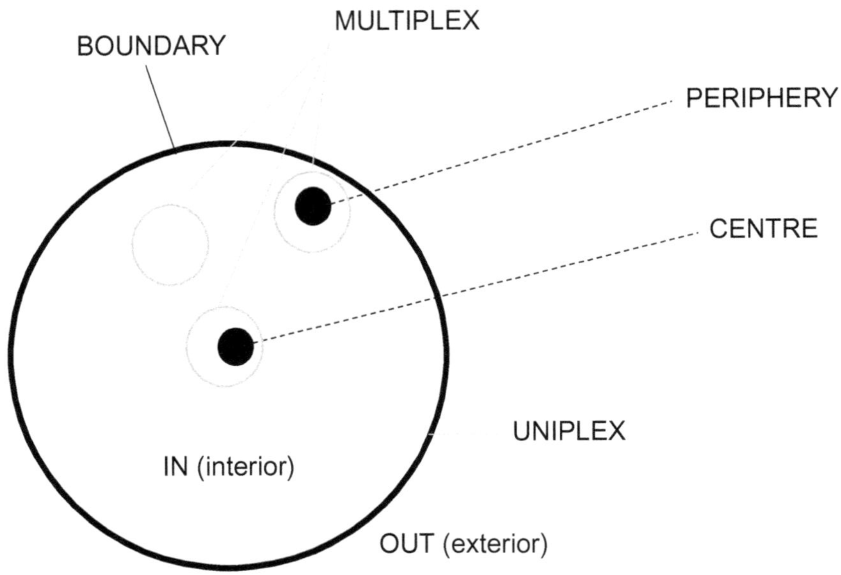

Figure 4.1 Structural components of the CONTAINER image schema.

Table 4.1 Prepositions in English and Image Schemas (based on Radden and Dirven, 2007, p. 310)

	Stative location	**Dynamic motion**		
Dimensions	**PLACE**	**SOURCE**	**GOAL**	**PATH**
0-dimensional POINT	*at, by, near, close to, with*	*from, away from*	*to, at, for, towards*	*by, past, via*
1- and 2-dimensional LINE/SURFACE	*on, on top of*	*off (of)*	*on(to), against*	*along, about, around*
3-dimensional CONTAINMENT	*in, within, inside, between, among*	*out of, outside of*	*in(to)*	*through, throughout*

[1] They jumped **into** the water.[2]

[2] They partied **throughout** the night.

[3] They live **in** fear.

The three sentences above activate the conceptual structure of a concrete or abstract CONTAINER when construing 'water', 'night' or 'fear'. Differences, however, can be seen in whether the container is bounded or not (e.g. 'in' vs 'throughout') or whether transformations are made so that an apparently static location ('water') is presented as the destination (GOAL) of movement. This is possible not only because image schemas can be transformed (Lakoff, 1987b, p. 442; Oakley, 2007, p. 217) but also because the conceptual structure of a container includes three dimensions: length, width and depth. A summary of how CONTAINMENT may be construed by prepositions in English and how this relates with the SOURCE-PATH-GOAL schema can be found in Table 4.1. In this table, other elements of the CONTAINER schema (e.g. SURFACE or LINE) also feature prominently. The PATH-GOAL-SCHEMA will be studied in more detail in the next two sections of this chapter.

The ideological effect of construing events as a CONTAINER has been previously explored. Two studies are of particular importance here. First, Chilton's (1996) study of security metaphors explores how conceptualizing international relations as a container presents a particular view of reality. Because of its three structural elements (and also because image schemas are bipolar in nature), containers involve separation and differentiation between what is inside and outside. This may be useful to impose restrictions and limitations to particular international relations. Because they are territorial in nature, nations can be construed as containers, that is, as bounded spaces (see Storey, 2001 for a more detailed discussion). As such, it is possible to legitimize defence or shielding policies or restriction of movement between nations depending on the elements of the bounded space which are highlighted. Likewise, it is possible to construe groupings of nations and states as being unitary or separated, or as being core (central) members of such group. This can be seen, for instance, in discursive constructions of the EU and how the existence of this entity is legitimized at times of crises (Filardo-Llamas and Perales García, 2022; Zappettini and Bennett, 2022). For example, the headlines reproduced in [4], [5] and [6] present EU(rope) in their own way: as a CONTAINER with/out borders (i.e. BOUNDARY being profiled), as a uniplex (e.g. in [4]) or as a multiplex entity (in [5]) depending on whether its constitutive elements (nations) are linguistically foregrounded, and in opposition to other (national) entities which are also construed as CONTAINERS (in [6]). These sentences show how not only (supra)national entities are presented as CONTAINERS but also that elements of the larger CONTAINER can be singled out and that internal relations can be established between those smaller (national) CONTAINERS embedded inside the larger (supranational) one. This kind of construal determines how entities are publicly perceived and the kind of (conflictual) relations they may be involved in.

[4] Covid: How is **Europe** lifting lockdown restrictions? (*BBC News*, 25 June 2021)
[5] Coronavirus: **EU** condemns Trump travel ban on 26 **European countries** (*BBC News*, 12 March 2020)
[6] Coronavirus: **North-South divide** clouds key **EU** meeting (*BBC News*, 8 April 2020)

Similar arguments can be found in another study, by Begoña Núñez-Perucha (2011), in which she explores the usefulness of the CONTAINER schema for explaining the construction of identities and how these are determined by a set of ideological beliefs. By focusing on the conceptualization of society as a CONTAINER, she shows how different social groups (men and women in her study) are construed as belonging to different types of smaller CONTAINERS – public or private – embedded within the broader CONTAINER that is society. Her study opens the way for two types of explorations of the CONTAINER image schema: first, the identification of diachronic changes in how ideological containers are construed at different times in history (i.e. the different waves in the feminist movement). Second, the analysis of the interaction between the CONTAINER image schema and other schemas (e.g. FORCE, BLOCKAGE, COMPULSION, VERTICALITY) in the construction of different discourse worlds. Similar findings about the conceptualization of identity labels as (abstract) CONTAINERS can be found in Filardo-Llamas and Roldán-García (2024). In their study of gender-identity labels in Tumblr, they show that BOUNDARIES of CONTAINERS can be challenged (e.g. shifted or opened) so as to account for multiple identities. All in all, these studies confirm the importance of exploring the CONTAINER schemas in CDS. Further arguments about how CONTAINER schemas relate to the maintenance or resolution of conflictual relations will be provided in the case studies included in this chapter.

Sequencing political life: The MOTION event

Political events and situations are a key component of political life, and it is necessary to identify how they are construed in order to reveal potential conflict situations. Events and situations shall be understood as a bipolar opposition, with the former foregrounding the dynamic nature of the action and the latter its stative features (Radden and Dirven, 2007). The structure of an event is complex, and it mostly 'consists of constituent events in a particular relationship' (Talmy, 2000b, p. 10). Two types of schemas (i.e. structural configurations) can be identified to explain the structure of an event: MOTION schemas (whose emphasis can be related to sequencing effects) and force dynamics (mostly related to causation, as will be explained in the following section).

MOTION schemas can be defined as 'a theme's change along a trajectory from a place at one time to another place at a later time' (Radden and Dirven, 2007, p. 278). This type of structural configuration involves a conceptual relation between space and time which tends to be related to directionality. As such, MOTION tends to activate three structural elements: a starting point (usually called origin, or SOURCE), a PATH and an endpoint (destination or GOAL) (Chilton, 1996, p. 52; Radden and Dirven, 2007, p. 278). These three elements, also known as the SOURCE-PATH-GOAL schema, show the focus of the motion trajectory followed by a moving entity, which can be placed on the initial, medial or final moment. It shall also be noted that the SOURCE and GOAL elements can also be construed as CONTAINERS, and that the emphasis can be on such positions or on the moving entities. The three elements in the SOURCE-PATH-GOAL schema form the Figure Event, that is, the action or situation which is profiled in discourse. Such Figure is usually constrained by relating it to a Ground, that is, the location against which motion takes place (Talmy, 2000b; Hart, 2025).[3] These basic structural elements are summarized in Figure 4.2.[4] SOURCE, PATH and GOAL – as the basic structural elements – frequently interact with two further elements that may also influence how reality is represented: MANNER AND CAUSE (Talmy, 2000b, p. 9; Hart, 2025). MANNER, which is frequently conflated with motion in verbs in English, tends to indicate the type of movement that is performed; CAUSE refers to the profiling or silencing of the agent initiating the moving action and is related to FORCE schemas, as will be explained in the next section.

While it is difficult to propose a one-to-one correspondence between lexico-grammatical choices and instantiations of the MOTION schema, some

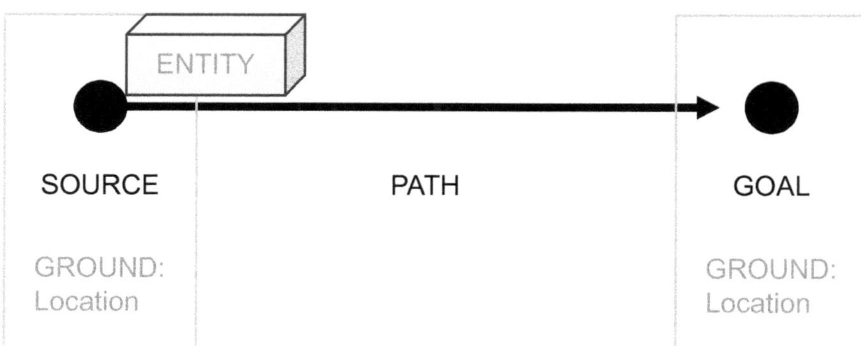

Figure 4.2 Structural elements of the SOURCE-PATH-GOAL schema (MOTION event).

patterns can be identified. These can be grouped along the different elements that compose the MOTION schema: first, those elements in the construction of a sentence that indicate a change of location (i.e. verbs indicating a physical movement) or that indicate a (metaphorical) change of state. It can be argued that these lexical choices signal a physical or abstract change in the defining properties of the source, which is presented as the profiled entity undergoing the motion. Variation can also be observed in how such properties are discursively constructed, with the focus being placed on the actual motion itself – by selecting an inchoative verb, that is, one that expresses the beginning (as in [7]) – or on the resulting state (as in [8]). As noted by Radden and Dirven (2007, p. 275), this is possible in English because 'many inchoative verbs are related to an adjective denoting the resultant state'. This can be observed in examples [7] and [8]. These sentences have been constructed for explanation purposes but are based on previous studies in which the MOTION event is applied to the study of immigration discourse (see Hart, 2025). In these sentences, the MOTION schema interacts with a construal of the source as a container. Manner can also interact and profile different properties of change (e.g. abrupt change, gradual, expected, controlled or uncontrolled), depending on the type of motion verb used or on the use of adverbials of manner (Radden and Dirven, 2007).

[7] The country **opened** its borders to refugees and asylum seekers.
[8] The country **is open** to refugees and asylum seekers.

Second, verbal choices can also be related to the representation of the moving entity as animate and human, and thus as having intentionality, or as a steady process which is inherently unchangeable (Radden and Dirven, 2007, p. 275). This distinction relates to the construal of motion as being human and agentive (regardless of whether it is caused by the self or the others), or as object and non-agentive. The distinction between agentive and non-agentive motion can be seen in sentences [9] and [10], which are explicitly created for explanation purposes to show structural configuration differences. These sentences are based on previous studies on immigration discourse (Hart, 2025) and descriptions of MOTION events in English (Radden and Dirven, 2007). In [9] movement is presented as if it were a natural, uncontrolled, phenomenon (similar to the one we can identify in weather forecasts) by using the verb 'pour'. In contrast, in [10] not only the agentivity of the moving entity is foregrounded but also the manner in which this movement is done (quietly and avoiding being seen).[5] As such, different construals of the PATH are activated by the two verbal choices.

[9] Migrants kept **pouring** into the country.
[10] Migrants are **sneaking** into the country.

Finally, MOTION events can be construed as foregrounding the GOAL (LANDMARK in Langacker's terminology (2008, p. 394)). Such landmark status can be conferred not only on physical locations but also on beneficiaries (as will be shown when exploring the relations between image schemas and causation), or on instruments. Likewise, the emphasis on the final stage of the motion trajectory can be observed when the focus is on the experiencer, defined as 'the participant that undergoes an emotional, perceptual or mental experience' (Radden and Dirven, 2007, p. 269). MOTION events can foreground the constructional properties of a given GOAL (destination), for example, in how borders of a country are perceived (either as being completely closed or as having a small opening in the boundary of an image-schematic CONTAINER). Variations in how MOTION is construed may be related, for example, to the preposition which indicates the destination of such movement or to the types of verbs used. As explained by Hart (2025), the use of the verb 'enter' signals entrance into a CONTAINER whose BOUNDARY is not closed. This can be contrasted with verbs like 'smash', which construes the landmark as a sealed CONTAINER whose BOUNDARY is broken with violence. The examples included in this section show the applicability of MOTION events to the study of how immigration is portrayed in discourse (Hart, 2010, 2011b, 2011c, 2025; Romano, 2019; Romano and Porto, 2021). Other studies have proved that MOTION and PATH schemas are also useful to explain separatist movements, such as Brexit (Martín de La Rosa, 2023) or counterterrorism discourse (Hampl, 2020, 2021). These authors present MOTION events as comprising not only the actual MOTION – that is, the image schema through which policies and political actions can be structured as being in an initial, medial or final stage – but also force dynamics – as the image schema through which agency (and causation) can be profiled. These two structural configurations are inextricably linked, as it is also the case of the sensory-motor experiences upon which they are based. Causation will be explained in the next section of this chapter.

Expressing causation: Force dynamics

As mentioned in the Introduction, conflicts can be explained as resulting from a 'binary opposition' (Van Dijk, 1998; Janicki, 2015; Filardo-Llamas and Morales-López, 2021) between (members of) an ingroup and an outgroup.

These binary oppositions can be discursively represented and constructed. Among the strategies used to do so, force dynamics influences reasoning about political processes, and it can conceptually structure a political situation. Force dynamics can be understood as an image schema explaining how a (human) agent initiates an action and directs it towards a GOAL (Radden and Dirven, 2007, p. 284). As such, they reflect a physical experience of FORCES, which can be pressures and resistances, and which can be, in turn, exerted and received (Chilton, 1996, p. 53). We can thus talk about the dynamics of forces and counterforces (Oakley, 2005, p. 8) which are prevalent in political discourse. This can be particularly useful to explain how we understand abstract social processes, such as causation and prevention, and epistemic and deontic positions, such as necessity, possibility, permission and prohibition. In this chapter, only causation will be analysed. While also related to force dynamics, it can be argued that epistemicity and deonticity (i.e. certainty and compulsion) are more complex reasoning process, and they are related to authorial sources of knowledge and inferential reasoning based on axiological values. This explains why they are covered in Chapter 7 in relation to the cognitive ability of perspectivization.

Similar to other image schemas, force dynamics is a bipolar construction. It requires two basic elements: an agonist (i.e. an active element exercising a force) and an antagonist (or the entity receiving such force). These elements are involved in four basic types of relationships between forces: (1) *causative pattern*: the antagonist 'moves' because of the force impelled by the agonist; (2) *weak despite pattern:* the antagonist 'rests' in spite of the force impelled by the agonist; (3) *strong despite pattern:* the agonist 'keeps moving' in spite of the existence of an obstacle; and (4) *causative hindrance:* the agonist is 'blocked' from moving further by another force (Chilton, 1996; Talmy, 2000a, 2000b; Oakley, 2005). Figure 4.3 presents diagrammatically such four types of force dynamics. Each circle indicates an entity (agonist/antagonist) and force relations are indicated with arrows (indicating FORCE being executed) or a small line on top of the circle (indicating lack of movement). This representation is adapted from a combination of Talmy's (2000a) representational model and the diagrams proposed by Hedblom et al. (2024).

The diagrammatic representation in Figure 4.3 shows two things about force dynamics: first, it stresses its bipolar nature, which clearly justifies its usefulness for explaining how social groups interact (see also Johnson, 1987, p. 43). As noted by Talmy (2000b, p. 438), an analogy can be established between physical FORCES and social FORCES, thus referring to a process he calls 'sociodynamics'.

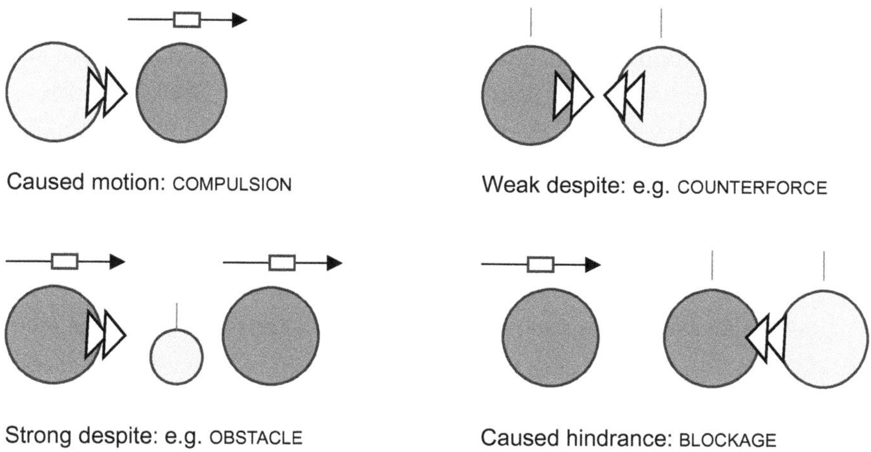

Figure 4.3 Force dynamics patterns.

Because of this, force dynamics allows us to explain how two FORCES interact with each other in the social realm – as seen in the use of the word 'pressure' when referring to social or peer pressure (Talmy, 2000b, p. 438) – or in the political one – for instance as observed in the use of words such as 'defend' or 'attack' (Chilton, 1996, p. 54). Likewise, the existence of two FORCES is of use for explaining which entity is the source and which is the target of such force, and also how this relates to causality (Johnson, 1987).

Second, there are multiple instantiations of the FORCE image schemas which reflect different types of interaction between such FORCES. Johnson (1987, pp. 43–8) identifies seven types of FORCES: COMPULSION (an entity is moved by external forces which cannot be resisted), BLOCKAGE (the existence of obstacles that block or resist a moving force), COUNTERFORCE (two equally strong forces which collide), DIVERSION (when a force vector is diverted as a consequence of the interaction with other forces), REMOVAL OF RESTRAINT (removing an obstacle, thus rendering a path open for the movement caused by a force), ENABLEMENT (an internal force compelling an entity to perform an action) and ATTRACTION (when there is some kind of physical or abstract gravitation towards another entity). These seven patterns can both foreground different aspects of reality and intensify the emotional impact of the discourses in which they appear (Talmy, 2000b; Martín de La Rosa, 2023).

While the analysis of image schemas is frequently related to the study of metaphor (Johnson, 1987), differences can be observed between them (see also Chapter 6). Via metaphors we obtain a more nuanced view of reality, frequently also related to evaluative purposes. FORCE image schemas, on the contrary, shed light on the type of (power) relations which can be established between different entities. The usefulness of analysing force dynamics in political discourse and CDS has already been tested (Chilton, 1996, 2010; Oakley, 2005; Hart, 2011a, 2025; Romano, 2019; Hampl, 2020, 2021; Martín de La Rosa, 2023). These studies have shown that identifying how FORCES interact in discourse can shed light on how political arguments are frequently construed as oppositional between two forces. As shown by Oakley (2005), different force dynamic patterns underlie what could be considered 'defensive' or 'offensive ideologies'. Likewise, different FORCES can be used to construe relations between countries. This can be seen, for example, in sentences [11] to [13], which have been taken from a speech given by Ursula Von der Leyen to the European Parliament on 9 October 2024.[6]

[11] Throughout the summer, hundreds of missiles **have rained** on Ukraine's energy infrastructure.

[12] There is no European language in which peace is synonymous with **surrender**. And sovereignty is synonymous with **occupation**.

[13] We must continue to **empower** Ukraine's **resistance** with political, financial and military support.

In these examples (inter)national relations are conceptualized via FORCE image schemas which present a partial construal of society. By using the word 'rain' in [11], the dropping of missiles is presented as being executed by an unknown external FORCE whose existence (as a natural force) cannot be prevented. This contrasts with the representation of the EU as an enabling force for Ukraine's blocking and defensive action (in [13]). Likewise, FORCE image schemas are of use for conceptualizing abstract political realities, as it is the case in the weak force unable to resist another stronger force (in the use of 'surrender' in [12]) or in the idea of CONTROL combined with FORCE as can be observed in the word 'occupation'.

These sentences also show that force dynamics is instantiated in different grammatical structures, including variation in sentence patterns (Radden and Dirven, 2007), that is, the use of transitive, ditransitive or intransitive verbs. A different conceptualization of agency can be observed if we compare the intransitive use of 'rain' in [11], in which the agent can be silenced, with other transitive options, such as drop, which would require an agent to be mentioned. This allows for the emphasis to be placed on the entity suffering from a negative external FORCE. On the contrary, a transitive verb – 'empower' – is used in [13] when the positive enabling actions of the self are to be stressed. A similar effect results from the use of the active or passive voice or when nominalizations are employed (see Chapter 5 for an analysis of nominalizations). These different construals can be explained by relying on what Langacker (2008, pp. 354–7) calls the action chain, which is of use to explain 'the role of nominal referents with respect to the profiled processes' (Langacker, 2008, p. 354). Such referents can be the participants (i.e. agonist and antagonist/agent and patient) and the location (i.e. the ground). The persuasive effect of verb choice and/or its combination with voice has been tested when exploring how violent protests are represented by newspapers (Hart, 2018). While not present in examples [11] to [13] above, other authors have emphasized the importance of analysing prepositions (e.g. because of, despite, against) or conjunctions (because, although) (Talmy, 2000b, p. 416). Modal verbs are also frequently associated with force dynamics, although as mentioned above these will feature prominently in Chapter 7. Most of these features will be exemplified and described again in the analysis section. The following analyses of the politics of NI, UK and the consequences of Brexit help to explain how political processes and actions are schematically construed within geographic and abstract political landscapes.

Case study 4.1: Brexit and the border in Northern Ireland

As explained in Chapter 3, the notion of the border is and has been of particular importance for understanding the NI conflict (see McCall, 2021 for an overview of the role of the Irish border throughout time and changes from a 'debordering' process to a 'rebordering' one). The idea of border (which can be perceived as being equivalent to the BOUNDARY element in the CONTAINMENT image schema) is necessary for conceptualizing space. Likewise, (national) territories are frequently defined as 'bounded spaces' (Storey, 2001, pp. 1–5), which explains why conflicts may arise when different communities claim the same space or when they have different perceptions on where the border – BOUNDARY of the CONTAINER – shall be placed. Multiple interpretations of borders and their relation to the configuration of identity can be observed in how NI organizes its sports teams: in rugby there is a 'single Irish team' which competes alongside the other three national teams (England, Scotland and Wales). In football, on the contrary, NI competes on its own in international contests alongside teams representing the Republic of Ireland, England, Scotland and Wales. The Olympic Games offer a different view, and only two representations can be found: the Republic of Ireland and the UK (Keating, 2021). This apparently simplistic example shows how sports teams are representative of different understandings of CONTAINERS which are defined by how their boundaries are perceived: as physical/territorial and delimited by the island (in rugby), a more abstract historical and national perception of space (in football) or a political configuration of states (in the Olympic Games). In all the cases, there is a single space – NI – whose existence is symbolically (and discursively) construed in different ways. This varied construction of abstract spaces can be linked to terminological distinctions between nation, states and to the perceived ethnic configuration of groups (see Coakley, 2012; Storey, 2001 for a discussion).

Our gestalt configuration of CONTAINERS (with all the associated image-schematic elements mentioned above) and links between them guide our understanding of politics and (inter)national relations. This could be seen in the 1998 Agreement, with three strands regulating not only internal affairs in NI but also external North-South relations within the island and East-West ones within the British Isles (NIO, 1998). Likewise, it can be argued that similar understandings of CONTAINERS underlie the process and regulations related to the UK withdrawing from the EU (known as Brexit) (see Martín de La Rosa, 2023, pp. 282–6 for a study of how the CONTAINER image schema featured in political discussions about Brexit). As noted by Storey (2001), identities are spatial in nature, and it is our understanding of such a space as physical, national, political, cultural and so on that determines how those identities unfold in discourse. Figure 4.4 seeks to summarize the multiple CONTAINERS which can be perceived as being invoked in sociopolitical discourse in NI. Visually representing them as being embedded within one another aims at showing the CENTRE-PERIPHERY/IN-OUT elements mentioned in the description of CONTAINMENT above. Dotted lines have been used to indicate containing entities with which parallel relations can be established. They are also aimed at foregrounding the idea that boundaries can be open or closed.

The process of UK withdrawal from the EU, implemented in 2021, can be discursively explained by relying on the notion of containers and how these are construed (Martín de La Rosa, 2023). This can be seen since the very beginning of the process in 2013, with David Cameron's reference to Britain as an 'island nation' in his so-called Bloomberg Speech (Parnell, 2023). This reference promotes a particular conceptualization of British identity as tied to an understanding of space as an island-container. How this container is construed could also be observed in discussions about how to implement Brexit and what this means for the configuration of the four nations within the UK. Examples of this include academic discussions on the role of the border in managing the relationship between Scotland and the EU (Hayward, McEwen

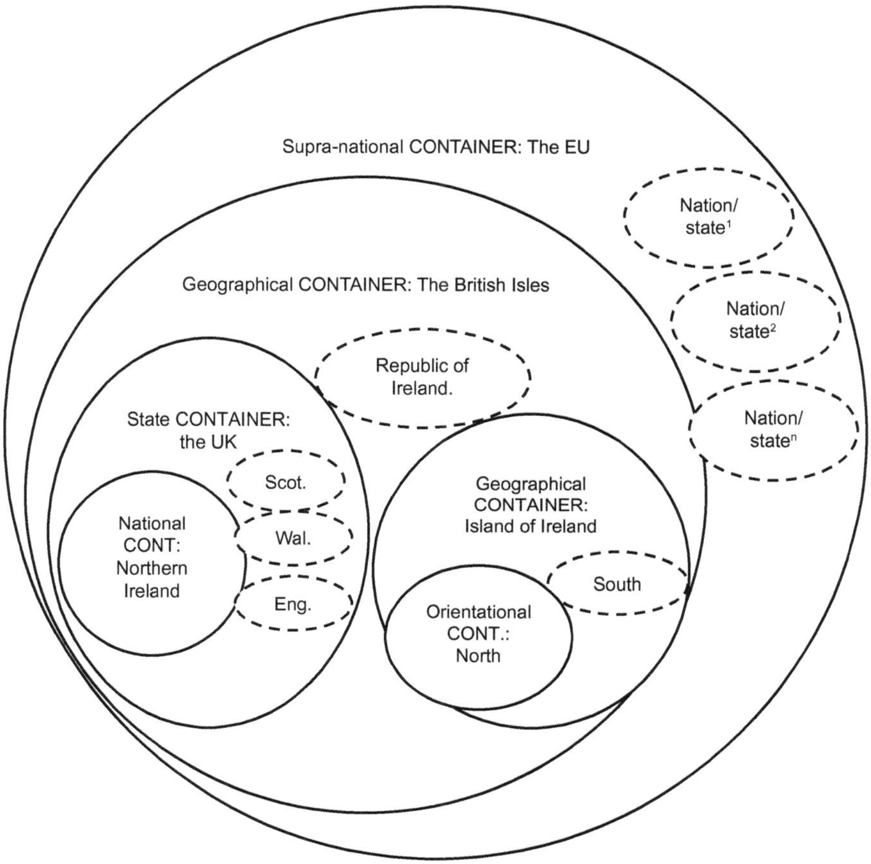

Figure 4.4 CONTAINMENT and discourse on NI.

and Komarova, 2022) or calls for the revision of the 1998 Agreement. While this document was initially conceived as guiding relations between entities within the British Isles, the UK's withdrawal from the EU incorporates an international dimension to these relations. As noted by Hayward (2023), 'Brexit exposed its [the Agreement's] roots to pressures that ran counter to the conditions in which it grew – divergence between states, border controls, unshared sovereignty.' The importance of the border in negotiations could also be seen in references to 'the Irish Backstop', discussions between whether a 'hard' or 'soft Brexit' were to be implemented, or the signing of the Protocol on Ireland and Northern Ireland in 2018 and 2019 (Considère-Charon, 2018; Keating, 2021; Parnell, 2023). The question of the Irish border became prominent because of the threats it posed to the Irish peace process, and in particular the risks Britain's proposals posed to 'hardening of the border, identity problems for Northern Irish citizens, [or] the loss of their fundamental rights guaranteed by the European Union' (Considère-Charon, 2018). Given that conceptualizations of space are inextricably linked to how people conceive their identity, in this case study the aim is to identify the (CONTAINER) image schemas which are activated by different political participants discussing how NI is to be treated in the Brexit negotiations. Given that the main controversy in negotiations of the UK Withdrawal Agreement was related to the movement between spaces, the significance of MOTION image schemas and force dynamics will also be considered.

Negotiations of the UK Withdrawal Agreement from the EU were complicated. Exploring and mediating the relations between NI and the two Unions (the UK and the EU) in which it is involved proved to be a key, and challenging, aspect in the negotiations (De Mars et al., 2018). To explore how these relations were discursively created, and the impact that such discourses had in maximizing or minimizing conflictual views, I have analysed the discourse around the Northern Ireland Protocol Bill (June 2022), a proposal by the British government to disapply some elements included in the NI protocol as reflected in the withdrawal agreement. This bill mostly addressed areas related to movement, such as trade and control. Eventually the UK did not proceed with this Bill, and a new deal – the Windsor Framework – was agreed in 2023 to regulate NI relations with the UK and the EU.[7] So as to account for the variety of actors involved, I have considered the debate held on the NI protocol Bill in the House of Commons on 27 June 2022. In it, different UK politicians standing for an array of political parties participated: Theresa May, Julian Smith, Bill Cash, Craig Macinlay, Robert Neill, David Simmonds standing for the Conservative Party; Hillary Benn, Tony Lloyd, Stella Creasy, Paul Bloomfield, Karyn Smith, Peter Kyle representing the Labour Party; Claire Hanna of the SDLP; Martin Docherty-Hughes of the Scottish National Party (SNP); and Carla Lockhart and Jim Shannon standing for the DUP.[8] Since all these politicians are members of the UK parliament, I decided to consider the position of Sinn Féin representatives as MEPs.[9]

CONTAINMENT image schemas feature prominently in how politicians construe the relation between the different entities involved in the EU withdrawal negotiations (as collected in Figure 4.4). Two types of containers can be identified: related to geopolitical spaces or to political life. First, the different construals of geopolitical spaces identified were frequently defined via the existence of more or less visible borders. These were at times invoked with the aim of emphasizing the isolation and difficult position of people in NI who designate themselves as British, as in [14]. By explicitly invoking the border in the Irish sea and referring to NI as a 'third country', the unionist politician Jim Shannon construes a container shaped by two boundaries: a geographical border – the Irish sea – which prevents the connection with the other political entities that make up the UK, and a symbolic cultural boundary which is related to the national identity with which members of the community identify. This stresses a sense of isolation – which is related to the unionist siege mentality (McKittrick and McVea, 2000; see also Chapter 3) – which legitimizes the call for a renegotiation of the NI protocol as a mechanism for safeguarding the constitutional status of NI as a part of the UK. Thus, geographical boundaries determined by the existence of two islands are to be minimized by 'removing' (a word which appears in many of the analysed speeches) checks, VAT or any other legal measure that stresses the existence of such border between the two locations.

[14] With **the border down the Irish sea**, it is clear to me that <u>we are not as</u> British as Finchley, but I want to be because I am very proud of my British heritage ... The protocol ... **makes Northern Ireland – my country – a third country** and undermines the Belfast agreement. (Shannon, 2022)

This can also be observed in how opposition relations between broader geopolitical CONTAINERS are construed by the other unionist politician, Clara Lockhart: NI versus the EU (in [15]). While NI is presented as an isolated container in this political opposition, it shall be noted that its existence is discursively presented as belonging to the broader container that is the UK, even if the fluid movement within this broader container is prevented by the sea border. The relation between both entities is not only shaped by their own geographical features but is also constructed as one of opposition between two FORCES (teams). One of these forces – the EU – poses a threat to the existence of the other one – the UK (and NI). This can also be seen in [16], where Jim Shannon (from the DUP) metaphorically presents the EU as a sponge. This lexical choice reflects the existence of a CONTAINER image schema whose BOUNDARIES are not only soft but also prone to change, depending on the amount of water (countries) it can absorb. Invoking this metaphor allows this unionist politician to stress not only the malleability and shifting shape of the EU but also its being a threat to NI being a part of the UK. It implicitly stresses that the lack of a political border between the Republic of Ireland and NI makes it easier for the broader container – the EU – to absorb the smaller one – NI.

[15] My party and now the Government are dealing with <u>the real problems caused by the protocol</u>: the huge administrative burden and associated costs foisted

on businesses **because of the sea border**; … the banning of items being *imported* **into Northern Ireland from other parts of the United Kingdom** … The transfer window is open: Members can switch from **team EU** to **team Northern Ireland**, and it is time they joined those of us whose intent is to resolve these issues. (Lockhart, 2022)

[16] The **EU is like a giant sponge**: it wants to take everything from you, but it does not want to give you anything. Tonight, we are asking for **the EU sponge to be lifted off our back** and for us to be given the same opportunities as the rest of the United Kingdom. (Shannon, 2022)

A similar emphasis on whether the boundaries of containers are discursively constructed as being political or geographical can be observed in SF's description of relations between the entities affected by the NI protocol: 'Ireland' (and the North of it), 'Europe' and 'the British government' (Anderson, 2022). The emphasis is placed on the existence of a physical continent – Europe – to which the island of Ireland belongs. This geographical boundedness can also be observed in references to the island of Ireland and parts within it (i.e. the north of the island or the existence of thirty-two counties), and it can be compared to the almost complete lack of references to the political institutions: the Republic of Ireland, Northern Ireland, the UK and the EU.

While the notion of boundaries/borders is important for understanding how geopolitical relations are construed, so is the CENTRE/PERIPHERY element of the CONTAINER image schema. The existence of multiple nations within the UK, all of which are allowed to have similar treatment, is stressed by some conservative politicians. As can be seen in [17], the similar political status of the four nations in the UK is stressed by comparing them. This central status of NI as part of the UK is appealed at when reflecting about the political role that the NI Protocol Bill could play in shaping the trading agreements between the UK and the EU. It is the political opposition to the centrality of NI caused by the NI protocol that was used to justify the need for a new bill. The centrality of all the British nations contrasts with perceptions by members of the SNP and their reference to some nations (NI and implicitly Scotland) being involved in a peripheric relation with what are perceived as core members, as exemplified by England. The explicit reference to opposition between central and peripheral members of the nation (in [18]) links up with the UP-DOWN image schema: peripheral elements in the container are subordinated to the control (sovereignty) desires of the core members, in spite of them not necessarily being the biggest entity in the container (i.e. the majority). Such central-peripheral opposition lies at the core of the SNP's delegitimization of the NI Protocol Bill because it would eventually damage one of the national members of the UK. Image schemas are thus of key importance for understanding how politicians construe intra- and international relations (Chilton, 1996, pp. 50–5).

[17] As we debate these issues, it is important to remain focused on the benefits that we expect future arrangements to bring to the people of **Northern Ireland, which is part of our United Kingdom.** ... The benefit of it has been felt **across England, Wales and Scotland**, but we are told that it is not possible for **Northern Ireland** to have that benefit. (Simmonds, 2022)

[18] that slowly drove a wedge between **England's interests and those of its periphery**. ... Be we in the 18th century or the 21st century, introducing legislation that damages the economic self-interest of **those on the periphery to benefit those in the core** will never end well, especially when, as in this case, it satisfies the desires solely of the parliamentary sovereigntist-fetishists, who do not represent any real majority, even in the core. (Docherty-Hughes, 2022)

Similar conflictual views can be seen if we analyse the type of BOUNDARIES that shape the containers. As noted above, human perception is characterized by closure, that is, we see entities as being ontologically complete (Evans and Green, 2006). Regardless of whether these are explicitly conveyed or not, when geopolitical entities (i.e. countries, nations or states) are conceptualized as CONTAINERS, these implicitly involve the activation of BOUNDARIES as one of its key defining elements. However, explicit lexical choices can result in different construals of such boundaries/borders, with them being more or less easily crossed. The role that such borders have in the creation and resolution of conflict can be observed in Tony Lloyd's – a Labour MEP – intervention: the reference to a 'hard border' located in different positions – either political (between the two nations in the island) or geographical (between the two islands) – stresses the existence of two distanced and opposed entities whose boundaries can be clearly defined (in [19]). For conflict between the UK and the EU to be solved (and for the 1998 Agreement to be safeguarded by maintaining symmetric North-South and East-West relations), such borders need to be minimized so that the two opposed and 'different systems' can occupy a consensually agreed unitary space.

Such agreed space is construed by some politicians as being defined by economic features, with references to the (European) single market as a means of safeguarding the relations established under the 1998 Agreement. Particularly interesting because of how politicians discursively minimize the existence of borders is the reference to 'dual market' by the representative party of the NI

SDLP, Claire Hanna (in [20]). Given the geopolitical in-between status of NI (see Figure 4.4), such reference to dual access – that is, the ability to enter the NI CONTAINER from both sides – stresses the desired PATH to be followed by goods moving between the three involved entities: the UK, NI and the EU.

Similar boundary oppositions and an implicit conceptualization of the relation between the EU and the UK as one between separate CONTAINERS can be observed in the opposition between the collocations 'hard' and 'soft Brexit', which were prevalent in the media at the time of negotiations of the UK's withdrawal from the EU. A study of how the media portrayed the process at the time of the 2016 referendum confirms this claim: the notion of 'soft Brexit' frequently triggered negative evaluations and was understood as being equivalent to 'weak' Brexit (i.e. with easily broken BOUNDARIES between CONTAINERS) or 'no' Brexit (thus stressing that the UK would still remain *inside* the EU) (Jeffries and McIntyre, 2018).

[19] The solution that guaranteed respect for the Good Friday agreement could be reached in only one way. It could **not** be done by having **a hard border across the island** of Ireland and it should **not** be done by having **a hard border down the Irish sea**. It has to be done through some form of negotiated solution that respects the fact that the two potentially different systems have to be brought as close together as possible. (Lloyd, 2022)

[20] End this toxic debate. That is what the people of Northern Ireland want. They do not want to have to hear about this day after day on the radio. They want **dual market access**, and they want our economy to prosper; and that is entirely achievable, with good will. (Hanna, 2022)

A similar conceptualization of the relation between entities can be observed in combinations of the CONTAINER and MOTION image schemas, particularly when discussing the economic relations between the UK and the EU. It shall be noted that, in such uses, what is discussed in most cases is the physical movement of goods (or persons) between two political/economic CONTAINERS. Particularly interesting is, as mentioned above, how BOUNDARIES in the CONTAINER determine the speed and type of movement. By echoing our knowledge of traffic regulation, references to 'red' and 'green' lanes in [21] and [22] foreground the existence or lack of checks or any other physical structures that may either prevent or slow down the movement of goods between locations. Other lexical choices in the co-text of the phrase 'red and green lanes' shall also be considered in these two speeches, which were uttered by Conservative politicians. In [21], a reference is made to the existence of borders, which shall influence how the movement of goods is regulated. Likewise, politicians rely on references to slow/difficult movement to legitimize the need for trust and confidence as the desired relation between geopolitical entities. This example reflects a common use of the CONTAINER image schema in international relations: it shows the need of defending or shielding a CONTAINER (the UK in the examples) and restricting movement to it (Chilton, 1996, p. 51). Inferentially, it also foregrounds the existence of another entity (country/state) from which the self has to protect itself.

[21] Clearly, when we in this House talk about **green and red lanes**, or any other part of the United Kingdom's international trading arrangements, it is important that we demonstrate that we have effective customs, and border controls in which people can have confidence. (Simmonds, 2022)

[22] I see some difficulties with the **red and green lanes**, because if the EU does not trust us now, I find it hard to believe that it is going to trust us in the future. We need mutual enforcement, where we trust it and it trusts us. That is what people do across borders. (Mackinlay, 2022)

These two examples show the usefulness of analysing the CONTAINER image schema – and its relation with other image schemas such as MOTION or force dynamics – for understanding how international relations and relations inside a nation-state are construed by politicians. Given the bipolar nature of image schemas, it is possible to present relations of opposition between two entities occupying different CONTAINERS, conceptualizing movement between them as more or less smooth, and presenting one of the entities as the one that is responsible for the lack of consensus. While the analysis in this case study focused on the relation between geopolitical entities (i.e. countries, nations or supranational organizations), similar uses of these image schemas can be observed for conceptualizing politics. This is particularly the case of MOTION and force dynamics. Given that the MOTION event profiles the existence of a (political) GOAL, politicians tend to rely on this schema for two main uses: (1) exploring multiple political PATHS to be followed (such as a process of negotiation between political forces (as in [23])), and (2) emphasizing the desired outcome of such political negotiations or stressing elements which could prevent reaching the desired (political) GOAL (as in [24]).

[23] they now say that the way to deal with the protocol is **through negotiation** … If they do, they will recognize that consensus is **the cornerstone** of our political **process**. We need to **get back to consensual progress**, as the reality is that no Unionist elected to this place or the Northern Ireland Assembly – not

> one – accepts the protocol. That ought to be of concern to all who value **the progress made in Northern Ireland**, so I make a sincere appeal to the Members and parties who have met Unionist opposition to the protocol with ridicule, sneering and ignorant dismissal to ask themselves whether they share that desire **to get us back on track to consensual progress**, and **to stop the slide** into division and the destruction of what we have achieved. (Lockhart, 2022)

[24] That is why we oppose the Bill. It takes us **further away from** the negotiated progress that is **the only way forward**. (Kyle, 2022)

Each of these functions relies on one of the elements of the schema: PATH or GOAL, respectively. Likewise, politicians sometimes provide detail in the co-text and/or metaphorically extend the idea of MOTION by focusing on the people involved in movement (i.e. other political parties) and the existence or lack of movement, for example. As seen in [23], this type of discursive strategy is used by Clara Lockhart, a representative of the DUP, to legitimize the NI Protocol Bill as a means of helping in maintaining the *progress* made in NI towards peace (as opposed to division), and the need for consensual movement in the future. By using the word 'consensual' as a premodifier of 'progress', she stresses the need for an active involvement of all political parties while silencing the DUP's individual role in the political negotiations. This type of metaphorical development echoes the conventional conceptualization of good politics as forward movement (Charteris-Black, 2005, 2014). The metaphorical framing of politics will be further explored in Chapter 7.

Relying on force dynamics may affect a sense of urgency or weight, but in this case it also relates to blaming and identifying a perpetrator (Hart, 2018). By emphasizing which FORCE is causing the political action, the other's negative actions can be stressed (as in [25]). Conflictual understandings also stem from the self being the entity receiving such negative political FORCE, and often by their impossibility to react to it. As shown in [25], others (the protocol in the example; the EU in the rest of the speech) are blamed by the DUP for what NI is suffering as a consequence of the UK's withdrawal from the EU. This explicit blame of the others allows politicians to legitimize their own political role as the party – DUP – or institution – the government – solving the problems caused by the others. Likewise, force dynamics also allows politicians to assign responsibility for the (lack of) political action and to stress which entity is, in their view, the one that has a prominent role in the (resolution of) political conflicts, as in [26]. A comparison of [25] and [26] shows the importance that choosing between active or passive voice plays in construing political responsibility and blame, and the relation that such grammatical choices have with the profiling of different elements in the action chain. This relates to the bipolar nature of image schemas, which is particularly prominent in the case of force dynamics as, by definition, it involves the opposition of forces and counterforces (standing for two groups, us vs them) in the physical or abstract (political) world (Chilton, 1996, p. 53; Radden and Dirven, 2007, p. 354; Langacker, 2008, pp. 355–7).

[25] While those who oppose this Bill deal with the unrealistic, my party and now the Government are dealing with **the real problems caused by the protocol**: the huge administrative burden and associated costs foisted on businesses because of the sea border. (Lockhart, 2022)

[26] Our challenge is to push **the EU to move beyond** the flexibilities it is proposing and to change the text, but we also need to be realistic about how changes will be made. (Smith, 2022)

More detail will be given in case study 4.2 on how the MOTION event and force dynamics are discursively employed to represent conflict or consensus between political FORCES.

Case study 4.2: Twenty-year commemoration of the 1998 Agreement

The analysis of image schemas proves to be useful for exploring how international relations (and those within nations) are construed, as shown in case study 4.1 and in Chilton (1996) or Martín de La Rosa (2023). In fact, given their pre-conceptual meaning, image schemas can also help when exploring other types of relations, such as those between social groups – as shown in studies of migration (Romano, 2019; Hart, 2025) or gender (Núñez-Perucha, 2011), or those involved in political activity (Oakley, 2005; Hampl, 2020, 2021). Departing from the findings summarized in case study 4.1, where image schemas featured prominently as a means of (de)legitimizing political actions, in this case study the focus is on speeches and statements uttered by different NI and British politicians to commemorate the twentieth anniversary of the signing of the 1998 Agreement.[10]

Three reasons justify this choice: first, the thematic and historical importance of the 1998 Agreement, which regulated relations between the different parties involved in the conflict and marks the beginning of a new process in the political life of NI (see Chapter 3 for a more detailed description). Second, the commemorative nature of the date implies that statements will be rather aimed at showing consensus (or lack of conflict) between parties. As noted by Achugar (2008, p. 171), the objective of commemorative speeches is to 'confirm or reconfirm how things are', and reflections on the meaning of a particular historical event can contribute to 'solidifying group identity and reaffirming group's values and norms'. The thematic emphasis of such speeches allows for construals to be built on more abstract patterns, related to either time or action. I thus believe that this type of speeches offers a chance to identify and explore different patterns in the use of image schema and their usefulness for the analysis of discursive construals of conflictual relations. Finally, the twentieth anniversary of the 1998 Agreement coincides in time with a suspension of the NI Assembly and negotiations of the UK's withdrawal from the EU. As such, a relation can be established with case study 4.1 and the other case studies included in this book.

The analysis of the statements shows how the type of speech event determines the prevalence of some image schemas over others. The commemorative nature relies on two main aspects: the importance of political action and the need to reaffirm a group's identity. As such, there are rarely references to geopolitical CONTAINERS, but CENTRE-PERIPHERY elements are exploited to stress the core values upon which different political actions and identities are based. Given that it is the 1998 Agreement that is commemorated, this document conceptually occupies the CENTRE of political life in the British Isles. It also has to be protected from other political actions, mostly those resulting from the negotiations surrounding the Brexit process. As such a clear relation can be observed between CONTAINER image schemas and force dynamics, as it is the content of the (political) containers that has to be protected from the threat of external FORCES (Chilton, 1996, p. 51; Cienki, 1997, p. 9).

More specific information on the entities to be protected can be found in different speeches. For most of the actors involved in NI political life, these include the political principles that regulate relations within the islands (as in [27]) or the value of consent (as in [28]). This contrasts with evaluations of the 1998 Agreement by the Workers Party, a party of Republican and Marxist views which was split from SF in the 1980s. With little political representation, the party supported the 1998 Agreement but, in their search for peace, they oppose the actions of the main political parties. This can be observed in a comparison of the different construals evoked by uses of the CONTAINER schema and CENTRE-PERIPHERY elements in [27], uttered by the representative of the SDLP, [28], by the UUP and [29], by the Workers Party. While in the first two examples it is the 1998 Agreement and related values that are at the centre, in [29] the use of the word 'blocs' triggers a clear division between two CONTAINERS. Such division ('sectarianism') is later profiled as the core value upon which the 1998 Agreement – as the political container – is based. This eventually delegitimizes the validity of this document as the framework upon which NI political life should be based.

[27] As change engulfs the islands of Britain and Ireland following the Brexit result, the three strands of relationships at the **heart** of the Good Friday Agreement haven't dated – they have truly come of age. (Eastwood, 2018)

[28] The Agreement was by its nature a compromise which did not give everyone all they wanted. It was certainly not perfect, but a **core value** was the principle of consent, where the constitutional future was placed firmly in the hands of the people of Northern Ireland, and was endorsed in a binding international agreement. (Stewart, 2018)

[29] After thirty years of miserable sectarian terror the participants **in the major sectarian blocs** began to establish the basis for a *settlement within* which nationalists and unionists could reach some form of accommodation … An Agreement constructed on the faulty foundations of sectarian division; an institutional framework which incorporates **sectarianism at its core** and an Assembly and Executive which effectively manages sectarianism. (Workers Party, 2018)

These three examples also show how the CENTRE-PERIPHERY schema interacts with the LINK schema. While CENTRE-PERIPHERY schemas construe entities as belonging (or not) to a particular structural configuration, LINK schemas rely on the physical experience of attachment to construe the relations between such entities (Chilton, 1996; Cienki, 1997). Given the bipolar nature of image schemas, LINK schemas can foreground the existence of consensual (linked) or conflictual (split) relations between political parties, communities, nations or institutions. Examples of this can be seen in the lexical choices referring to relations between communities in NI: with 'compromise' or 'binding' (in [28]) stressing the consensual nature of the Agreement and its political prevalence, and 'sectarianism' (in [29]) invoking a similarity and closeness relation only between members of the ingroup, who are often opposed to some other group.

Similar construals can be observed in these politicians' description of relations between communities in NI and the British Isles. Some lexical choices foreground the necessary LINK between communities if peace is to be maintained, as can be seen in references to relations being organized in the spirit of 'power-sharing, partnership and cooperation' (Eastwood, 2018), or political stability and reconciliation being maintained through 'mutual trust' (Stewart, 2018).

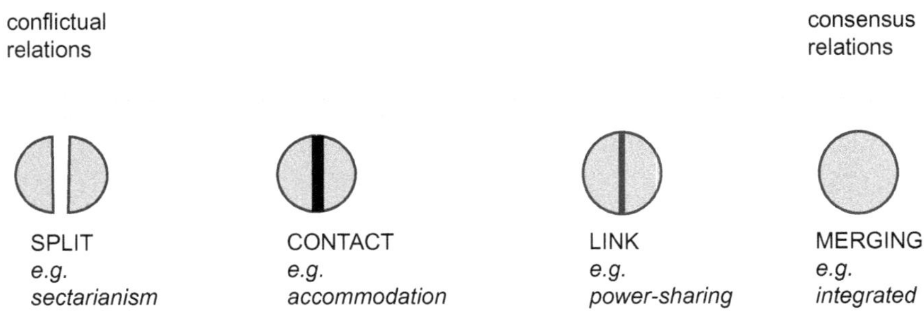

Figure 4.5 RELATION schemas and inter-community relations.

Image schemas shed light on how relations between parties are conceptualized. A summary of how conflictual relations can be structurally configurated via RELATION image schemas is included in Figure 4.5.

A continuum of 'process' schemas (Cienki, 1997, p. 12) could be established, with them ranging from SPLITTING – as the most conflictual schema – to MERGING – as the one where members of different communities are construed as belonging to a single (broader) entity. Such MERGING schema is activated in descriptions of NI as a 'shared' and 'integrated' place resulting from the 'spirit of the' 1998 Agreement (in [30]).

[30] Twenty years on, let's return to the spirit of the GFA, while reforming the structures for our current needs, restoring sustainable political institutions and most importantly of all, recapturing the vision of a **shared, integrated** and prosperous Northern Ireland at peace with itself and its neighbours. (Long, 2018)

The emphasis of this chapter is on image schemas; however, a clear link can be established between image schemas and some primary metaphors which convey similar meanings, such as ORGANIZATION IS PHYSICAL STRUCTURE, IMPORTANT IS CENTRAL, SOCIAL DISTANCE IS PHYSICAL DISTANCE, or SIMILARITY IS PROXIMITY, among others (Grady, 1997; Goatly, 2007). Such primary metaphors are based on basic cognitive mechanisms and frequently have an image schematic component. Thus, it could be argued that a parallelism can be established between the analysis of image schemas and primary metaphors in their ability to conceptually provide a structural configuration to the discursive construction of events. Further details about the usefulness of (resemblance) metaphors as part of the judgement construal operation will be provided in Chapter 7. However, primary metaphors will not be further considered in this book. Mentioning them here aims at stressing their possible inclusion as an analytic tool in future studies of the structural configuration of sociopolitical events in discourse.

While the LINK and CENTRE-PERIPHERY schemas shed light on how politicians configure entities and relations between them, uncovering the activation of MOTION events and force dynamics can help us understand how politicians present their role (and the role of others) in the achievement and success of political actions. As explained above, three elements form part of the MOTION event: SOURCE, PATH and GOAL. Such motion interacts with FORCES, which typically follow a single (usually forward) path of motion (Cienki, 1997, p. 10). Both force dynamics and MOTION events feature prominently in the analysed statements: the former stresses the agency of politicians; the latter contributes to construing policies.

Two aspects can be highlighted when exploring how MOTION is exploited to construe political events. First, existence or lack of MOTION is relevant to understand politicians' conceptualizations of political processes. As shown in [31], different events can be foregrounded by focusing on the source of movement (or lack of it as can be seen in the reference to the 'stalemate') or the type of movement. The phrase 'drove a coach and horses' metaphorically extends the meaning of the image schema and foregrounds the arguably violent and uncontrolled 'manner' in which such MOTION (political action) took place (Hart, 2025). The GOAL of such movement – that is, subsequent negotiations of the 1998 Agreement which were later agreed upon by the political forces on the extremes (SF and the DUP) – is thus delegitimized.

[31] Sadly, the 'behind closed doors' deal by the DUP/Sinn Fein at St Andrews in 2006 **drove a coach and horses through** the principles of the Belfast Agreement and <u>turned</u> every subsequent election into a top dog competition over the First Minister post that encourages sectarian division and has left us with the **political stalemate** we now find ourselves in. (Stewart, 2018)

The MOTION event also allows politicians to construct certain political deals as the PATH towards peace. Focusing on those two elements (PATH and GOAL) legitimizes the political validity of given political documents, and mostly the 1998 Agreement, as a mechanism for achieving a destination which is positively evaluated. As is frequently the case in political discourse, such PATHS are activated via metaphorical extensions of elements in the MOTION event which foreground the role of political means (or policies) as PATHS in achieving a destination (Chilton, 1996, p. 52; Grady, 1997). Besides the legitimization of the 1998 Agreement, by presenting it as the 'roadmap' to be followed by 'getting back to it', extract [32] exemplifies two further uses of MOTION events in political discourse. First, it shows the dynamic and bipolar nature of image schemas: PATHS and movement foreground the opposition between states and processes and activate our experience of (political) CHANGE as MOTION (Grady, 1997, p. 292). Second, the example also shows how the structural configuration activated via image schemas can be further evaluated through interaction with other lexical choices. Thus, references to 'broadness' (compared to 'minor') stress the intensity of movement by combining motion with a SCALE schema. This allows for paired comparisons between different political events (Clausner and Croft, 1999). As such, it can be argued that the SCALE image schema foregrounds the politicians' judgement of the situation (see also Chapter 7). As will be shown in Chapter 5, scalar configurations are also related to attention as a construal operation.

[32] It would seek to show that the narrow issues that we now contend with are very minor compared with the broadness of **progress** and possibility which was **mapped out** for us in 1998. It could provide **a roadmap** for the restoration of the Executive and finally provide the North with a voice and answers to the **looming** Brexit threat. The review wouldn't be about pulling the Agreement apart, it would instead be about **getting back** to it. (Eastwood, 2018)

The analysis of MOTION events cannot be separated from the study of force dynamics (Hart, 2025). As noted in Cienki's (1997) classification of image schemas, a distinction can be made between PATHS (as explained above) and FORCES (see also Chilton, 1996, pp. 52–3). The latter, however, allow for a clearer construal of agency in political life. It has been found that such agency is highlighted when referring to positive political action, which is usually presented as self-propelled (Grady, 1997). This contributes to legitimizing the actions of the political parties involved in achieving the desired GOAL (or political destination). As such, politicians present themselves as having performed an active role in the negotiation and signing of the 1998 Agreement, thus legitimizing their political existence and performance throughout time, as can be seen in [33].

[33] The **efforts** for peace **by** the community were equally invaluable. Even in the darkest of times community groups in West Belfast **sought to engage with** our unionist neighbours, including unionist paramilitary organization. (Adams, 2018)

The explicit mention of 'the community' as the agent exercising the FORCE in [33] contrasts with the reference to abstract FORCES, such as 'division and violence', which are to be 'blamed' for social and political conflict in NI (in [34]). This last example shows how a combination of multiple strategies apparently results in a less conflictual construal of society. First, NI is presented as the main entity by relying on the CONTAINER image schema. This interacts with a RELATION schema, and the past is negatively evaluated by presenting what should have been a unitary entity as a split one (in 'torn apart'). Second, while our understanding of politics is modelled upon our embodied experience of the opposition between two FORCES (an agonist and antagonist), such force dynamics is shifted to an abstract level and presented as a counterforce relation between 'politics' and 'violence'. While counterforce relations imply the existence of two equal colliding FORCES, the stronger nature of 'politics' is foregrounded in the use of the verb 'triumphed'. This allows for a subsequent configuration of the Agreement as the source of 'forward' political movement, whose positive effect is intensified through the activation of the SCALE schema in 'huge'.

[34] The Agreement that was reached twenty years ago was one of historic magnitude, a landmark in the history of Northern Ireland, of Ireland and of these islands. It was an occasion when **politics triumphed over** the **division and violence that had torn** Northern Ireland **apart** over the preceding two decades. ... There's little doubt that as a result of the Agreement Northern Ireland has taken *huge* strides forward in the past twenty years. (Bradley, 2018)

Example [34] also shows that construals of sociopolitical events do not only result from the structural configuration inherent to the use of one single image schema. Rather, such configuration results from the interaction with other discourse strategies and therefore from the combination with other construal operations. This can be observed in the use of abstract lexical choices and nominalizations ('politics', 'division', 'violence'). As will be explained in Chapter 5, such words contribute to directing attention towards specific aspects of reality and to backgrounding the role of others. As such, no specific political party is presented as the agent of change or the cause of violence in [34]. This allows for multiple audiences to align with the 1998 Agreement as their core identity value, regardless of their political position as Unionists or Nationalists, and it also stresses the historical meaning of such document, as would be expected from a commemorative statement.

Summary: Gestalts in conflict discourses

This chapter has focused on the role of the cognitive ability of gestalt creation, understood as the conceptual configuration of an event in its most basic level.

As shown throughout the chapter, such basic structural configuration results from the discursive activation of image schemas, that is, basic experiential or embodied preconceptual structures which are directly meaningful. Given the bipolar nature of such image schemas, the analysis of structural configuration strategies proves to be useful for explaining how conflict unfolds discursively. This is so because construals resulting from the use of different image schemas – or elements within them – can maximize or minimize the opposition between entities (i.e. politicians or the communities they stand for). The examples in the case studies have shown that no finite list of linguistic cues can be provided for the identification of structural configurations. Still, some grammatical patterns shed light on how basic relations between entities are constructed, as is the case of prepositions, transitivity or voice. Likewise, some lexical choices are inextricably linked to the activation of basic conceptual structures and/or may stress the prevalence or absence of conflictual relations between entities.

Findings from the case studies show that it is not only one image schema on its own that triggers a construal. Rather, it is the interaction between a few of them that may result in more or less conflictual views. As such, via the CONTAINER image schema different configurations of inter- and intra-national relations can be discursively constructed. Such a schema proves to be useful in cases of ethnonationalist conflicts, or of any other conflict that results from a clear anchorage of an identity to a physical or abstract ground within which it can be contained. Structural configurations based on the CONTAINER image schema are flexible, and different relations can be construed depending on whether the CONTAINER is discursively presented as maximally or minimally encompassing and on whether it is shaped by open or closed boundaries. CONTAINER image schemas can thus shed light on the structural configuration of geopolitical and social entities as figures. Such construals may be modified via the interaction with the CENTRE-PERIPHERY schema, which (as shown in the case studies) can foreground the existence of specific relations between such entities (as in case study 4.1) or the values upon which an identity is constructed (as in case study 4.2). As shown in the analysis, it is frequently the contextual meaning of such schematic elements that can result in conflictual or consensual representations of an event.

Besides entities, the analysis of image schemas can shed light on how relations between such entities are construed, thus giving more insight into their potential (in)compatibility. Such relations can be of two types. First, these can be just based on the actual connection (rarely physical, but mostly abstract) between communities and entities. The continuum of basic conceptualizations associated with the LINK image schema plays a prominent role in this, as shown in case study 4.2. All these elements – SPLIT, CONTACT, LINK, MERGE – can be grouped under a broader RELATION schema, which can be of use to conceptualize not only political contact but also broader social and community-building processes. Second, relations between entities can be defined as being connected to political activity. As shown in both case studies, MOTION events and force dynamics are of particular relevance when exploring construals of policies and of the political role of the self and the other. Via the MOTION event, and particularly elements related to the SOURCE-PATH-GOAL image schema, a basic conceptualization of policies can be presented. As shown in case study 4.2, focusing on PATHS allows politicians to stress political achievement throughout time by mentioning destinations (GOALS) which have been met. Likewise, the MEANS and MANNER of political action can also be foregrounded, thus minimizing political responsibility and hence allowing for more consensual discourses. This is possible because the bipolar nature of the PATH image schema is built around the direction of movement.

Force dynamics, on the contrary, can be perceived as being more conflictual as, by definition, it implies the antagonistic relation between two FORCES. Conflict can be maximized or minimized depending on the process followed by the political FORCE in their attempt to achieve political success. Such action can be of different types, as seen in both case studies: self-propelled COMPULSION, BLOCKAGE by others, or the existence of strong or weak COUNTERFORCES. Because of this, force dynamics functions as a useful discourse strategy in the attribution of positive responsibility, usually to the self or to a group of entities within which the self is included. Negative responsibility can be equally ascribed, frequently to the others, thus stressing the entity that is to be blamed for political failure or for any other action that could be threatening to the self's identity. All in all, the analysis of the structural configuration of reality may be of use for uncovering both the (de)legitimization of the existence of entities (i.e. political parties, social groups or communities) and the nature of the bipolar relations established between such entities.

5

Attention and salience

What do we mean by attention and salience?

As explained throughout this book, the study departs from the notion of construal, and its definition as 'our ability to conceive and portray the same situation in alternate ways' (Langacker, 2019, p. 140). Cognitive linguists and psychologists have tried to explain this by identifying a variety of systems (Talmy, 2000a), dimensions (Langacker, 2019) or operations (Croft and Cruse, 2004) upon which such alternative conceptualizations are based. The cognitive ability of attention is one of them. As noted by Talmy (2007, p. 295), in any speech situation, 'a hearer may attend to the linguistic expression produced by a speaker, to the conceptual content represented by that expression, and to the context at hand'. Given the impossibility of representing a situation in a single way, construals may (re)distribute a participant's attention in a specific way, or they may (re)direct such attention towards certain aspects of the situation. A construal, thus, 'reflects the user's ability to adjust the focus of attention by altering what tends to be called the *mental imagery* associated with a situation' (Divjak, Milin and Medimorec, 2020, p. 38).

When explaining attention as a cognitive system, Talmy (2000a, p. 257) relies on a viewing metaphor: language functions as a window through which we see – and experience – a given situation. The cognitive process of attention, thus, refers to how we view such scene, or 'event frame': 'the portions [of it] that are foregrounded by inclusion are *windowed*, and the portions that are backgrounded by exclusion are *gapped*' (Talmy, 2000a, p. 257). This highlighting or silencing of particular aspects of a situation is done through language. Croft and Cruse (2004, pp. 47–8) explain attention not only as a cognitive ability, but they also emphasize how this results in (aspects) of such reality having more salience to someone's attention. Thus, three notions shall be emphasized here: the cognitive ability (attention), its non-linguistic effect (perceptual salience) and its linguistic realization (or syntactic and lexical accessibility) (Tomlin and Myachykov, 2019, p. 52). Two further things shall be mentioned when exploring this construal operation. First, even if the focus of this chapter is on attention, linguistic cues related to it could also be studied as related to some of the other construal dimensions, such as perspective, judgement or structural configuration (Langacker, 2019, p. 141). The decision to focus on attention and salience as key factors in the configuration of discursive construals is determined by the need to expose and explain the arguments included in this book in a systematic way. Second, descriptions in this chapter rely prominently on textual choices. However, a clear relation has been established between construal operations as realized via language and their relation with other semiotic modes (Divjak et al., 2020; Hart, 2025; Langacker, 2019, p. 141). This decision is likewise motivated by the research needs of this book. Because of this, the linguistic cues included in this chapter are not to be understood as an exhaustive list.

When exploring the relation between attention and construal, CL has frequently relied on grammatical and syntactic features. Early studies on attention mostly focused on the sentential role of the salient referent, that is, on the syntactic position. It was argued that the more salient referents tended to occupy the most prominent syntactic role, that is, the subject position (Tomlin and Myachykov, 2019, p. 46). Based on this, studies were conducted looking at the difference of attention activated via syntactic choices related to voice – active versus passive – or the attribution of semantic roles through transitivity choices – for example, subject versus direct object (see Tomlin and Myachykov, 2019, for a description of studies in different languages). The importance of syntactic roles also underlies Talmy's (2000a, pp. 262–78) description of the relationship between how events are construed and the structure of the sentence, with a particular focus on the role of the complement and adjunct in determining how much attention we devote to different participants in the event frame. A similar idea underlies Divjak, Milin and Medimorec's (2020) analysis of dative alternation, though their experimental tests showed this had no significant influence on how much attention is devoted to participants as represented in the clause. Examples of this could also be seen in Chapter 4, where the use of different grammatical forms triggered varied structural configurations. The choice of an image schema can also result in different elements of an event being highlighted. Thus, focusing on individual construal operations in each chapter does not mean that they are meaningful on their own. Rather, it is their interaction that contributes to the creation of a discourse world, understood as a partial representation of reality.

For example, the relationship between attention and perspective as cognitive abilities and how they both are linguistically realized can be better seen in Divjak, Milin and Medimorec's (2020) study of how the manipulation of prepositions can lead to different entities being made salient via language. They tested the perceptual difference between typical and atypical prepositional uses in sentences. Typical sentences were understood in this study as those which located the more easily moveable item with respect to the less easily moveable one. Their experiment showed that selecting one preposition over another does have an effect in how we view reality; atypical prepositional uses were found to make elements less salient.

A very complete description of the morphological and grammatical choices which are related to the attention system can be found in Talmy (2007), where he identifies ten categories of attention-related phenomena together with their linguistic realizations. Still, most of the studies mentioned above are based on the manipulation of individual variables in isolated syntactic clauses, as it is usually the case in theory-advancing texts on CL. These sentences have been usually created by researchers based on their introspection and reflection about how language works. In this book, I rather explore how lexico-semantic choices in an instance of discourse can contribute to a coherent representation of reality in which particular entities or processes are made salient.

Attention and salience in context: Nominalization

Discourse-based studies of attention and salience, as reflected in actual language, can be found in Hart (2025) and Schröter (2013). These two authors represent different approaches to the study of how parts of reality can be foregrounded or silenced. In her study, Schröter (2013) focuses on the effect of what happens when politicians consciously fail to speak out in response to public demands. As she notes, previous studies on deliberate attempts at concealment have mostly focused on the study of presupposition and implicature (see also Polyzou, 2014, for a description of the methodological challenges of studying presupposition). This approach thus just focuses on the performative effect of textual and spoken silences, which may eventually result in entities not necessarily being concealed but foregrounded due to a variety of inferential processes.

A different approach is followed by Hart (2025) in his study of reports of violence in the Gaza Strip. He explores four main aspects which can help us explain how events are presented. Departing from the notion of 'action chain', he looks at how choices of transitive verbs, voice, preposition and subject/thematic position in the clause have an effect on the profiling and silencing of the role of particular entities in a scene. A clear relation can be observed in his analysis between attention-related strategies and structural configuration as explained in Chapter 4. Besides those syntactic choices, the notion of mystification is of particular relevance for the study of attention. Mystification can be defined as the readerly effect resulting from particular linguistic expressions which 'downplay or altogether avoid reference to the role or intentions of social actors in the representation of actions and processes' (Hart, 2025, p. 81). Mystification has also been the object of some research within CDS, most notably because it points towards the absences one can find in texts (O'Halloran, 2005; Hart, 2020). Mystification, I would argue, is the effect of our cognitive ability of attention: depending on the linguistic choices we make, sociopolitical actors and processes may not be discursively salient, which could result in those actions/actors being legitimized because they are perceived as natural.

While not explicitly related to mystification, other linguistic choices have been studied because of their backgrounding/highlighting potential. Among them, nominalization can be mentioned. This refers to the process of rendering abstract nouns from other word classes (Radden and Dirven, 2007, p. 79). Nominalization has not only been one of the most widely studied tools in CDS (see, for example, Fairclough, 2003, pp. 134–54; Fowler, 1991; Fowler et al., 1979), but it has also been the subject of debate between scholars on its effect and interpretation (Billig, 2008; Fairclough, 2008; Van Dijk, 2008a). Following the trend initiated by the East Anglia school (Fowler et al., 1979), it has been argued that nominalization and passivization have an effect on how texts are construed: (1) agency is deleted, that is, not all the information about the action and whom it is performed by is given; (2) processes are reified, that is, they are discursively presented as entities whose existence is assumed; and (3) reified entities can be presented as agents, hence silencing the actual actors and attributing responsibility to unidentifiable entities (cf. Billig, 2008, pp. 785–6).

CL-informed explanations of nominalizations shed light on how this linguistic strategy functions, mostly by relying on the notions of specification, quantification and grounding (Heyvaert, 2003, p. 62). Nominals, as referential expressions, function as an access point into the discourse world and they specify the entities – and their prototypical features – which are to be representative of this particular category. Likewise, the existence of such entities is emphasized, hence making them salient. The use of nominals also implies the choice between a singular and plural form and the use of given determiners. As will be explained in detail later in this chapter, both are important because they provide information on how the entities are grounded – that is, how they are related to the speech event and context in which they are produced – and on the quantities associated with those entities. Such quantification does not mean a reference to the number of instances; it is the size of the instantiated entity that is profiled (Heyvaert, 2003, p. 63; Langacker, 2008, pp. 259–309). Size is to be understood here as metaphorically indicating the magnitude occupied by such entity in the mental space. Magnitude is usually defined in relation to the maximal scope occupied by all the virtually existing prototypical instances of the entity referred to. As will be argued below, quantifying has an effect in how world views are construed as they can be linguistically made salient, hence gearing the discourse participants' attention towards those entities. The importance that these linguistic choices can have in the way the world is construed can be seen when looking at the following examples. All of them are headlines taken from news about the war between Israel and Palestine in December 2023.

[1] Netanyahu warns Hezbollah after cross-border attack kills Israeli civilian. (*AlJazeera*, 8 December 2023)
[2] Fearing attacks, Jews in Egypt cancel public Hanukkah celebrations (*The Times of Israel*, 10 December 2023)
[3] US sanctions individuals implicated in West Bank attacks. (*BBC News*, 6 December 2023)

In all three examples we can see a nominalization used to refer to the action of attacking. When presented as an action (through the verb), two participants are semantically required: the subject, as the actor inflicting hurt or damage, and the object, as the entity or actor suffering from that hurt. However, via deverbal nominalization, 'attack' is reified as an event noun. While arguably its argument structure is preserved (Park and Park, 2017), it becomes easier to background – if not silence altogether – the actors committing the attack. Besides, the use of a singular or plural noun also has an effect on how the events are construed: the plural nouns in [2] and [3] clearly intensify the act of violence, which is perceived as being bigger and repeated. A further thing shall be noted about the examples above. In [1] and [3], attack as a noun is premodified. Both cases – 'cross-border' and 'West Bank' – ground the event to a particular location, hence highlighting not only the existence of those attacks but also where they took place. The lack of premodifier in [2] and the noun following the verb 'fear' project something that might happen in the future. In this case, the use of the noun has two effects: on the one hand, its being plural maximizes the magnitude of violence as it refers to more than one instance, hence highlighting the idea of repetition throughout time; on the other, its being a noun presupposes the existence of such violence, as nouns indicate types of entities 'that have an autonomous and stable existence in the world as we see it' (Radden and Dirven, 2007, p. 61). In spite of it referring to future and hypothetical events, the use of the nouns makes salient the existence, likely immediacy and repeated nature of such violence. In contexts where conflict is deeply ingrained, it would be likely for a reader to infer that actors performing the attacks are those with whom they do not align, that is, the others. This can be explained by our understanding of conflict as necessarily involving an opposition between two actors and by the influence of the ideological square in our thinking about society: those which do not belong to the ingroup are frequently perceived to be the ones carrying out the negative actions (Van Dijk, 1998).

Attention and salience in context: Metonymy

Closely related to nominalization, although having received less attention in CDS, is metonymy (Meadows, 2007; Hart, 2011c, 2025; Catalano and Waugh, 2013; Filardo-Llamas and Roldán-García, 2024). The centrality of metonymy in our conceptual system has been already attested, together with its pervasive use in communication and its ubiquitous nature (Panther and Thornburg, 2007, p. 236; Cienki, 2013, p. 299; Dancygier and Sweetser, 2014, pp. 4–5). Likewise, the relationship between metonymy and nominalization has already been explained in CL (Langacker, 2008, p. 119). Metonymy can be defined as a cognitive operation which is based on a relationship of correlation. This means that we associate things which occur together in experience, and that 'salient parts evoke their wholes, and salient subcategories evoke the larger categories of which they are part' (Dancygier and Sweetser, 2014, p. 5). Metonymy is thus a cognitive process which is based on mappings established within one single conceptual domain.[1] An example could be seen when we refer to a person via physical attributes – as in 'she's just a pretty face' – where the word 'face' activates the conceptual domain of the body or person. This relationship of contiguity is frequently equated with a part standing for the whole, or the whole standing for the part, but it also includes any other type of contiguity relationship whose part-whole relation may not seem as prototypical, such as trait standing for object, bodily reaction standing for emotion, or cause standing for effect (see Dancygier and Sweetser, 2014, pp. 100–25; Panther and Thornburg, 2007 for a more detailed description).

While slight variations could be found in how different authors define metonymy,[2] authors tend to agree that one of the properties of metonymy is that 'it highlights or foregrounds its target content and, accordingly, backgrounds its source content' (Panther and Thornburg, 2007, p. 242). The target domain is discursively made salient and hence it may attract more attention. Given the indexical nature of metonymy, we can claim that via metonymy specific aspects of entities in the real world can be made salient for political reasons, thus directing the audience's attention towards them. Interesting examples of this can be seen in Meadows (2007), where metonymy is explained as a mechanism for constructing social groups in political discourse. As shown in that article, in the 2004–5 campaign on military intervention in Iraq, former President Bush constructed very specific enemies by relying on metonymy and providing very concrete examples of who could be considered the enemy. Inferentially equating an unknown and vague concept such as 'enemy' with particular groups helped former President Bush legitimize his intervention policies on Iraq. For this, a framework was discursively constructed in which the word 'enemy' was used to index particular groups of individuals which were signalled to justify the existence of a broader enemy. A specific type of metonymy is mentioned in the article: 'domain reduction' (Ruiz de Mendoza Ibañez and Díez Velasco, 2002; Meadows, 2007) as a type of foregrounding a specific segment of a larger group as indicative of the group. Thus, in the analysed examples a correlation was established between 'rejectionists, Saddamists and terrorists' as members of the Iraqi population and the enemy (Meadows, 2007, p. 7). This type of metonymic use has further consequences as it does not only make particular social groups salient, but it also allows for an inferential generalization whereby the profiled social groups are presented as prototypical of broader social groups. Individual features of members of such groups are silenced and this may result in a depersonalization of people via metonymy (Reisigl and Wodak, 2001).[3]

Domain reduction metonymies are identified in the literature as one of the metonymy types we can find. This, also known as TARGET-IN-SOURCE metonymy, is characterized by the metonymic term being part of the referent, that is, causing a reduction of the larger domain to only one segment of it. They compare this with SOURCE-IN-TARGET metonymy whose main characteristic is that the referent is part of the metonymic term (Ruiz de Mendoza Ibañez and Díez Velasco, 2002). Other more detailed classifications of metonymy have been proposed in the literature (see Littlemore, 2017), in an attempt to explain the contiguity relation between the referent and the metonymic term. As noted by other authors (Hart, 2025), the semantic associations activated by metonymy can be explained as being intrinsic or extrinsic. Intrinsic relations are those that highlight inherent features of the indexed entity, such as fixed attributes of a person. Extrinsic relations are those based on 'contingent relations' (Hart, 2025), that is, those established between people and places or institutions. A detailed analysis of the different kinds of semantic associations that are metonymically activated in the description of immigrants by the media can be read in Catalano and Waugh (2013).

The importance of metonymy in explaining how conflict unfolds discursively is related to two theoretical premises. First, the role of shared knowledge in successful communication, which has also featured prominently in previous chapters of this book. Such activation of shared knowledge is also necessary for explaining how metonymy works: through lexical choices an Idealized Cognitive Model (ICM), or frame, is activated. ICMs are the mental representations that people have about prototypical situations in life, and their activation depends on cultural knowledge being shared by discourse participants (Littlemore, 2017, pp. 409–10). As explained in definitions of context included in Chapter 2, context is not objective but constructed by discourse participants as based on 'subjective participant interpretations, constructions or definitions of such aspects of the social environment' (Van Dijk, 2006, p. 163). The subjective nature of such interpretations is frequently related to the role that opinions play as part of the shared knowledge that forms part of the context (Van Dijk, 2008b). Thus, how participants in a communicative event understand metonymies is situated, that is, mediated by their knowledge and interpretation of the profiled features of the entity and of the entity's relation with the activated frame.

Second, metonymy does not only have an indexical function in discourse whereby certain features of the referent are profiled. In some contexts, metonymy also has an evaluative function; it can convey specific social attitudes on the part of the speaker, and it can function as a marker of group membership (Littlemore, 2017). Examples of how metonymy works to profile different aspects of reality can be seen in the use of names (Lewin-Jones and Webb, 2013) to refer to different locations, people or even policies. The indexical function of metonymic names in NI and all the inferences and beliefs that these activate can be seen in the following headline, found in an opinion article after a leader of the SDLP rejected to participate in an official investigation over a march to commemorate Bloody Sunday. The march had been allegedly not notified:[4]

[4] Eastwood sounding like a Drumcree Orangeman over Bloody Sunday Walk.
(*The Irish News*, 20 December 2023)

The reference to Drumcree is a PLACE FOR EVENT metonymy (Littlemore, 2015), and understanding it requires knowledge about historical events in NI. On July 12, the Protestant community celebrates parades commemorating the victory of King William of Orange at the Battle of the Boyne (see Chapter 3). This day is known as The Twelfth and parades are commonly held by the Loyal Order Institution, known as the Orange Order, a conservative and religious British Unionist organization (for more information, see Kaufmann, 2007). One of the contemporary controversies over these parades is associated with Drumcree, a parish in the county of Armagh. Conflict erupted between Orangemen and the Catholic population of Portadown – the town where the Drumcree church is located – over the route of the parade which would originally cross Catholic streets in the area. From 1995 to the early 2000, different attempts were made to solve this dispute, which was also characterized by inflamed speeches and rioting (Bryan, 2000). The metonymic reference to Drumcree in [4] does not only activate knowledge about such historical events but is also evaluative as it foregrounds the existence of violent and conflictual relations between the communities and the extreme positions adopted by some sociopolitical groups. How the audience of the newspaper interprets such evaluation depends, however, on their values and on their alignment with members of the communities involved in the Drumcree dispute. Metonymy, thus, highlights a particular sociopolitical behaviour by inferentially associating that behaviour to a location in NI at a concrete moment in time.

Salience and granularity: Scalar adjustment

A final dimension in the study of salience involves exploring how users discursively adapt the scale of attention (Croft and Cruse, 2004, p. 52). References to 'scale' (Tenbrink, 2020, pp. 119–23) or 'scalar adjustment' (Croft and Cruse, 2004, pp. 51–3) are closely linked to the notion of 'granularity', also explained via alternative terms such as 'specificity' or 'resolution' (Langacker, 2008, p. 55). Following a metaphorical conceptualization, granularity can be defined as a 'cognitive zoom' (Tenbrink, 2020, p. 118), thus reflecting the different perceptions of reality we could get by (discursively) using a magnifying glass. Coarse-grained views, which are general, are different from fine-grained views, which would allow discourse participants to see finer details. Studies of granularity in CDS have been related to the use of noun phrases (NPs), and mostly the distinction between singular and plural nouns (Hart, 2025) and their visual counterparts in newspaper images. This analysis aligns with Van Dijk's (2011, p. 397) explanation of the semantic component of granularity as involving a distinction between preciseness (usually related to the negative characterization of the others) and vagueness (usually about the self's negative actions). Vague language has been previously studied as a strategy used in political discourse with the aim of avoiding controversy, and it has been shown that it offers speakers the possibility of expressing many degrees of truth without having to adopt a clear compromise with a single position (McGee, 2018).

The study of precise versus vague language in terms of degrees of truth allows me to stress two further ideas about the importance of scalar adjustment for studying how cognition mediates the relation between discourse and conflict. First, the study of granularity and scalar and vague language features prominently as one of the epistemic structures that can be identified when studying discourse semantics (Van Dijk, 2014, p. 313). This activation of knowledge via discourse structure is based on a variety of cognitive strategies, such as specification, selection or inference. As noted by Van Dijk (2014, p. 255), these structures may be manipulated discursively so as to convey the importance or salience of given properties of particular situations or entities.

Second, one possible way of manipulating the speaker's attention is through the use of scales, which can be generally understood as providing more or less details along a continuum (see also the brief explanation of SCALE as an image schema in Chapter 4). Scales consist of a 'set of linguistic alternates, or contrastive expressions of the same grammatical category, which can be arranged in a linear order' (Levinson, 1983, p. 133). They can be used as tools to measure 'weight, distance, volume, wind force, and other things, depending on their nature' (Tenbrink, 2020, p. 119). In spite of these measures being done in units, our conceptual understanding of a scale is rather qualitative and tends to be based on subjective perceptions whose understanding is contextually determined. Scalar attributes are thus relative, and they do not have any concrete value of their own. This may lead to conflictual interpretations depending on the contexts, the associated world knowledge and how these are construed by different communities. Previous studies on conflict and disagreement in everyday conversation have implicitly identified scales as a source of conflict, mostly in relation to absolute language (such as the pronouns 'everything' or 'everyone') (Scott, 2002), or extreme summaries and generalizations (Zhao et al., 2022), which function as two discursive strategies which would lean towards the maximal end of a scale. An example can be seen in the controversy which arose over one of the slogans used in 2019 by Ryanair in an advertisement campaign. This is reproduced in [5].

[5] Europe's lowest fares, lowest emissions airline.

This campaign was banned by the Advertising Standards Authority (ASA) in the UK after complaints had been filed. Among accusations of greenwashing by Ryanair,[5] it is interesting to read how ASA justified this ban[6] by making references to the scales used by Ryanair to measure carbon emission (compared to those used by the Civil Aviation Organization) and to how these could be differently understood by consumers depending on the knowledge they had. This lack of clear definitions of procedures, contextual features and units of measures makes it complicated to understand the word 'lowest', hence making it prone to contextual variation. This example also proves that, given their subjective and contextual nature, scales could render different aspects of reality salient, hence resulting in controversy and conflict.

Within CL, different linguistic cues have been studied when looking at granularity or specificity (Langacker, 2008).[7] Particularly relevant, in my view, are scalar implicatures, that is, the use of linguistic cues which can trigger contextual inferences based on different points in a scale. Scalar implicatures, also known as 'generalized quantity implicatures' (Levinson, 1983, p. 132), arise when a form of a scale is asserted. This implies the negative of all forms higher on such scale (Yule, 1996, p. 41; Tenbrink, 2020, pp. 121–2). Scalar implicatures, which can be cancelled depending on the context, are useful for explaining the meanings triggered by words related to quantities (as in [5] above or in words such as 'all', 'most' or 'some'), time (e.g. with words like 'after', whose meaning is dependent on context, or with variation in verbs tenses and aspect) or space (establishing different relations depending on the prepositions used) (Croft and Cruse, 2004, pp. 51–2; Tenbrink, 2020, pp. 122–3).[8]

The last three sections of this chapter have covered the three main linguistic cues which will be the object of analysis in the case studies that follow: nominalizations, metonymy and scalar adjustment. As mentioned throughout this explanation, it is not the aim of this chapter to claim that these strategies are only related to the study of attention as a construal operation, but they have been identified in the literature as featuring more prominently in it. Still, it cannot be forgotten that these are further related to other operations, such as perspective or framing, and that other linguistic processes (e.g. schematization or metaphor) may also result in particular features of the world view being made more salient.

Case study 5.1: Conflict over the police service. The Patten Report

As explained in Chapter 3, one of the controversial aspects of the 1998 Agreement was related to policing and justice. The Agreement recognized that these were emotive questions and hence provided for the opportunity of a new beginning to policing in NI, which would be monitored by an Independent Commission. The first report by this Independent Commission was released on 9 September 1999, and it included 175 recommendations, among which there were several controversial ones, such as changing the name from the Royal Ulster Constabulary (RUC) to Police Service of Northern Ireland (PSNI), adopting a new badge and symbols free of British or Irish association, or making a major effort to recruit more Catholics (ICPNI and Patten, 1999). These recommendations obtained different responses. The SDLP accepted them, SF welcomed them cautiously and the Unionists were generally hostile to them (Albert, 2008). In spite of the question of policing being wide and complex (as can be inferred from the 175 recommendations), the fact that controversies were mostly related to some of them helps me explore the role of salience when looking at the relation between discourse and conflict. This also ties in with perceptions in each community about the police and the role that policing had in previous evaluations of the 1998 Agreement by NI politicians (Hayes and McAllister, 2001, p. 176). Examples included in this case study are obtained from the statements and reactions by the four main NI political parties to the release of the Patten Report.[9]

Nominalization proves to be a strategy which is used by politicians to foreground aspects of the Patten Report that would render it (il)legitimate for a party's aspirations. As explained above, via nominalizations politicians mystify information, that is, they linguistically endow more attention to some aspects of reality than others, hence contributing to delegitimizing the adoption of given policies (such as those resulting from recommendations in the Patten Report) or the social and political role of groups which are directly related to the implementation of those policies (such as the RUC). Of particular interest in the analysed statements is the use of nominalization in referential expressions which foreground the existence of violence. While this type of nominalization can be found in the statements by SF, the UUP, and the DUP, they foreground different aspects of reality, as can be observed in examples [6], [7] and [8]. All the examples share, at least apparently, a mystified entity: the actor of violence.

This actor, however, is not suppressed from the discursive representations, but just backgrounded (Van Leeuwen, 1996). Because we find references to it in the co-text or because shared knowledge about the nominalized actions is activated, audiences of the statement make the necessary inferences about the backgrounded aspects of reality – that is, who has committed violence – while construing events as reified process.

[6] After one year of taking submissions and listening directly to the public, many of whom have been *victims* of **RUC violence**, the Patten Commission has produced a very detailed, and wide-ranging report on policing. (SF, 1999)

[7] Beyond that the only change that is really needed is to have many more Catholics serving the community in the police. All that is needed to achieve is **an end to intimidation**. (UUP, 1999)

[8] The law is to be changed so that the composition of the Police force will be built on *a quota system* to produce a guaranteed 50% Roman Catholic force. **Deliberate discrimination** against Protestants is to be legally engaged in. (Paisley, 1999)

Unionist parties (in [7] and [8]) rely mostly on deverbal nominalization where the nouns 'intimidation' and 'discrimination' are derived from the verbs 'intimidate' and 'discriminate'. When used as verbs, in both cases a complex relationship is established between two entities which are involved in a process that evolves throughout time (see Figure 5.1a). However, when nominalized, the process is reified and is presented as a thing, that is, a cognitive unitary schema (Langacker, 2008, p. 105) (see Figure 5.1b). It shall be noted, however, that deverbal nominalizations still retain the verb's argument structure (Park and

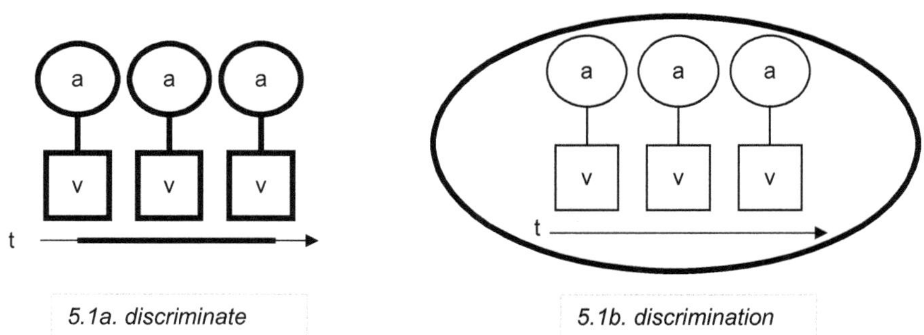

Figure 5.1 Salience in verbs and deverbal nominalization (based on Langacker, 2008, p. 119).

Park, 2017), but this is just backgrounded, as shown in the comparison between Figures 5.1a and 5.1b.

Examples [7] and [8] are interesting for explaining how nominalization contributes to delegitimizing political actions. Both the UUP and the DUP opposed the Patten Report, with different degrees of intensity, as it can also be observed in those examples. As noted above, since both 'intimidation' and 'discrimination' derive from verbs, their argument structure is retained (Langacker, 2008; Park and Park, 2017) and the involvement of actors in those processes can be retrieved inferentially. It is here that the co-text and shared knowledge by members of the community play a significant role. In both cases we have co-textual marks that allow the audience to infer that the republican/Catholic community is the one performing the negative actions. In example [7], where the emphasis is on the need for recruiting more Catholic members as part of the police force, it can be inferred from the previous sentences that 'intimidation' takes place within the Catholic community: it is Catholics that intimidate other Catholics, hence preventing them from joining the police forces. This emphasis on the Catholic community – as the ones who need to perform an action – aligns with the not-so-extreme position of the UUP and clearly shows how via nominalization the negative actions of the outgroup are (inferentially) highlighted (Van Dijk, 1998). Because of their inferential nature, such claims could be negated by the uttering politician. Likewise, via nominalization a different view of the action chain – as resulting from force dynamics – can be observed. Thus, it is necessary to stress the inextricable link between image schemas (explained in Chapter 4) and attention-related linguistic strategies (as exemplified in this chapter).

A similar inferential process can be observed in example [8]. Those suffering the 'discrimination' process are explicitly mentioned in the postmodifier position of the noun: 'against Protestants'. Those who are to be blamed for the discrimination process can be inferentially related to the Catholic community, which appears in the previous sentence, and which are the internal outgroup to whom Unionism is opposed. The use of the adverb 'legally' in the same system and the phrase 'a quota system' in the previous sentence metonymically highlights the existence of legislation upon which such discrimination would be based. It is the situational context that can help the audience infer which document is discursively blamed for such action. Nominalization and metonymy contribute here to making salient the threat posed by the Patten Report to the Protestant community, hence delegitimizing the validity of this document.

What is important in both [7] and [8] is that the actions mentioned, which would be sequentially scanned (Langacker, 2008, pp. 118–19) as a process taking place along time, are now construed as a unitary, holistic and stable entity (Heyvaert, 2003, p. 51; Radden and Dirven, 2007, p. 79). Because of this, I would argue, the existence of such negative reified actions is presupposed. It shall also be noted that both 'intimidation' and 'discrimination' are mass nouns, hence construing such processes as steady situations, that is, 'situations that are thought of as lasting indefinitely' (Radden and Dirven, 2007, p. 84). While both nouns are very similar in their grammatical behaviour, it is via inferential processes that different aspects of reality are highlighted by the two unionist parties. Both delegitimize the validity of the Pattern Report, but they do it for different reasons. The UUP seems to imply that reforms within the police force are not necessary because unequal representations of both communities are due to Catholic intimidation (and hence not to Unionist discrimination). A more extreme position is held by the DUP, which delegitimizes the report because recommendations included within it will render discrimination against the Protestant Community legal.

The existence of violence is also presupposed in example [6]. In this case, the noun 'violence' does not derive from an identifiable verb, so we cannot talk about a deverbal nominalization, but about nominalization coming from an adjective (OED, 2024). As in the other examples, the use of this noun construes a reality in which a complex process is conceptually grouped as a unitary entity (Langacker, 2008, p. 35). This use of the noun does not necessarily fit within more traditional analyses of nominalizations in CDS which have focused on deverbal nominalization (Billig, 2008; Hart, 2014, pp. 30–3). However, the use of 'violence' as a noun has the same effect as the one of the previous examples (cf. also Radden and Dirven, 2007, p. 79): it makes salient the existence of a sustained negative process throughout time – exercising physical force (OED, 2024) – while apparently silencing, or at least backgrounding, the agency of particular sociopolitical groups. It likewise construes this process as a steady situation with an indefinite duration in time and foregrounds the violent quality, as expressed in the adjective, as an immanent feature of NI society.

In NI the noun violence could be interpreted as the one being exercised by and to both sides of the social divide. Thus, looking at the NP in which 'violence' appears can shed light on how SF construes violence and why: 'the public, many of whom have been *victims* of **RUC violence**'. Two types of relations are linguistically construed in this phrase. First, the use of RUC as a genitive premodifier (in spite of not having the formal <'s> mark) functions as a qualifying relation which profiles the role of the RUC as the entity owning violence. Because the RUC is the access point in that NP, its role as possessor is

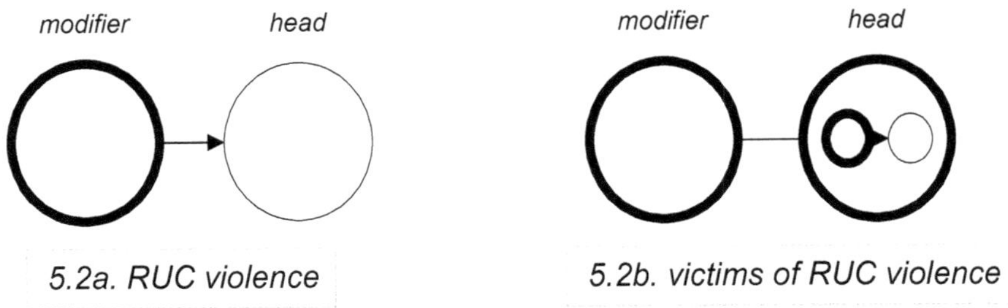

Figure 5.2 Salience in qualifying relations within the NP (based on Radden and Dirven, 2007, p. 160).

highlighted (as depicted in Figure 5.2a). Second, 'RUC violence' appears as part of an 'of phrase' which establishes an intrinsic relation between two participants. These are also made explicit in this phrase: 'the public and victims' – as a general term indexing those suffering from violence – and the 'RUC' as the participant executing it (Radden and Dirven, 2007, pp. 141–66). The construal of the scene in this phrase contributes to legitimizing the need of the Patten Report, as the continuation of the RUC – as the existent (violent) police force in NI – is to be revised.

Examples [6] to [8] show how nominalization has been employed by political parties in NI to construct different world views which can eventually justify the party's positions towards the Patten Report and the reforms of the police system. The three parties have relied on the use of abstract – nominalized – nouns related to negative processes involving the execution of some kind of physical or emotional force. Via nominalizations they have presented this process as a steady situation. Further features about these steady, violent, situations have been made salient via three linguistic strategies: (1) premodification (in [6]), hence establishing an association between such violence and the alleged participants causing it (the RUC), whose existence is delegitimized; (2) co-textual references (in [7]), hence foregrounding existing problems within the police, and allowing for inferences that would set the blame on a section of the social divide while minimizing the need of the suggested policy; and (3) co-textually activating shared knowledge by members of a community (in [8]), hence presenting the document as a threat to the existence of a core entity (the RUC) in the community and delegitimizing the document where recommendations are made to change it. As shown in the examples, the abstractness of the nouns can be made more specific by relying on grammatical patterns. By making them specific, attention is laid on concrete social entities (usually sociopolitical actors).

A similar delegitimizing effect of the Patten Report can be observed in examples [9] and [10]. Both of them clearly show how lexical choices construe a violent world view in which the intensity of violence is modulated – that is, intensified or downplayed – depending on the agent inflicting it.

[9] Changes to policing in Northern Ireland will flow from **an end to terrorist violence**. Those changes are set out by <u>the RUC's own Fundamental Review of Policing</u> and various reports of Her Majesty's Inspector of Constabulary. (UUP, 1999)

[10] To be told by a Minister of the Irish Republic that we must accept the Patten Commission's Report for **the destruction of the Royal Ulster Constabulary** is insulting. Indeed, it is **an unconstitutional attack** upon the democratic rights of the Ulster people. (Paisley, 1999)

Looking at examples [7] to [10] shows the prevalence of nouns related to the execution of physical force (as explained in the analysis of force dynamics in Chapter 4): 'intimidation' and 'violence' by the UUP, and 'discrimination', 'destruction', 'attack' by the DUP. The fact that all these nouns are deverbal nominalizations, which present a reified abstract entity, explains how they are used to profile different degrees of violence and how this relates to the relation established between such processes and different social actors. Previous studies on cognitive grammar have argued that adjectives – such as violent – and verbs are gradable and can be intensified (Radden and Dirven, 2007, p. 149). This allows both actions and properties to be placed along a scale, which is called 'scalar property' and can be defined as 'an open-ended scale which involves an implicit norm' (Radden and Dirven, 2007, p. 365). Scalar properties can be placed along two kinds of scales: comparison (more violent, the most violent) and intensity (very violent, awfully violent). While this has been traditionally studied in isolated sentences, I would argue that similar intensity scales are reproduced discursively in the analysed examples, with different lexical choices foregrounding more or less physical (and non-physical) FORCES being executed. Premodification plays again an important role in the discursive construction of the UUP: 'intimidation' (in [7]) – as describing an internal process within the police force – was not related explicitly to any social actor in the NP (but only inferentially to the Catholic community). However, violence is premodified by the word 'terrorist', hence foregrounding who is to blame for violence (in [9]). The use of the word 'end' – once again a nominalization – does not only presuppose the steady situation of violence but also implies a call for action to be made by terrorist groups,

Figure 5.3 Attention and the profiling of scalar properties.

which members of the unionist community will metonymically equate to the IRA. Changes to the police system are, in the view of the UUP, not necessary but dependent on actions to be done by Republicans. Such discursive profiling is depicted in Figure 5.3.

A similar degree of intensity in violence can be observed in the DUP's discourse (in [10]), though in this case it is not the agents, but the victims, that are explicitly foregrounded by the use of modifiers in the NP. Two things shall be noted in the violence-related nominalizations used by the DUP: first, the intensity of the physical force is higher than in the words used by the UUP, and it increases throughout the statement (discrimination$^{\uparrow}$ → destruction$^{\uparrow\uparrow}$). This difference in intensity relates to them being different kinds of nominals which profile different parts of the action chain (see Chapter 4): 'discrimination' can be grouped under ACTION/EVENT ones, hence profiling the existence of a reified discriminating process, whereas destruction can be characterized as a RESULT nominal whose focus is the outcome of the event described by the 'destroy' verb base (Melloni, 2011). Second, nouns are, in this case, followed by prepositional postmodifiers. When combined with abstract nouns, postmodifiers foreground an intrinsic relation with a reified thing. As relational terms, both 'discrimination' and 'destruction' imply a relation between two participants in a situation. By mentioning the Protestant community or the RUC, these participants are made salient, and hence the threat to their existence is stressed. This eventually contributes to delegitimizing the validity of the Patten Report, as this document would cause such threat. Likewise, because the selected nouns involve a negative relation between two participants, the existence of conflictual – opposed – relations between them is foregrounded: it is them – the outgroup – that is causing us – the ingroup – to feel threatened. As explained throughout this chapter, the interaction between strategies related to two construal operations is to be mentioned here. The choice of violent-related terms activates a FORCE schema (as explained in Chapter 4). However, via nominalization some elements in the action within which forces are embedded – that is, the agonist and the antagonist – are silenced or backgrounded, and it is the existence of a particular type of situation that is emphasized.

Further insights into what political parties make salient when talking about the police can be observed in how they refer the existent and new police force (Table 5.1). An analysis of these NPs sheds further light onto how construals may vary depending on what is discursively made salient, and also on the reality to which such forces are anchored, which can either be factual – when the definite article is used – or hypothetical – through the indefinite article. While all the political parties refer to the RUC via their acronym (as shown in Table 5.1), a difference can be observed between its use as a collective noun (by SF, the SDLP and the DUP) in which its nature as a collective group is profiled, hence construing it as 'an object, except for the fact that its internal composition does not consist of parts but of individual members' (Radden and Dirven, 2007,

Table 5.1 Referential Expressions for the Existing and New Police Force in NI

Patten Report – contents	SF	SDLP	UUP	DUP
Existent police force	The RUC The armed guardians of the union with Great Britain and the armed wing of unionism A repackaged RUC	The RUC	All those brave RUC officers The police	The Royal Ulster Constabulary/ the RUC The entire Royal Ulster Constabulary Reserve The Ulster Special Constabulary The Ulster Defence Regiment The Government police service
Changes/ new police force	A policing service A new democratically accountable policing service A proper democratically accountable policing service	A police service The neutralization of the police service A routinely unarmed police service A balance in the police service		IRA-controlled police services

p. 75). This uniplex construction of the police – versus the multiplex one evoked by nouns in the plural – de-individuates the police force. By depriving it of its humanity trait, it also silences the identities and motivations of its members (cf. Hart and Marmol Queralto, 2021, for a detailed analysis of uniplex and multiplex constructions in immigration discourse). This construal contrasts with commemorating references by the UUP to 'all those brave RUC officer**s**'[10] and with SF's characterization of members of the RUC as 'armed guardian**s**' of the Union.[11] In both cases, it is the existence of individuals within the group that is made salient, either as a means of delegitimizing their existence (by SF) or as a means of justifying their actions in the past (by the UUP). It shall be noted here that while these examples have been analysed as being related to the cognitive ability of attention, connections can be established with schematization and gestalt creation (as explained in Chapter 4) and perspectivization (in Chapter 7). Discursive uses by the DUP when referring to the RUC are equally significant, mostly because they provide a more fine-grained view, with higher resolution onto what the RUC is (cf. Langacker, 2008, p. 55). First, the discourse of the DUP is constructed along a strategy of elaboration which renders particular details about the RUC salient. Elaboration is successfully exploited by Ian Paisley when he explicitly mentions all the forces that are part of the RUC ('the entire Royal Ulster Constabulary Reserve', 'the Ulster Special Constabulary', 'the Ulster Defence Regiment'). This provides further details and evidence of the claim he is making (Tenbrink, 2020, p. 124): the recommendations included in the Patten Report are unacceptable because they will imply the disappearance of many different forces. Like uniplex constructions above, this elaboration provides a more specific construal of the components of the RUC. With this, he reacts to the Patten Report's proposal of 'amalgamation' of the different sections that composed policing in NI in one single force (ICPNI and Patten, 1999, secs 12.12–12.18). When Paisley discursively highlights their disappearance, he also refers to all these forces with their complete names, hence highlighting the centrality of 'Ulster' in the name. The word Ulster does not only foreground one of the traits of the existing forces, it also has an emotive value because it indexes the imagined homeland (Billig, 1995, sec. 108) of the unionist/Protestant community. This also contributes to inferentially stressing the threat that the recommendations in the Patten Report pose to entities which lie at the core of the unionist identity.

Elaboration is in these uses closely related to metonymy. A multiplex construal of the police service is provided and the existence of different forces within it is made salient. Likewise, discursive attention is placed on a distinguishing trait – Ulster, which also stands out in the name of the existent force.[12] The problem of this name being so politicized and enregistered to one side of the social divide is also acknowledged in the Patten Report, where proposals are made to change it to a more inclusive one: Northern Ireland Police Service (ICPNI and Patten, 1999, secs 17.4, 17.6). In spite of a new name (and subsequent acronym: PSNI) being proposed and legally adopted, it cannot be forgotten that lexical choices can be discursively re-signified by a community, hence rendering even the most 'consensual' forms 'conflictual'. To do this, all they need to do is explicitly mention, so as to make them salient, controversial aspects of reality or opposed beliefs. This is the case of the supposedly neutral PSNI. This acronym was used a few years later in a mural in the Republican community as standing for 'Patten Still Not Implemented' accompanying an image of two contraposed – but similar – police officers whose only difference was in the helmet where the names RUC or PSNI could be read.[13] Likewise, the Unionist community has also recontextualized (Wodak and Fairclough, 2010) the acronym in graffiti in the streets, where their criticism of this new police force can be observed in the phrase 'Proactively Supporting Nationalist Ideology'.[14]

Similar coarse-grained versus fine-grained construals (Langacker, 2008, p. 55) can be observed in references to the new police force. While Republicans (SF) and Nationalists (SDLP), who mostly welcomed the proposals in the Patten Report, refer to the resulting change as a 'new' policing (or police) service, the DUP again makes salient one of the traits of the new service: there will be more than one force (as seen in the reference to 'service**s**' in Table 5.1) and they will be controlled by the 'IRA'. Foregrounding the intrinsic relation between the new police service and the outgroup stresses the lack of legitimacy of the new force. This fine-grained conflictual view clearly contrasts with the coarse-grained one triggered by the more generic unmodified NP 'police service', with which both sides of the divide could feel aligned.

Case study 5.2: The question of weapons

Besides policing, another major source of disagreement between NI communities was related to the question of weapons and decommissioning by paramilitary groups. This was particularly important with regard to the inclusion of the republican party SF in the new NI institutions set-up by the 1998 Agreement, and it was a major source of conflict and accusations between the different political parties. Conflictual relations around this are partly due to how issues related to weapons are worded in the 1998 Agreement. The ambiguity of the document has caused an openness of interpretation which is, at least slightly, responsible for the political developments taking place in NI in October 2003. This is the focus of the analysis in this case study. In its article 25, the Agreement states that 'those who hold office should use only democratic, non-violent means, and those who do not should be excluded or removed from office under these provisions' (NIO, 1998). Explicit reference is made to weapons in article 3, about decommissioning, which states the following:

> All participants accordingly reaffirm their commitment to **the total disarmament of all paramilitary organizations**. They also confirm their intention to continue to work <u>constructively and in good faith</u> with the Independent Commission, and to use any influence they may have, to achieve **the decommissioning of all paramilitary arms** within two years following endorsement in referendums North and South of the agreement and in the context of the implementation of the overall settlement. (NIO, 1998; my emphasis)

Such wording allowed both sides of the social divide to justify their sociopolitical actions: by relying on the phrase 'constructively and in good faith', nationalist and republican parties justified that they were working towards the decommissioning of republican paramilitaries, even if actual decommissioning had not taken place. On the contrary, it is the reference to the quantity of arms to be decommissioned – in 'total' and 'all' – which served to justify the position of Unionists and their demand of a complete disarmament. The importance of such words cannot be dismissed as it is by studying which quantitative elements political parties make salient that the role of scales in analysing the relation between discourse and conflict can be explained.

Disagreement between NI political parties has frequently resulted in suspensions of the NI Assembly, often following demands and actions by the NI political parties (see Chapter 3 for further details). On 14 October 2002, a suspension took place. Decommissioning became particularly important in justifying unionist reactions to the lack of power sharing, as their arguments were mostly related to the end of paramilitary activities. To solve this, a sequence of events was agreed on 21 October 2003. This involved Westminster calling elections for the NI Assembly for 26 November, a statement by Gerry Adams saying that the full implementation of the Agreement would provide for the closure of conflict, an endorsement of it by the IRA and an act of decommissioning. Two previous acts of decommissioning had already taken place on 21 October 2001 and 8 April 2002. Nevertheless, the sequence collapsed after Gen de Chastelain's – chair of the Independent International Commission on Decommissioning (IICD) – vague report on the process of decommissioning failed to meet Unionists' demands for transparency. The reason for failure revolved around the quantity of weapons that was decommissioned, which was described by the IICD in the following terms:

> The commission has witnessed a third event in which **IRA weapons** are put beyond use in accordance with the government scheme and regulations.
>
> The arms comprise light, medium and heavy ordinance and associated munitions.
>
> ...
>
> The quantity of weapons involved was **larger than the quantity put beyond use in the previous event**. I do want to make the point – and that is why we have indicated this time – that the amount of arms put beyond use was **larger** – I would say **considerably larger** – than the previous event. (de Chastelain, 2003)

This vague wording caused a negative reaction by Unionists – mainly led by David Trimble, who considered that the act of decommissioning did not correspond to the required standards for the process to continue. Disagreement between the parties can be explained by relying on the notion of scale and its role as a discursive strategy for creating and maintaining conflict.[15]

The analysis of the wording of John De Chastelain's statement shows that coarse-grained construals of reality are provided. First, information related to the type of arms which have been 'put beyond use' has not been elaborated, hence not providing a specific and detailed view about the decommissioning process (cf. Tenbrink, 2020, pp. 123–5 for a description of elaboration). Second, the question of weapons is construed around two scales – time and quantity – which are measured by a (vague) intertextual comparison with other political events: the two previous acts of decommissioning by the IRA. The importance of both time and quantity as mechanisms for scalar adjustment has been previously acknowledged in the literature (Croft and Cruse, 2004; Tenbrink, 2020). Similar uses of scales feature in politicians' reactions to the decommissioning act, as shown in examples [11] and [12], taken from David Trimble's statement.

> [11] Then we were expecting to have a report from General de Chastelain on **transparent acts** of decommissioning and there was clear agreement between us and republicans when we were talking that there should be **greater transparency.** (Trimble, 2003)

[12] I am sorry I have to say that in view of the failure of the IICD to create the necessary **confidence** and because of what the IICD has done we probably have **less confidence than** we had an hour ago, because of that **I** regret **I** am not in the position to make those statements. (Trimble, 2003)

Such vague, coarse-grained construals of reality allow political actors to further justify their sociopolitical role in relation to different aspects, depending on their understanding of these discourses. Thus, lack of specificity about the IRA's behaviour allows the UUP to delegitimize the IRA decommissioning act, among calls for 'greater transparency' (in [11]), and justifying their putting the agreed sequence of call as a consequence of their having 'less confidence' in the IICD (see [12]). The actions of the IICD are thus measured along the UUP's implicit norms, which function as an open-ended scale along which quantities are constructed. By relying on comparison strategies (Radden and Dirven, 2007, p. 365), the other's political actions are delegitimized, hence justifying the self's (undesired) ones. The use of comparisons here makes salient the existence of norms and expectations and evaluates desired and current political actions in relation to them (as shown in Figure 5.4). It shall be noted that an overlap exists between scales as an image schema (see Chapter 4), their ability for making meaning salient, and their role as part of perspectivization (see Chapter 7), mostly because these also imply a positioning of the speaker in relation to particular social norms and expectations. Thus, references to this kind of strategies have been made in the previous chapter and will also be made later when exploring proximization strategies (Cap, 2010, 2013, 2017).

A similar strategy can be seen in example [13] when positively evaluating the self's actions by making their validity salient in comparison to those of the others. A scale is activated in comparative form of the adjective, 'easier'. Gerry Adams relies on this to justify the current actions of the republican community

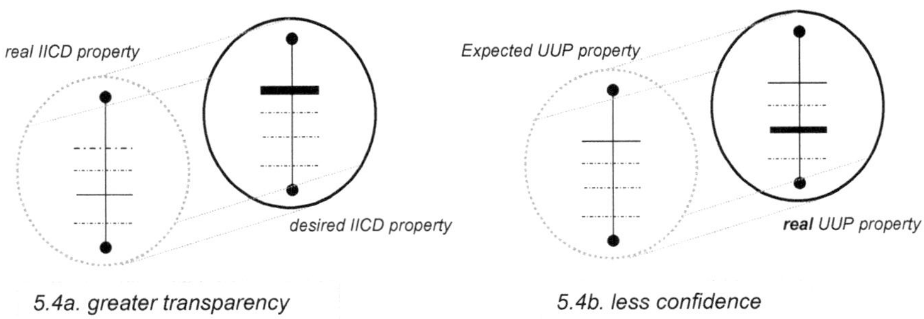

Figure 5.4 Scalar quantification and salient meaning.

by comparing them to those made by previous historical figures in the group. These examples show how scales help in managing discursive representations of the ingroup and the outgroup because they can be of use for making salient perceived evaluations of given properties in relation to the (desired) implicit norm.

[13] It is always **easier** to begin a journey. The **hard** thing is to finish it. Sinn Féin is in this process to the finish. (Adams, 2003)

Lack of transparency and confidence in Trimble's statement, which eventually caused the collapse of the agreed sequence of events, is clearly related to conflictual interpretations about the quantity of arms to be decommissioned. In English, a distinction can be made between set and scalar quantification in the NP (Radden and Dirven, 2007, pp. 117–19). Set quantification invokes a construal which makes salient the relation between a collection of elements and the whole set of which they form part, whose existence is presupposed (see Figures 5.5a and 5.5b). Prototypically, it is expressed by 'set quantifiers, such as *most, all, every, each* and *any*' (Radden and Dirven, 2007, p. 117). Scalar quantification, on the contrary, invokes 'a quantity relative to an implicit norm on a scale' (Radden and Dirven, 2007, p. 117). This scale may be related to expectations or may be (inter)discursively constructed, and it is 'expressed by scalar quantifiers such as *many, much, few, little* and numerals such as *three*' (Radden and Dirven, 2007, p. 117) or by comparison to a norm which functions as the reference point (see Figure 5.5c).

Using different types of quantification allows politicians to make salient different aspects of reality, which vary depending on what is to be magnified: (lack of) achievement in the decommissioning of weapons (by

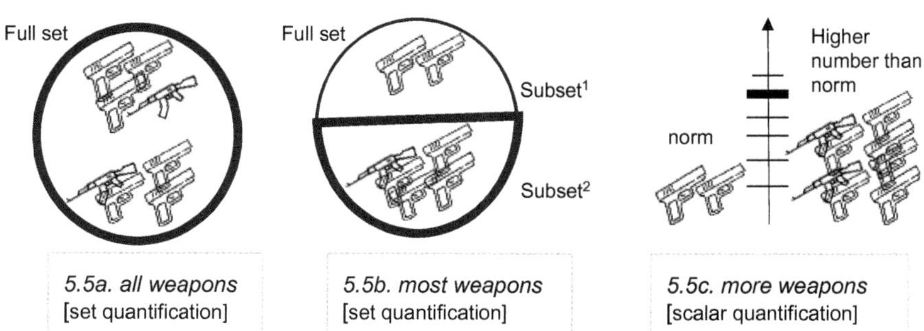

Figure 5.5 Set versus scalar quantification (based on Radden and Dirven, 2007, p. 118).

profiling (vast) numbers of weapons being put beyond use) or measurement of such actions in relation to the politician's desired norms. Likewise, different types of quantifiers allow for more coarse-grained (less detailed) or fine-grained (more detailed) representations of such reality, depending on whether specific figures are provided. The use of quantifiers ties in with previous studies on political discourse and social expectations about it. These have shown that the use of concrete numbers makes audiences perceive statements as more reliable and objective (Chilton, 2004; Hart, 2025). In order to understand how scalar quantification contributes to construing conflictual and opposed views of reality, it is useful to compare how the political actors involved in the October 2003 agreed sequence of events construe the magnitude of decommissioning (in examples [14] to [18]):

[14] **All participants** accordingly reaffirm their commitment to the total disarmament of **all paramilitary organizations**. … to achieve the decommissioning of **all paramilitary arms** within two years. (NIO, 1998)

[15] The amount of arms put beyond use was **larger** – I would say **considerably larger** – than the previous event. (de Chastelain, 2003)

[16] We have authorized our representatives to meet with the IICD … with a view to proceeding with the implementation of a process to put **arms** beyond use at the earliest opportunity. (IRA 2003a)

[17] The leadership of Óglaigh Na Éireann (the IRA) can confirm that a further act of putting **arms** beyond use has taken place under the agreed scheme. (IRA, 2003b)

The analysis of NPs referring to weapons in these examples shows why and how conflict arises. While the 1998 Agreement relies on set qualification ('all arms') and establishes a clearly bounded set of weapons to be decommissioned, this is not what is reflected in the statements uttered by politicians. The IICD relies on scalar quantification 'larger', but the reference point upon which the quantity is to be measured – that is, the implicit norm – is specified through reference to previous (unspecified) events. This event is construed with a clear lack of specificity, and the comparison can only be understood inferentially by relying on a scale whose knowledge is not shared by all the participants in the communicative situation. Likewise, the analysis of the IRA statements does not shed light on the number of weapons decommissioned. They only refer to generic 'arms', without any quantification ([16] and [17]). The use of a plural noun only construes a multiplex entity (i.e. one with more than one component) (Talmy, 2000a; Radden and Dirven, 2007), but for it to be meaningful in this situation finer-grained distinction quantifiers would be necessary. As the IICD and the IRA contravene Grice's (1989) cooperative principle by flouting the quantity maxim (i.e. by not providing enough information), communication can be broken (see also Tenbrink, 2020, p. 121). This would explain the UUP's breach of the agreed sequence of events on the call of 'greater transparency' (in [11]). Conflict can be here explained as a consequence of required information being silenced via a coarse-grained representation of events.[16]

SF addresses this by relying on set quantification as part of a desirable future (in [18]). However, contemporary events are backgrounded with the use of nominalizations (example [19]). As explained above, deverbal nominalization allows Gerry Adams to background the complexity of the process in which the IRA should have been involved while presenting it as a situation – 'implementation' – whose existence is presupposed. It shall be noted that this is combined with a set quantification of a noun whose semantic scope is vague, and which could be interpreted in multiple ways by different audiences: 'all its aspects'. Likewise, example [19] shows how quantifiers can also be used to redirect attention to different entities. By using the set quantifier 'all', Gerry Adams reconstrues reality and contrasts two discourse worlds: the one of the media where the focus is on the paramilitary division of the republican movement, and the supposedly real one, in which focus should be placed not only on republican paramilitaries but on all the political actors involved in the peace process. The responsibility of the others is thus highlighted and blame for the collapse of negotiations is implicitly redistributed between multiple actors.

[18] The IRA leadership wants the full and irreversible **implementation** of the Good Friday Agreement in <u>all its aspects</u> and they are determined that their strategies and actions will be consistent with this objective. (Adams, 2003)

[19] In recent months, and especially in the last few weeks, the Sinn Féin negotiating team has been involved in intense discussions with the Ulster Unionist Party and the two governments. Much of the media focus has been on the IRA. The reality is that **all of the participants**, and the two governments have significant contributions to make if the institutions are to be restored and the Good Friday Agreement made to work efficiently and effectively. (Adams, 2003)

The analysis of how quantification is worded in the 1998 Agreement shows that the significance is placed on two entities: the quantity of weapons and the participants involved in the process (as seen in references to 'all participants' in [19] and to 'all paramilitary organizations' in [14]). Based on clear parameters within set quantification, the use of 'all' does not allow for multiple interpretations. This strategy was also exploited by SF in October 2003. As the 'blame' for the conflict not being solved could be placed on them, they minimized it by construing the IRA as one of the participants in a multiplex representation of political life which involved other actors. In this way, the actions done by the IRA are to be assessed relative to those of other entities in the same set: political participants. In this way attention is shifted from the IRA alone to the responsibility of all participants in NI political life. How these participants are to be interpreted is discursively elaborated and specified in the co-text via a reference to the UUP and the two governments (in [19]). As members of the same set, the fact that all these participants share equal responsibility is made discursively salient.

Case Study 5.3: Seeking consensus: Power sharing in 2007

The questions of policing and decommissioning played a key role in the process of implementation of the 1998 Agreement (Dixon and O'Kane, 2014). Conflictual views about these issues – among charges of mistrust – are important for understanding political behaviour and how events developed. Different attempts were made at establishing and restoring the Northern Ireland Assembly, which collapsed on 14 October 2002. A close look at the events and political statements in NI between October 2002 and May 2007, when the NI Assembly is restored, shows the importance of both policing and decommissioning (as also explained in Chapter 3 and the other two case studies in this chapter).[17] Eventually, an agreed date was set for the restoration of devolved powers to NI, and the NI Assembly was resumed on 8 May 2007. In the previous case studies in this chapter, the focus was on exploring how discursive strategies related to the construal operation of attention were managed by politicians and how they contributed to maximizing conflictual views. This section explores how attention and salience are managed when politicians try to legitimize political actions while seeking consensus and acceptance by different groups within the social divide. To do so, the analysis is based on speeches and statements pronounced by Gerry Adams (as leader of SF), Martin McGuinness (as SF representative and elected deputy prime minister in the 2007 NI Assembly) and Ian Paisley (as leader of the DUP and elected prime minister for NI in 2007).[18]

The attempt to maintain consensus can be seen in how representatives of both communities silence (or at least background) controversial aspects of reality, which could be opposed by members of both the outgroup and of the community they represent. Ian Paisley mostly focuses on the economic benefits that restored institutions would bring to NI. This is discursively achieved by the constant use of verb phrases or nominalized action verbs which foreground sequential activities throughout time. This can be seen when comparing examples [20] and [21], with references to the present and future action in the active voice and via deverbal nominalization (in [20]) and past events construed via abstract nouns. It shall be noted that such nouns – 'horrors' and 'tragedies' (in [21]) – are not nominalized but refer to bounded states, as morphologically indicated by the use of the plural noun (Radden and Dirven, 2007, pp. 81–6). These nouns construe past events in NI as episodic situations, and most notably as episodic states. As such, their temporary, transient nature is foregrounded, and their being presented as states contributes to silencing their heterogeneous complexity and most notably the involvement of particular individuals in them. The temporary nature of such events can be compared to former construals of violence by Ian Paisley as being permanent and explicitly caused by given individuals (as shown in case study 5.1). A similar use of abstract nouns indexing episodic situations in a way which easily allows for a silencing of the involved participants can be found in Gerry Adams's construal of the past, in example [22].

[20] In the period of devolution we will **participate** fully with the other parties in the executive ... With hard work and commitment to succeed, I believe we can **lay** the foundation for a better, peaceful and prosperous future for all the people of Northern Ireland. (Paisley, 2007a)

[21] We must not allow our justified loathing of **the horrors and tragedies of the past** to become a barrier to creating a better and more stable future for our children. (Paisley, 2007a)

[22] The relationships between the people of this island have been marred by **centuries of discord, conflict, hurt and tragedy.** (Adams, 2007)

[23] We have all come a very long way in the process of **peace-making and national reconciliation**. (Adams, 2007)

Besides the difference in the use of nouns related to the violence semantic domain, further insight on how the new devolution agreement is discursively constructed can be gained from looking at examples [20], [21] and [23]. In those, several verbs have been nominalized, either by conversion and derivation – 'work', 'commitment', 'reconciliation' – or via gerundives – 'peace making' and 'creating' (Heyvaert, 2003, 2008; Melloni, 2011). The use of such nominalized forms allows ACTIONS to be presented as situations, hence backgrounding the role of specific political actors while foregrounding the existence of such actions which are to be positively evaluated by society. Such positive evaluation is closely related to the use of RESULT nominalized nouns – as 'reconciliation' – which are discursively construed as the desired outcome of the political process in which actors are involved.

Metonymy also plays a key role in backgrounding and silencing actors who are deemed responsible for such work. Besides the constant use of shifting referential uses of the pronoun 'we' (Filardo-Llamas and Boyd, 2017; see also Chapter 7), in three of the speeches uttered by the politicians at this stage we can find references to the 'Executive'. Both the pronominal and lexical choice foreground the role of the totality of the participants involved in the political negotiation. This focus on the whole rather than on the parts does not feature prominently in Ian Paisley's first speech as first minister of NI (Paisley, 2007b), where an emphasis is placed on the wrong actions suffered by him (and other members of the Unionist/Protestant community) in the past, as shown in examples [24] and [25].

[24] I well remember the night when the Belfast Agreement was signed I **was wrongly arrested and locked up** on the orders of the then Secretary of State for Northern Ireland. (Paisley, 2007b)

[25] It cannot and will not be erased from our memories, nor can we forget today those who continue to bear the scars of suffering and whose bodies **have been robbed** of sight, **robbed** of hearing, **robbed** of limbs, yes and we must all shed the silent and bitter tear for those whose loved ones have not yet **been returned**. (Paisley, 2007b)

The difference between the two speeches uttered by Paisley in March and May 2007 can be explained by looking at their function in the broader sociopolitical context. The speech uttered in March seeks to advance the political process, with the aim of eventually restoring devolution. Thus, all social groups are part of the intended audience, including the unionist and the republican and nationalist community. This can be seen in the agreed sequence of events, with Gerry Adams's (2007) speech explicitly referring to the one previously uttered by Ian Paisley. This would also explain the use of discursive strategies where political actions are made salient while backgrounding the (past) actions of the republican community which had been delegitimized on previous occasions (see the two case studies above and Filardo-Llamas, 2008a). Still, it cannot be forgotten that Ian Paisley – and the DUP – had traditionally opposed power sharing with Republicans, and that their joining the Executive in 2007 was not easily accepted by some members of the unionist community (Dixon and O'Kane, 2014). The need to emphasize that he had not 'changed' his 'unionism'

(Paisley, 2007b) proves that, when uttering his speech as first minister, Ian Paisley was directly addressing sceptic members of the unionist community. A close linguistic analysis of examples [24] and [25] shows the importance of adjusting salience so as to minimize the discursive construal of opposed and conflictual relations.

In both examples ([24] and [25]) we can also observe a use of the passive voice. As in the case of de-verbal nominalization, the passive voice involves the use of a transitive verb, which signals a relation between two participants: an agent and a patient (Divjak, Milin and Medimorec, 2020). In the active voice attention would have been placed on the agent, which first appears presented as the Figure.[19] However, by using the passive voice it is the patient (the victim in this case) that is made salient and hence presented as the primary focus. Actors performing such negative actions – 'robbed of' – are silenced because the agent phrase is not explicitly mentioned in the speech.[20] By relying on their shared knowledge, the unionist community can inferentially understand that it is Republicans that have performed such actions. Still, not zooming on the role of Republicans allows Ian Paisley to simultaneously address the broad nationalist/republican community when saying that he believes that 'Northern Ireland has come to a time of peace' in which relations between communities are to be based on 'neighbourliness' (Paisley, 2007b).

A similar attempt to shift salience from specific actors – such as those who had been formerly referred to as 'IRA/Sinn Fein' (Filardo-Llamas, 2010) – to more generalizing and encompassing construals of social and political actors can be seen in example [26]. Power sharing with SF is justified by Paisley through a coarse-grained construal of this group via the collective noun 'community'. By using such kind of nouns, the individual identities of members of a multiplex entity (i.e. a group) are backgrounded (Radden and Dirven, 2007, p. 74). In Paisley's speech the primary focus is on 'a community' characterized by their former opposition to policing, hence silencing the role of specific individual actors. Still, background knowledge shared by members of the unionist community makes it possible to identify the reference to the republican community in this phrase. By using the indefinite article together with a NP indicating a description of an entity, the existence of only one referent that would fit that description is emphasized (Langacker, 2008, p. 287). As such, attention is laid on the defining characteristic of the community – demonstrating hostility for policing – while inferential processes allow the audience to establish the equivalence 'Republicans = community that were hostile to the police'. A similar backgrounding of individual actors can also be observed in [26] in the use of the de-verbal nominalization 'support'.

> [26] Winning **support** for all the institutions of policing has been a critical test that today has been met in pledged word and deed. Recognising the significance of that change from a community that for decades demonstrated hostility for policing has been critical in Ulster turning the corner. (Paisley, 2007b)
>
> [27] We will continue to rely on that support as we strive towards **a society** moving from division and disharmony to one which celebrates our diversity and is determined to provide a better future for all of our people. One which cherishes the elderly, the vulnerable, the young and all of our children equally. … **A society** which remembers those who have lost their lives. (McGuinness, 2007)

The use of collective nouns seems to work as a strategy aimed at presenting more consensual views of reality, as similar practices can be seen in Martin McGuinness's first speech as deputy first minister. By referring to the people of NI as 'a society', its multiplex nature is silenced and the uniplex construal evoked by the term contributes to silencing the individual nature of people belonging to such society. A metonymic lexical relation is later established in the speech, when members of such community are mentioned: 'the elderly, the vulnerable, the young and all of our children'. The use of nominalized adjectives – 'the elderly, the vulnerable, the young' – allows McGuinness to index 'generic human groups' who are metonymically described via a salient property that characterizes its members (Radden and Dirven, 2007, p. 110). Presenting such members of society as belonging to a class emphasizes its generic component and construes them as a uniplex group. A similar effect is achieved via set quantification in 'all of our children' and 'all of our people'. The quantifier 'all' construes two sets of people – one embedded within the other – as benefiting from the new future that is to be provided. Such focus on the totality of the beneficiaries makes it easier for politicians to legitimize the policies that are discussed, such as the new agreement on devolved government in this case study.

Summary: Attention and salience in conflict discourses

This chapter has focused on the role of salience and attention in managing discourse in conflict situations. As shown in the case studies, via linguistic choices politicians construct the sociopolitical situation in such a way that they emphasize or minimize conflictual relations between groups. Conflict may arise from the focus being placed on different – and opposed – aspects of reality, which at times seem to reflect even a paradoxical view of reality. The use of particular linguistic choices contributes to this. The examples in the case studies have shown how by relying on nominalizations, metonymy and scalar adjustment, different construals of conflictual realities are presented by each political party. These construals further contribute to legitimizing sociopolitical actions which are either perceived as beneficial for the ingroup or as protecting it from the threat posed by the outgroup.

Findings from the analysis section of this chapter show that fine-grained representations of society – usually achieved via part-for-whole metonymy, pre- and post-modified deverbal nominalizations and (ambiguous) scalar quantification – result in conflictual representations of reality. Such choices lead to a minimal viewing frame and allow politicians to zoom into potentially conflictual actions, which are discursively made salient. The examples analysed in case studies 5.1 and 5.2 have also shown how such discursive choices were frequently related to the activation of the semantic domain of violence and specific events associated with it, most notably when referring to the actions done by members of the outgroup. As discussed above, such fine-grained constructions of reality are also shaped to conform to the intended audience of political communication as they mainly appear in speeches addressed at people belonging to the same (ideological) community as the uttering politician.

On the contrary, more coarse-grained views of reality, with which particular details can be silenced, may result in wider social and inter-communal agreement. Examples of this have been seen in the use of set quantification, adjectival nominalization or the use of abstract nouns and whole-for-part metonymy (if any is used at all). Likewise, words from the semantic domains of violence show a lower degree of intensity and are never premodified, hence not associating such violence to any specific community. These linguistic choices result in a maximal viewing frame which allows politicians to present a general picture of political events while backgrounding controversial aspects and silencing the negative actions of the outgroup. As shown in case study 5.3, this is the strategy used by politicians which were formerly at the extreme – SF and the DUP – to legitimize their involvement in the power-sharing institutions which they had formerly rejected. By cognitively zooming out and presenting a wider picture of a society in which members of both communities can be involved, their political involvement in the devolved institutions is legitimized, not only in front of members of their own community but also to audiences belonging to the other side of the social divide. Variability in granularity and discursively making salient different aspects of reality thus prove to be a useful strategy for managing conflictual discourse. It is through linguistic choices that politicians master their need to bring certain elements of reality to the audience's attention, hence allowing for different political actions and decisions to be legitimized.

6

Judgement and comparison

What do we mean by judgement and comparison?

As mentioned in Chapter 2, judgement is a cognitive ability which is realized via comparison (Croft and Cruse, 2004, p. 54), which in turn involves establishing a predicative relation between entities. Although Langacker did consider comparison as a construal operation in his early descriptions of the theory (Langacker, 1987; Croft and Cruse, 2004), this has been included under what he calls 'prominence' (i.e. salience) in later accounts (Langacker, 2019). However, I believe that, even if they are closely related, comparison and salience allow us to focus on different aspects of the relation between discourse and cognition: while salience helps us explain which entities and actions are foregrounded in discourse, comparison focuses on how such entities are discursively constructed via the discursive attribution of qualities. As will be claimed below, alternative construals result from the use of different lexical choices which may result in different qualities – and associated connotations – being discursively ascribed to any aspect of reality. Comparison strategies thus help political speakers *construct* reality (inter)subjectively while at the same time evaluating it. Inferential processes are of particular importance for understanding how such judgements – or evaluations – function. It is through the conceptual comparison of observable facts with shared knowledge that different – and conflictual – views of reality can be spread (Hart, 2014, p. 111; Tenbrink, 2020, pp. 142–53).

Previous work on CL-CDS has explained the comparison construal operation as being related to framing strategies (Hart, 2014, p. 111, 2025), which provide a 'filter' through which a particular situation is to be understood. As noted by Hart (2025), framing strategies add richer and more specific information to the discursive structural and schematic configuration of reality activated by image schemas.[1] The notion of 'frame' has been widely used in different disciplines, and most notably in the social sciences and linguistics.

Definitions of the term do not always coincide (see Tannen, 1993, pp. 18–21 for an overview), so in this chapter understandings of frame reflect how this term is widely used in linguistics and particularly within 'Frame Semantics' (see Cienki, 2007). Frames can be defined as '"prefab" chunks of knowledge structure' (Dancygier and Sweetser, 2014, p. 17). This knowledge structure is characterized by it being concerned with particular aspects of the world about which it generates expectations and inferences in communication. Frames also tend to be associated with given lexico-grammatical choices (Semino, Demjén and Demmen, 2018, p. 627).

Two possible applications can be found when looking at frames in sociopolitical contexts (see Dancygier, 2023 for a discussion). On the one hand, some studies have focused on identifying broad frames which function as pervasive patterns of conceptualization in the political landscape. One of the best-known examples of such cognitive approaches is Lakoff's (2002) identification of two main frames in the US political landscape: the Strict Father morality (associated with republican discourse) and the Nurturant Parent morality (associated with the Democrats). The reference to morality in the identification of such frames stresses, in my view, one of the key aspects of framing strategies: they inferentially activate some kind of evaluative judgement based on the associations that utterers and audiences make with the activated knowledge.

More interesting for this book are those studies which identify instantiations of frame activation in discourse (Dancygier, 2023) via the analysis of textual cues. Examples of this are wide and varied, but an interesting discussion of terminological differences can be found in Cienki (2007), Dancygier and Sweetser (2014) and Kövecses (2017) while methodological insights can be obtained from Semino et al. (2018) and Hart (2008). The importance of analysing framing strategies in political discourse has been also widely attested in the literature, and previous studies have discussed how the activation of particular frames (most notably via metaphors) can influence persuasion and result in specific affective responses (Brugman, Burgers and Vis, 2019; Hart, 2021, 2023).

Framing strategies, as a term encompassing categorization and metaphor (Croft and Cruse, 2004; Hart, 2014, 2025), relate to the cognitive ability of judgement and comparison. While in the definition of judgement and comparison mentioned above no reference to the evaluative potential of the cognitive ability of comparison has been made, it is important to reflect about it here, also given its relevance for the analysis of political discourse (Van Dijk, 1997, p. 28).[2] The explanation of the evaluative potential of frames becomes even more necessary because 'judgement' features prominently as one of the categories of analysis of Appraisal Theory (Martin and White, 2005), one of the most widely used frameworks for the study of evaluation. Evaluation is, thus, understood as the discursive representation of subjective opinions while attempting to achieve intersubjective consensus towards it (Hart, 2014, pp. 43–69). Both in Appraisal Theory and in CL, judgement implies ascribing particular characteristics to a given entity (or action). While such characteristics are related to moral values in Appraisal Theory, they are to be understood as being more general in CL. In the latter, I would argue that it is the inferential association with shared beliefs about the source category that allows for those characteristics to be judged along a good-bad continuum, hence resulting in evaluation of the target entity. Previous studies on metaphorical language in political discourse (Charteris-Black, 2004, 2005, 2014) have also stressed its evaluative potential. Evaluation, however, does not only feature when framing is realized via figurative language but also when it is not figurative, as will be explained below (see also Hidalgo-Downing et al., 2024 for a discussion of evaluative language).

The distinction between figurative and non-figurative frames can be observed in Hart's (2014, 2025) identification of framing strategies as categorization and metaphor. This distinction is largely based on Croft and Cruse's (2004) proposal of the linguistic construal operations which underlie the cognitive ability of judgement. The reference to categorization and metaphor is likewise related to frames displaying 'various levels of specificity, complexity, and cultural embeddedness' (Dancygier and Sweetser, 2014, p. 18). As will be explained below, comparison features prominently both in categorization and metaphor, although it is realized in different ways. These two strategies are of key importance in this book's approach to the analysis of framing categories when looking at discourse and conflict. These two strategies are largely based on the existing literature. However, I believe that a third strategy shall be added when exploring the cognitive ability of judgement: the evaluation via the activation of intertextual frames. This aligns with Dancygier and Sweetser's (2014, pp. 11–12) identification of three key tenets for the analysis of figurative language: (1) the prominence of 'category structure' as an object of study in cognitive science, (2) the frame-based nature of human cognition and linguistic meaning (as explained above), and (3) the blend of metaphoric and non-metaphoric spaces in the mental representations activated by a given instance of discourse. All in all, as argued by Hart (2025), it is via framing strategies that discursive links with socio-historical and intertextual knowledge are activated, hence resulting in inferential evaluations of policies and entities and their subsequent (de) legitimization.

Comparison through lexical knowledge: Categorization

The relation between categorization and framing departs from Fillmore's (1985) Frame Semantics, in which meaning is explained as being related to understanding rather than to truth values (Croft and Cruse, 2004; Cienki, 2007). In his explanation, Fillmore proposes that lexico-grammatical choices evoke a particular understanding, called frame. Similar beliefs lie at the core of theories of categorization in social psychology, and their explanation of it being based on the attribution of shared features to entities belonging to a particular category (Croft and Cruse, 2004; Cienki, 2013).

Underlying the definition of categories are two core beliefs in CL. First, symbols (understood as words and their depictions) are internal representations of an external reality (Lakoff, 1987, p. xiii). Second, such representations are not necessarily the real world, but they are an encoded and perceptual version of such reality. This perception of reality is based on convention and is acquired mostly through social interaction (e.g. via learning or interaction with peer members of a community) (Taylor, 1995, p. 2). Categories are thus a central process in our linguistic and cognitive ability, and they are the entities designated by linguistic or semiotic symbols. Such categories can certainly refer to physical entities in the world (such as table or elephant), but they can also refer to activities or abstract things – for example, singing or government. The linguistic symbols – the words – acquire meaning if the designated entities share a number of properties, which are understood as 'the necessary and sufficient conditions for defining the category' (Lakoff, 1987, p. xiv). These properties, however, are not to be seen as objectively defined but rather as resulting from experience.[3] While the meaning of concepts tends to be generally stable, it is possible for it to be redefined following exposure to different kinds of experiences (Janicki, 2006, p. 59). As shown in Figure 6.1, it is some of the entity's defining properties that are profiled. Thus, how an entity is categorized differs, and diverse properties may be highlighted in different usage events (Langacker, 2008, pp. 47–50). As

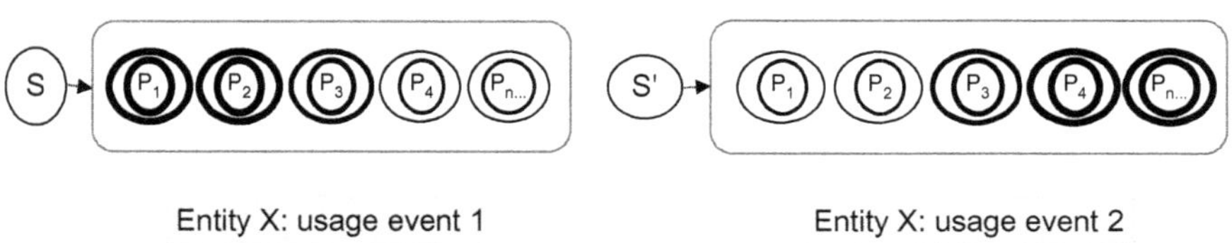

Figure 6.1 Categorization and meaning variation (based on Langacker, 2008, p. 50).[4]

noted by Lakoff (1987, p. 8), categorization is not only an essential and basic human capacity, but it is a 'matter of both human experience and imagination – of perception, motor activity, and culture on the one hand, and of metaphor, metonymy, and mental imagery on the other'. As such, via categorization we access a world view: the use of one category activates a given conceptual domain, which reflects how we construct discursively such conceptual structure as a unit and which triggers multiple conceptual associations. As shown in Figure 6.1, specific defining properties of that entity can be foregrounded in different contexts via variability in lexical selection.

In Lakoff's (1987) description of categorization a clear distinction can be made between non-figurative and figurative perception. Non-figurative understandings of categorization – as being related to perception, motor activity and culture – clearly link to the notion of lexical frames, that is, those 'prefab' chunks of knowledge which are paired with lexical item(s) that represent them (Dancygier and Sweetser, 2014, p. 17). Such lexical frames are often evoked through lexical expressions, and they frequently interact with more complex frames conjuring the role of particular entities and the relations established between them. As mentioned above, frames reflect shared knowledge between participants in the communicative situation.

Categorization is a term which has been previously used in CDS, particularly when explaining how social actors are represented in discourse (Van Leeuwen, 1996, 2008). In this sense, this process is defined as the identification of social actors via reference to the functions and identities (i.e. the properties) they all share. In Van Leeuwen's (1996) understanding, categorization is contrasted with nomination, which involves the reference to a single individual by referring to their unique identity. In my view, however, a clear connection can be observed between categorization strategies and the analysis of naming practices (Jeffries, 2010) or between referential and nomination strategies as explained by the Discourse Historical Approach in CDS (Reisigl and Wodak, 2002; Wodak, 2007). A majority of the examples focusing on such use of nominals – and how via given lexical choices particular defining properties are conceptualized – have focused on explaining the effect of naming practices when talking about migration (Goodman and Speer, 2007; Taylor, 2019). As claimed by some of these studies, names are important and 'they fulfil the central role of discourse in both reflecting and shaping perceptions of social realities' (Taylor, 2019, p. 130).

The significance of studying nominals (or NPs) in political discourse analysis has also featured prominently in proposals based on DST (Chilton, 2004; Filardo-Llamas, 2010), as it is through NPs that the existence of entities as part of a mental space is profiled, that is, they are presented as belonging to the speakers' discourse world. In my view, nominals thus perform a double function: they index given entities in the real world hence presupposing their existence, and they present them as belonging to a given conceptual category. It can be argued that categories have both a referential and conceptual function. This is important in political discourse as it is such categorizing ability that allows speakers to communicate a given (and subjective) conceptualization of the world which involves not only the attribution of given qualitative (defining) properties but also of specific roles in the political landscape (Chilton, 2004, pp. 201–4). Referential expressions – or NPs – thus have an indexical function, and how this is interpreted arises through shared background knowledge conformed by both social knowledge and values (Chilton and Schäffner, 2002, p. 33). Such understanding of nominals relates to representational semantics, which explains how individuals take into account their mental representation of reality to interpret the link between words and symbols. That is, the way we report reality is influenced by the conceptual structures we have conventionalized within our language, and meaning derives from language being a reflection of our conceptual structures (Saeed, 2015, p. 24). This explains one of the possible relations between categorization and conflict, which Charlotte Taylor (2019, p. 128) describes as 'conflict about naming'. Since nominals are not neutral and they convey representations of reality, how social groups are referred to is frequently negotiated, at times even aggressively, and conflict may erupt over such naming practices. Examples on immigration discourse would involve the debate about whether to use the term 'migrant' and/or 'refugee', as the latter would imply a legitimization of such forced movement from the country of origin. Likewise, debates about naming practices in NI have frequently been a source of conflict, not only in references to this geographical area ranging from 'Ulster' to 'the North' but also to sociopolitical actors with different terms such as 'terrorists' or 'freedom-fighters' (Dunn and Dawson, 2000; Gillespie, 2009). Choosing between those terms conveys a particular view of reality which reflects and shapes specific world views. This is why whenever I am not explicitly quoting or consciously reproducing how political actors view reality, I have opted for (at least apparently) more neutral terms such as 'Northern Ireland' for the geographical area or 'paramilitary groups' for social participants directly involved in violence.

Two aspects shall be borne in mind when studying categorization. First, this is often equated to the study of nominals, which involves analysing the denotation and connotation triggered by the nouns chosen. Likewise, pre- and post-phrasal modification of that noun shall also be considered (Jeffries, 2010).[5] The analysis of NPs, including also proper names, can help us identify the entities which speakers construct as belonging to their discourse worlds. Such entities are categorized via linguistic choices which construe them as having certain defining qualities and as being involved in given relationships, usually with other entities (Werth, 1999).

When talking about entities, some authors mostly focus on references to social actors, that is, those participants involved in the sociopolitical circumstance. This is important for conflict studies, as groups are frequently described by the binary comparison between the self and the other and the legitimization of the self frequently presupposes the delegitimization of the other (Taylor, 2019; Van Dijk, 1998; Zimbardo, 2007). Prior work on the representation of social actors has tried to propose a 'sociosemiotic inventory of the ways in which social actors can be represented' together with their linguistic realization (Van Leeuwen, 2008, p. 23). However, I believe that underlying that taxonomy of uses is a process of categorization, regardless of whether the prototypical properties associated with particular entities are related to the activity they perform (i.e. functionalization in 'guardians') or their ethnic properties (e.g. identification in 'nationalists'), among other traits. By analysing categorization, I am thus advocating for a study of how non-figurative lexical choices activate frames which contribute to placing entities as belonging to a particular category, and how this results in potential evaluation of the said entities.

Second, categorization has been widely applied to the analysis of the representation of social actors and discursive group construction.[6] However, the discursive construction of a world view – or a discourse world – does not only involve analysing who is involved in sociopolitical action, but it requires considering as well the actions that are done, when and where (Werth, 1999; Chilton, 2004). As such, the analysis of nominals shall involve not only the identification of participants but also of any other element that conforms a social practice, including activities (i.e. core sociopolitical actions), performance indicators, times, places, tools and the materials used to carry out actions, dress and grooming, and eligibility conditions that are necessary for any social practice to exist (see Van Leeuwen and Wodak, 1999, pp. 94–6 for a thorough discussion and definition of these entities). I thus propose to adapt Van Leeuwen and Wodak's (1999) identification of elements of a social practice to the analysis of political events, and that lexical choices used to refer to any of its constituting elements can have a categorization and framing effect. In Table 6.1, references to the political life surrounding the 1998 Agreement and to the contents of this

Table 6.1 Elements of a Social and Political Practice: An Example

Van Leeuwen and Wodak's (1999: 94–96) elements of a social practice	**Political elements for the analysis of nominals**
Activities: • habit, convention • activity sequence • social goal	(Activities in political process) *Main policy*: 1998 Agreement *Specific sub-policies:* Prisoners, decommissioning, policing, security or other safeguards
Participants and roles	Political parties within NI Political participants outside NI (Members in) NI communities NI social and political groups
Performance indicators	Feelings about: • peace process • relations between participants Characterization of peace
Times	Context of utterance Historical events
Geographical areas	Geographical areas
Tools and materials	Political solutions Forms of government
Dress and grooming	Cultural components of communities
Eligibility conditions	Eligibility conditions for inclusion

document are used as an example for the proposal, hence pairing such elements with the different entities featuring in the discursive representation politicians made of this accord.

The importance of analysing categorization in conflict situations can be observed in the following example, taken from the headline of an article written by Solcyré Burga and published in *Time Magazine* (13 November 2023). In the article, the author follows up on ongoing media debates and reflects on how we should describe violence in Palestine:

[1] Is What's Happening in Gaza **a Genocide**? Experts Weigh In. (Burga, 2023; my emphasis)[7]

The article reflects on definitions given to the noun 'genocide', hence questioning implicitly its categorizing potential. What the article and the experts' arguments quoted in it show is that meaning – or rather our understanding of words – depends on contextual factors, and that these influence how a lexical unit is defined (e.g. legal source document vs colloquial definitions, narrow vs broader understanding of prototypical defining properties, etc.). This is so because concepts are imprecise and their meaning is contextually dependent on usage by members of a community or at a particular event (Janicki, 2006; Langacker, 2008). Thus, we cannot underestimate the importance of analysing categorization in conflictual contexts or of its framing effects (Janicki, 2015, p. 48). Doing so cannot only shed light into which entities have been brought into existence via linguistic choice, but it can also help us underpin the ideological and attitudinal views of users. Eventually this may have sociopolitical – or even legal – implications as the existence of groups and policies can be (de)legitimized via such lexical choices.

Comparison between domains: Metaphors

Metaphors are one of the most widely researched areas in CL-CDS (Charteris-Black, 2004, 2005; Chilton, 1996; Hart, 2008; Koller, 2004; Musolff, 2012; see also Hart, 2017 for a discussion). Metaphors shall be considered when explaining how cognition mediates the relation between discourse and conflict. First because it is a pervasive and key cognitive mechanism in our everyday life (Lakoff and Johnson, 1980), and second because such conceptualizations can be exploited by speakers to achieve specific rhetorical goals (Semino, 2008). As such, metaphor is not to be considered a 'rhetorical flourishing'. Rather, it is a cognitive mechanism which is conceptual in nature and 'essential for the creation of social realities' (Musolff, 2012, p. 302). Following Chilton's (1996) seminal study on security metaphors, we shall not understand metaphors as misleading or manipulative, but rather as an intrinsic part of human cognition and communication. Metaphors are thus constitutive of reality, and their use reflects the way in which a speaker, or a community, understands the world. This is why metaphors are important for the study of political language, also in conflict situations. In such contexts, they can be either contested, hence increasing conflictual perceptions, or can also leave room for the negotiation of specific meanings and references (Chilton, 1996, pp. 68–71). This is consistent with previous studies, which have proved that politicians use metaphors to 'characterize themselves, their opponents, and their political agendas, and use metaphorical language in policy debates to steer the public toward a certain viewpoint' (Boeynaems et al., 2017, p. 118).

Metaphor is a key framing strategy (Croft and Cruse, 2004; Hart, 2014) which could be successfully exploited for transmitting particular images of reality. As such, metaphor is based on our cognitive ability to compare experiences. Thus, metaphors can be defined as involving a relationship between a source domain – that is, the source of the literal meaning of the metaphorical expression – and a target domain – or the domain of experience being described by the metaphorical expression (Croft and Cruse, 2004, p. 55). Domains are by definition conceptual and shall be understood as rich mental representations which are portions of our background knowledge. Among such portions of knowledge, aspects such as elements, relations and patterns of inferences are included (Semino, 2008, pp. 6–7). Other terms used to refer to such mental representations are 'scripts', 'schema', 'frame' and 'scenario' (Musolff, 2006; Semino, 2008; Semino, Demjén and Demmen, 2018). Some authors establish a difference, however, between conceptual domains – understood as more general and overarching conceptual structures – and frames – which are more specific. In their view, one conceptual domain (e.g. JOURNEY) could include more than one frame (e.g. SPEED, VEHICLES, etc.), and these are reflected in different linguistic expressions (compare, for example, 'we navigated through our last years of marriage' with 'our marriage was a crazy ride').[8] Regardless of the terminology used, metaphor 'resides in a set of connections among a source space, a target space and a blended space' (Langacker, 2008, p. 51).[9] By comparison, a new conceptually blended frame, or integration network, is created. In it, an entity in the real world acquires the properties of the entity in the source frame, as shown in Figure 6.2 (based on Langacker, 2008, pp. 50–54; Hart, 2014, pp. 137–61).

Taking as a point of departure the text and identifying metaphorical linguistic expressions, we can access a conceptual mental representation whereby elements of the source domain are mapped onto elements of the target domain (cf. Charteris-Black, 2005; Goatly, 2007; Semino, 2008; Semino et al., 2018, among others).[11] The emphasis on the text (or instance of discourse) as the object of analysis is methodologically important as it seeks to explore the use of metaphor in authentic discourse and explain how construals resulting from the use of such metaphors are inextricably linked to the context in which they are used. Such linguistic expressions – or *metaphorical expressions* – connect large networks of knowledge – or interrelated *frames* – which influence the understanding of the sociopolitical situations and events described. Such connection with background knowledge is contextual, and it is what allows alternate linguistic expressions 'to construe the target scene in alternate, ideologically vested ways – a process broadly captured by the term framing' (Hart, 2023, p. 3). As a consequence of the correspondences established between the source and target conceptual structures, inferential processes are produced of both a logical

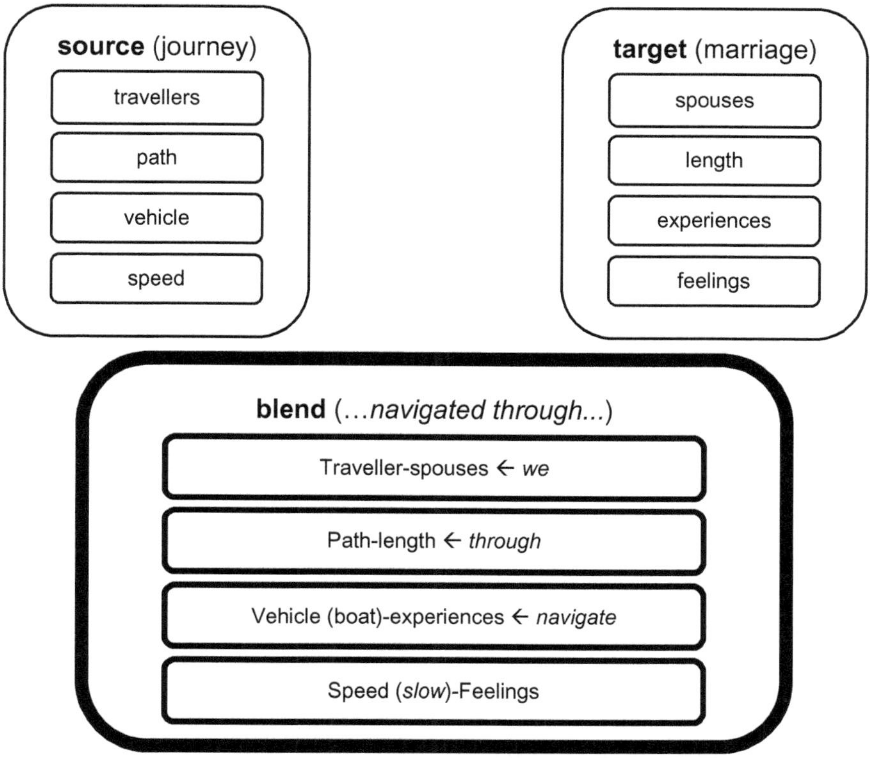

Figure 6.2 Conceptual blend for the metaphor MARRIAGE IS A JOURNEY.[10]

and affective type (Chilton, 2004, p. 52; Hart, 2023). Metaphors, thus, do not only construe alternative views about reality in which different aspects of that reality are foregrounded or backgrounded; they may also trigger evaluative and emotional associations which may eventually lead onto the (de)legitimization of the actions done by given sociopolitical groups and which may be useful for justifying subsequent behaviour by both the speaker and the audience (Semino, 2008; Semino, Demjén and Demmen, 2018; Hart, 2023; Hidalgo-Downing et al., 2024).

Previous studies on the persuasive power of metaphor have sought to analyse metaphorical framing effects. A difference can be observed between those which focus on the cognitive effect, that is, experimental studies based on response-elicitation approaches or studies considering recurrent patterns of conceptual representations, and those which stress the discursive effect of different mental representations.[12] For this book, it is the emphasis on discursive effects that is of particular interest. By exploring in which political contexts politicians rely on specific metaphors (understood as the linguistic expression activating a given conceptualization), we can gain insight into the possible effects and consequences of their use. Since metaphorical mappings are used for reasoning (Chilton, 2004; Musolff, 2004), it is the 'entailments' that they trigger that are of interest because they impose a conceptual representation of reality on the target event. Such entailments lie at the core of the derived inferences, which are also dependent on the cultural, historical and experiential knowledge shared between discourse participants.

Given the dynamic nature of metaphor – as meaning is negotiated and co-constructed in interaction (Chilton, 2004, pp. 201–4; Cameron, 2011; Semino, Demjén and Demmen, 2018), conflictual relations between participants could arise for different reasons: (1) a communication breakdown caused by lack of knowledge of the activated frames, (2) the conceptualization of members of the outgroup (and their actions) in negative terms and as being opposed to the ingroup, (3) the misalignment with the evaluative connotations of the source frame, and (4) a negative affective response to the activated frame. Most of these reasons are covered in the concept of 'polarizing metaphors', defined as those which 'polarize in particular social contexts by conceptualizing "Us", the ingroup, positively, and/or "Them", the outgroup, negatively' (Peterssen and Soares da Silva, 2024, p. 2). Likewise, how conflict may arise as a consequence of metaphorical framing can be explained by its (de)legitimizing function, which is the result of three main dimensions: (1) metaphors communicate political arguments via reasoning, (2) they help in establishing the ethical integrity of entities by relying on shared moral values, and (3) they could heighten the emotional impact of discourse as they draw on the participants' systems of beliefs, which are also culture-specific (Charteris-Black, 2005). These claims are of applicability to multiple contexts. A clear instance of the polarizing and conflictual potential of metaphor can be observed in the following example, taken from a speech given by Donald Trump in a political rally in Ohio on 17 March 2024.[13] He was talking about migrants at the southern US border:

> [2] in some cases they are not people, in my opinion, but I'm not allowed to say that because the radical left says that's a terrible thing to say. These are bad … These are **animals**. (Trump, 2024)

By conceptualizing migrants as animals, Trump is figuratively creating correspondences between a specific group of people and non-humans, as is explicitly mentioned in the example. Such metaphorical framing negatively conceptualizes the outgroup, which is dehumanized. Since metaphor is dynamic and negotiated in interaction, this metaphor could be received by the audience in two different ways. On the one hand, when viewers of the speech align with the ideological beliefs that have motivated the metaphorical framing, this may result in the delegitimization of migrants whose presence in the United States is not welcome (see also Hart, 2021; Porto, 2022; Taylor, 2021). Consistent repetition of such metaphor – that is, it becoming extended within one speech event and/or a systematic metaphor[14] as part of the discourse of a given community (Cameron, 2011; Oswald and Rihs, 2014) – can render such views more acceptable and, by accumulation, increase their evaluative and emotional impact.[15] On the other hand, when the audience does not align with the evaluative inferences triggered by the metaphorical framing, emotions might also come up, although in this case they would not be directed at the metaphorically framed outgroup (i.e. migrants) but at the speaker (i.e. Trump). The evaluative potential of metaphor can thus help us explain how the interpretation of some metaphorical framings results in conflict and polarization, with variation on what they cognitively perceive as the entity to be opposed. As noted throughout this book, conceptualizations and reactions to them are influenced by contextual variables, including not only the situational dimension but also the role of shared background knowledge.

From the explanation above, we can argue that 'metaphoricity can only in practice be identified relative to particular sociocultural groups and discourse contexts' (Cameron 1999, p. 105). Acknowledging the role of metaphor in context is of particular importance when studying the relation between discourse and conflict as it does not only allow us to explore the cognitive dimension – that is, the prevalence of particular conceptual metaphors – but also to take into account the pragmatic effect of such uses in different contexts – that is, the discourse dimension (see Semino et al., 2018). The indexical relation between metaphors and sociocultural (and political) groups is thus of importance when analysing political discourse in NI. By looking at the metaphors used by each political party we shall be able to gain insight into how they understand the different components of society and how those components are characterized in the discourse world constructed by different politicians.

Comparison via cultural knowledge: Intertextual frames

While accounts of framing strategies in CDS have mostly (if not only) focused on the study of categorization and metaphor (Hart, 2014), I believe that a further element should be included in the analysis. Two reasons support this decision: first, previous accounts of the structural configuration of mental representations have identified a hierarchy of levels of metaphoricity, which go from the most schematic ones (e.g. image schemas or metonymy) to the least schematic ones, that is, those which provide richer details (Dancygier and Sweetser, 2014; Kövecses, 2017). Second, definitions of framing strategies stress that it is at this level that language connects with socio-historical and intertextual knowledge, which also influences how events are conceptualized (Hart, 2025). In my view, this intertextual dimension is not always explicitly acknowledged by CL studies focusing only on metaphor. Still, the need of including the role of historical and cultural knowledge in the study of discourse in conflict situations has been previously emphasized in the literature. The Discourse Historical Approach in CDS (Reisigl and Wodak, 2002) has stressed the importance of interdiscursivity and intertextuality as a means of explaining how instances of discourse are related to prior discursive products and the effect that such interdiscursive references have in legitimizing particular world views. Likewise, storytelling, or mythopoesis, has been identified in the literature as a key legitimization strategy (Van Leeuwen, 2007) which relies on two main (or intertwined) possibilities: it creates a moral cautionary tale and it can rely on symbolism. The importance of symbolism and myths for the creation of different communal mentalities in NI has been explained in Chapter 3 of this book.

The affective effect of symbolism and storytelling, and its legitimizing impact (Reyes, 2011), has been accounted for in Kelsey's (2017) proposal for the incorporation of a Discourse Mythological Approach in the analysis of political discourse. While focusing on myths as analytic categories, this approach clearly stresses the importance of considering historical intertextual knowledge in political discourse. Even if they are presented as naturalized, references to historical events can serve an ideological function as their interpretation is not neutral but culturally constructed (Kelsey, 2017, p. 13).[16] The use of historical and cultural myths implies the activation of some kind of (shared) knowledge which triggers evaluative inferences about sociopolitical actors and events. This can, and shall, also be considered a framing strategy, as such myths may result in richer conceptual structures being construed. A parallelism can also be observed with the notion of metaphoric scenario explained above: when discussing how metaphors work, we can talk about the construction of metaphoric mini-narratives which carry with them some kind of evaluative stance (Musolff, 2006, 2017). Likewise, historical and cultural frames function as evaluative mini-narratives which are determined and influenced by shared intertextual knowledge. If metaphors are framing strategies because there is a comparison between different kinds of (physical and abstract) experiences/domains, intertextuality is likewise a framing strategy based on the comparison of experiences coming from different social and historical times or from the activation of different mental models (Van Dijk, 2006, 2008, 2014). The validity of this claim has been previously tested in an analysis of framing strategies deployed for explaining Brexit by Spanish media (Filardo-Llamas, 2021).

Analysing the activation of intertextual knowledge in discourse is likewise an attempt to reflect in the analysis the multi-layered nature of cognition and the constructive and dynamic nature of discourse. As shown in previous studies (Filardo-Llamas, 2019), one lexical cue could activate at the same time multiple knowledge schemata. These may include, for example, socially shared generic knowledge about prototypical categorization, partially shared interpersonal knowledge about specific events or experiences, or even personal private knowledge (Van Dijk, 2008, 2014, p. 225). All these frames, or knowledge schemata, influence how lexical cues are interpreted by the audience, and construals may be richer in detail depending on the amount of knowledge shared by the participants in the communicative situation: the more knowledge is shared, the more likely it is that complex inferences are activated. This complexity results from the creation of detailed mental spaces which reflect how construals vary in specific usage events. Such mental spaces do not only borrow their structure from frames but also from the generic structures activated by such frames and specified in context. Thus, 'mental spaces can be structured by one or several different frames. That is, they can be the realizations of a single frame or they can rely on a combination of roles and relations from several distinct frames' (Kövecses, 2017, p. 326).

As noted above frames are related to different types of knowledge, and all of them combined can trigger more or less complex conceptual blended spaces – or mental representations – which are the result of different input spaces – types of knowledge – being activated (see Filardo-Llamas, 2019 for an example). The likely complexity of such mental representation is pictorially represented in Figure 6.3. Input spaces reflect the different types of knowledge which may be activated by a lexical cue. The blended space results from the combination of features coming from each of the activated conceptual domains. Whereas multiple input spaces are included in this idealized figure, their impact on the blended mental representation will depend on the knowledge shared by discourse participants, as mentioned above. Lack of knowledge being shared and/or different evaluative connotations being triggered by each participant can possibly result in conflictual mental representations.

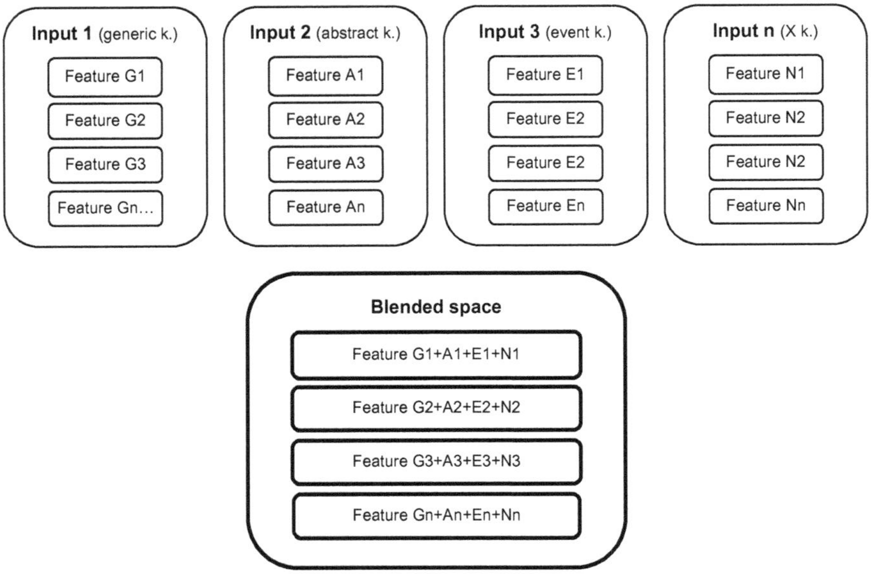

Figure 6.3 Blended space resulting from the activation of multiple frames.

The use of the word 'genocide' to categorize contemporary political violence in example [1] above reflects how the activation of intertextual frames related to knowledge about previous historical and political events works. Two layers of meaning can be identified in such lexical choice: a general one related to prototypical conceptual properties and a more specific one based on historical knowledge. Both of them are based on a comparison cognitive process and both are also of importance in the adoption of a particular frame. Thus, 'genocide' activates generic knowledge which is related to the foregrounding of particular defining features about the situation – for example, the killing and persecution of people being 'deliberate and systematic' and it having the purpose of 'partially or wholly destroying that group' (OED, 2024). However, using that word can also have an evaluative and emotional effect as it can trigger further associations to similar historical events, as can be seen in sentence [3]. A double-layered comparison operation can be observed in this example: first, violence is construed as meeting the defining properties mentioned above; second, it is evaluated by implicitly activating a comparison with the Holocaust (the systematic killing of Jews during the Second World War). This intertextual reference to a historical event thus has framing effects as the situation in Gaza – which is what the news piece was about – is to be evaluated in the light of social views about the Holocaust.

[3] Charging Jews with genocide is to declare them guilty of precisely what was done to them. (Howard Jacobson, *The Guardian*, 3 December 2023)

While the example above shows how the activation of historical frames is related to non-figurative categorization, other examples can shed light on the figurative framing of intertextuality. For example, interesting uses of historical references could be observed at the time of the Covid-19 pandemic. Metaphorical conceptualizations at the time frequently relied on the WAR domain, with politicians referring to the 'fight against the virus' and framing it as being related to other historical conflicts, such as the Second World War or the Spanish Civil War (Filardo-Llamas, 2021a). In spite of such war against the virus being metaphorical, further and richer inferences were triggered by referring to other historical events. These, in my view, shall also be considered part of the framing strategies as participants in the communicative situation are relying on those past events for judging present and contemporary ones. Such judgement, understood as the cognitive ability, is realized via comparison. These comparisons are frequently activated via explicit references in the near co-text of a categorizing nominal or a metaphorical frame. The inferential process and evaluative potential of those intertextual frames, however, depend on the knowledge shared by participants. As noted by Kelsey (2017, p. 167), the importance of socio-historical and cultural knowledge shall not be forgotten in CDS, as it can help us better understand 'some of the deeper affective qualities that make certain stories and narratives more powerful than others'.

Case study 6.1: Binary oppositions and the 1998 Agreement

As explained in Chapter 3, the Peace Process culminates in NI with the signing of an Agreement in 1998. This document was carefully drafted in such a way that it would not 'imply radical change to the ideologies and goals of the parties concerned' (Hayward, 2008, p. 6). This allowed politicians to legitimize the document without apparently compromising the interest of the people they represented. Political parties responded to the accord in multiple ways, and they adopted different positions during the endorsement referendum: Sinn Féin, the SDLP and the UUP were mostly in favour of the Agreement – although a majority of UUP ministers voted against it; the DUP was against the document.[17] Although the 1998 Agreement was mainly a document aimed at reaching peace in NI, the speeches uttered by politicians at the time show the discursive existence of a paradoxical reality (Aughey, 2002; Filardo-Llamas, 2010). Such paradoxical reality is related not only to the discursive representation of apparently opposed worlds but also to such discursive construals reflecting the prevalence of conflict based on an understanding of society as based on opposition. As noted by Klar, Bar-Tal and Kruglanski (1988) in their socio-cognitive approach to the study of conflict termination, it can be argued that a CONFLICT schema exists when there is underlying knowledge about the existence of incompatible goals between two parties (or communities). In my view, this is reflected in discursive choices which manifest an intrinsic binary opposition between two communities.

This binary opposition can be identified in the analysis of categorization and framing practices by NI politicians when campaigning in favour or against the 1998 Agreement, and particularly in relation to controversial aspects within it. The analysis below is based on speeches uttered by the four political leaders in the initial stages of the campaign during the 1998 NI Agreement referendum. This analysis does not intend to provide an overarching view of the strategies used by each party but rather to reflect on how the linguistic choices made construe particular world views.[18]

A clear example of conflictual categorizing choices can be seen in the NPs selected by politicians to refer to the constitutional status of NI. Such constitutional status can be perceived as a complex process which is difficult to understand by citizens. In the 1998 Agreement, it was discursively designed as one which could allow for multiple forms to be adopted, as shown in the phrase 'whatever choice' in [4]. Given that constitutional status is a key defining element in how each of the NI communities constructs their identity and that politicians need to legitimize any political activity that would affect NI citizens (see Table 6.1), I believe that exploring how politicians categorize the constitutional status can shed light on how the cognitive ability of judgement works in this conflict situation. Because such constitutional status is inextricably linked to geographical locations and because these are of particular importance in political discourse (cf. Table 6.1), the names given to NI by different politicians have been also analysed.

[4] recognize the legitimacy of **whatever choice** is freely exercised by a majority of the people of Northern Ireland with regard to its status, whether they prefer to continue to support the Union with Great Britain or a sovereign united Ireland. (NIO, 1998)

[5] I outlined our view that British policy in Ireland has manifestly failed, that **partition** has failed, and that the days of <u>unionist rule</u> are gone forever. …

We cannot and we will not recognize as legitimate **the six county statelet.** And we can and we will continue to reject **partition** and British rule. That is our credo. (Adams, 1998)

[6] The Government of Ireland Act 1920 which establishes the supreme authority of the British Parliament over Northern Ireland is abolished. In return for the total abolition of this legal claim, **Dublin's illegal claim** is merely to be amended … this **Province** can be saved through a massive unionist 'no' vote next month. (Paisley, 1998)

As can be seen in examples [5] and [6], both Ian Paisley and Gerry Adams refer to the status of NI, an area which is named in different ways. In example [6], Ian Paisley refers to the area as 'the Province', hence activating historical knowledge about the four traditional provinces of Ireland: Connacht, Leinster, Munster and Ulster. The use of the term 'the Province' refers to the latter, and it inferentially establishes an intertextual link to the origin of unionism being inextricably linked to Ulster, as this word appeared in the name of most unionist parties (Arthur, 1996, p. 70). It shall be noted that Ulster was originally composed of nine counties, only six of which are part of NI. Such inferences contribute to anchoring unionist identity as being not only British but Ulster-British while also claiming for more land to be part of NI. This identity feature was a core value which the DUP was determined to defend (Tonge, 2014, p. 120). A similar reference to core values and beliefs can be seen when Adams categorizes NI as 'the six county statelet' (in [5]). With this phrase not only is he activating the frame of a single nation – which is inferentially understood as a united Ireland – within which the six counties are contained, but he is also delegitimizing the existence of NI by presenting it as a 'small political state' (OED, 2024) whose existence can be understood as being dependent on a larger country (Collins, 2024). Comparing references to the same location as a 'province' or a 'statelet' shows a different categorization procedure whereby NI is constructed as being prototypically defined by what can be perceived as opposed features. Such categorization is not figurative, but it still has evaluative potential, also resulting from the addition of a further layer of meaning that stems from its current state being judged as resulting from past actions.

When referring to geographical locations politicians are categorizing them in such a way that they activate frames that would align with the core identity traits of the community they represent. These are emphasized by the co-textual and inferential activation of historical and intertextual frames. Both aspects are even more obvious if we focus on references to the current status of NI as 'partition' by Gerry Adams (in [5]). This choice frames the island of Ireland as a whole divided in (two) parts (see also the explanation of the LINK schema in Chapter 4), and it does so by establishing a historical connection with the origin of such division being the Anglo-Irish Treaty signed in 1921 and which resulted in an Irish Free State in the south of the island and Home (British) Rule in the six north-eastern counties (Bardon, 1993; see Chapter 3). While both the categorization and the intertextual frame are present in the use of the noun 'partition', this is stressed by the co-textual reference to unionist and British Rule. Both events have been previously identified in the literature as being significant in the configuration of the victim mentality that characterizes the republican community (Alonso, 2001). The importance of this historical event can also be seen in Paisley's speech, who ties the legitimate and legal existence of 'Northern Ireland' to the 1920 Act (in [6]). A difference can be observed between this reference to the legal political entity through its official name, and the affective and evaluative dimension implicit in the use of the phrase 'the Province' as the location to be defended. It shall be noted that these historical frames are intertwined in the speeches with references to what each community perceives to be 'legal' (or illegal). Such legal framing functions as the moral judgement upon which policies included in the Agreement are to be considered (Entman, 1993; Van Leeuwen, 2007).

A similar categorization process can be seen when we analyse politicians' construals of the relationships between political parties (and the communities they represent) as established in the 1998 Agreement (examples [7] and [8]). In the document, provisions are made for a possible change in the constitutional status of NI and for the approval of policies in the NI Assembly. In the case of the former, such changes are only possible if they count with the 'consent of the majority of' the people in NI. In the case of the Assembly, decisions have to be approved either with parallel consent, described as the majority of designated unionist and nationalist members present and voting, or with a weighed majority of 60 per cent of people voting requiring at least 40 per cent of each of the designated members in each community (NIO, 1998). Consent, understood as agreement by a number of people to a policy or plan, activates notions of 'harmony, concord, affinity' (OED, 2024). However, this type of relation aimed at ensuring consensus between the communities is categorized by both Gerry Adams and Ian Paisley as a 'veto'. This categorization frames the relationship between communities as being based on opposition, with one having power to 'prohibit' the other by rejecting legislative measures and proposals (OED, 2024). With this lexical choice, politicians are eventually delegitimizing the agreement because it allows representatives of the other community – whose existence is foregrounded via premodification (see Chapter 5) – to reject social and political measures. Different inferences about how relations between parties are to be understood are thus drawn from 'consent' (as construed in the 1998 Agreement) and 'veto' (as recategorized by the two political representatives). As explicitly shown in example [7], using veto as a categorizing mechanism also allows for an intertextual framing by comparing the perceived veto in the agreement with past historical situations. Consent was introduced in the agreement as a measure aimed at ensuring protection for all groups in a power-sharing system so that inter-ethnic tensions could be minimized (McEvoy, 2013, p. 254). However, the lexical choices made by politicians representing the most extreme political parties construe this measure in such a way that it is power of one group over another that is inferentially profiled. An attempt to counteract this focus on opposition is seen in example [9], taken from the UUP's rebuttal of DUP's claims about the Agreement.[19] When referring to the DUP's claim about the Assembly containing a 'nationalist veto' (UUP, 1998), they follow two strategies: rechannelling attention to both communities being able to exercise such veto via premodification, and reframing this as 'nationalist consent', hence stressing the need for concordial consensus between the communities.

[7] We knew from the outset that other parties, had already subscribed to **a unionist veto** described euphemistically as <u>'consent'</u>. We disagree with that position. The reason we cannot subscribe to a unionist **veto** is quite simple. That **veto** led to partition and to great suffering by nationalists under Stormont. It was a great historical wrong which allowed a national minority to veto progress by the Irish nation. (Adams, 1998)

[8] The <u>Trimble/Adams agreement</u> will destroy the Union. It repeals the Government of Ireland Act 1920 which gives the United Kingdom parliament its authority over matters in Northern Ireland. It provides for the release of terrorist prisoners including murderers and the restructuring of the RUC. The Assembly set up under the agreement gives nationalists **a veto** over any Assembly decision. (Paisley, 1998)

[9] There are **vetoes** on key issues for Unionists and Nationalists. All sensible people know that a degree of <u>nationalist consent</u> – 40% of Nationalist Assemblymen – is required if the Assembly is to work. (UUP, 1998)

As shown in examples [7] and [8], the DUP and SF frame the Agreement in such a way that binary opposition between the two ethnic communities is stressed. Their categorization choices show that policies and proposals within the Agreement result in an inferential negative evaluation of the document. This is often emphasized by the co-textual activation of intertextual frames, mostly related to former historical events which had a negative impact on the community politicians represent. Such categorization, thus, does not only result in a delegitimization of the political action – the Agreement – but it also stresses the existence of conflictual relations between the two NI communities.

A slight difference can be observed in the discourses of both SF and the DUP after the St Andrews Agreement: they refer to the NI political situation as participating in 'power-sharing and all-Ireland political institutions' (Adams, 2006) or 'devolved government founded on sound democratic principles' (DUP, 2006). Two things shall be noted about these categorization strategies: first, they do not frame politics as linked to the opposition between the two communities, as could be seen in examples [4] to [9].[20] Second, intertextual references to historical events are minimized and the focus is placed on local politics and institutions (i.e. anchored in NI). Still, while both categorization practices stress that there is a relation between various political entities, differences in construals can be seen: 'power-sharing' (as used by Adams (2006)) stresses the need of both communities to be equally involved in local government whereas 'devolution' (as prominent in DUP discourse (DUP, 2006)) foregrounds that power is to be exercised by NI politicians instead of by the British government.

Similar construals can be seen in the metaphoric framing of the 1998 Agreement. Some metaphors, such as those activating a WAR frame, are not only pervasive in political discourse but also particularly prone to presenting adversarial relationships between two sides (Semino, 2008; Flusberg, Matlock and Thibodeau, 2018). Besides construing such adversarial relation, war metaphors also tend to activate emotions and mostly those related to fear as a result of a potential threat. This can be clearly seen in example [10]: the validity of the Agreement is to be assessed not in relation to its policies but also to the perceived actions of members of the outgroup and how these could impact on the self. Likewise, war metaphors also have an evaluative potential which could be useful for delegitimizing both policies and the actions of other political parties. As seen in example [11] our knowledge about the structure of WAR (Charteris-Black, 2004, p. 69; Flusberg, Matlock and Thibodeau, 2018, pp. 7–8) activates evaluative inferences about political action: if the other unionist political parties (e.g. the DUP) have deserted the negotiation talks ('the battlefield' in the example), then they are not working in favour of the community, and thus their political legitimacy is minimized. By inferential opposition, the validity and political legitimacy of the uttering political party (the UUP) are highlighted. This self-representation in positive terms can also be observed in the second part of the example with a clear focus on mappings related to the defensive nature of war. These lexical choices are not only meaningful because of their figurative framing of the political situation in NI. Given that metaphor is dynamic and that inferences are contextually dependent (Cameron, 2011; Flusberg, Matlock and Thibodeau, 2018), such framing choices can also be inextricably linked and understood as being not (only) metaphoric. This is the case of references to 'opponents and enemies' in example [10] or 'defend' (in [11]). Rather, these words can also relate to more literal perceptions of members of the other communities. Besides, in both examples we can observe that lexical choices activating the WAR frame are repeated, hence contributing to the discursive construction of a metaphoric/intertextual space which serves as the narrative basis – that is, the scenario – upon which political actions are to be judged.

[10] On Easter Sunday all of our speakers called on all republicans to examine the document in great detail. … It needs to be examined in **the context of strategy and struggle**. And in preparing for the next phase we need also to examine the positions and **strategies of our opponents and enemies**. (Adams, 1998)

[11] those voices who cry out 'treachery', and accuse us of selling the Union, whose primary objective is the destruction of this party. … They are the very people who have **deserted the battlefield**, who have no vision for a NI secure within the UK. … Unlike others, who ran away from the **fight**, the UUP attended the talks because we felt that the best way to **defend** and **promote** the cause of the Union was not by abstention but by fighting for our cause. (Trimble, 1998)

Attempts to counteract the adversarial nature of such metaphorical framing can be observed in explicit negations of the WAR frame. This can be seen in example [12], understood as referring to the non-figurative end of the ongoing violent conflict in NI and presenting a metaphoric outcome of the political negotiations. Negation is important in this extract. First because it functions as framing instantiation mechanism, that is, it activates the frame in our mind (Stockwell, 2020, p. 110), and second because negation could work co-textually as a mechanism for challenging generally accepted views which, in this example, are subsequently reframed by providing an alternative categorization of reality (Stockwell, 2020, p. 163). The WAR frame as a mechanism for conceptualizing reality is rejected (not a 'victory' or 'defeat') and an alternative frame ('success') is proposed. A further discursive opposition is co-textually constructed: the opposition implicit in the WAR frame (and explicit in the attention-grabbing premodifiers 'sectional' or 'partisan') is equally rejected and the idea of the agreement being an achievement (OED, 2024) that is to be mutually attributed to both communities (in the use of 'common' as premodifier) is profiled.

Example [12] shows one of the most distinguishing feature of discourses by the SDLP: their attempt at providing a conceptual framework within which members of both communities could be accommodated (Filardo-Llamas, 2008a, 2010; McLoughlin, 2008).

> [12] The Agreement challenges all of us but the Agreement threatens none of us. The Agreement did not involve, and its provisions do not offer, **sectional victory or partisan defeat**. Instead it represents common success for unionist, nationalists and others as we try to create new relationships … Nobody's aspiration is thwarted by the Agreement. The integrity of nobody's position has been **surrendered** in this Agreement. (Hume, 1998)

In order to understand how metaphor relates to conflictual discourses, it is also important to reflect about how some metaphors are inextricably linked to the core values of some of the political parties. For example, in NI, such is the case of those figurative uses of language which activate a religion frame, which are most prominent in the case of the statements uttered by Ian Paisley (see example [13]). The DUP is described in the literature as an 'ethno-religious organization' whose defence of the Union is fused with a particular religious approach. The DUP emerged from Paisley's Protestant Unionist Party in the 1960s and its appeal is partly related to their fusion of politics and religion (Tonge, 2014, pp. 132–62). Religion thus features prominently in Paisley's discourse, and it does not only function as a means for metaphorically evaluating political actions. It also activates intertextual inferences which render those metaphorical uses evaluative. Thus, religion functions as a frame which triggers a moral judgement (Entman, 1993). As in examples [10] and [11], a very rich metaphoric scenario is discursively created in [13], hence allowing for multiple negative emotions to arise from the activated correspondences: God is mapped with the IRA and the sacrificed lamb is mapped with the RUC. Intersubjective beliefs about the IRA and the RUC and how these relate to the core beliefs of the DUP and the unionist community allow for this frame to reproduce conflictual relations between the two communities in NI.

> [13] In one of the most despicable aspects of the deal, all terrorist prisoners are to walk free within 2 years whilst the RUC **is to be put on the altar and sacrificed to keep the IRA happy**. (Paisley, 1998)

While the metaphorical examples analysed above are not to be understood as an exhaustive analysis of all the frames activated in politicians' responses to the 1998 Agreement (see Filardo-Llamas, 2008b for a more detailed description), these extracts show how such metaphorical framing works in this conflictual context.

First, correspondences between domains stress the existence of adversarial relations between social and political participants. Second, they usually rely on co-textual activations of intertextual frames which are usually related to historical events, features of the situational context or core knowledge shared by members of a group. Both features render metaphorical framing useful for evaluating and (de)legitimizing given policies, such as the 1998 Agreement, and they do so by relying on the discursive function of frames as mechanisms upon which moral judgement can be based. Such oppositions can be diluted by relying on other frames, such as JOURNEY and particularly on the possibility to move 'forward' (Adams, 2006; DUP, 2006), which feature more prominently in responses to the St Andrews Agreement in 2006. In spite of metaphor being dynamic and its meaning being dependent on context, these differences in framing resonate with discussions of framing effects in other contexts. Examples of these studies include Hart's (2023) analysis of the WAR frame in media discourses about social movements or Semino et al.'s (2018) comparison of the framing effects of the WAR and JOURNEY metaphorical domains when talking about cancer.

This section has focused on the analysis of categorization, metaphor and the activation of intertextual knowledge as specific types of framing strategies. The examples have shown how all of them rely on the cognitive ability of judgement as a mechanism for construing different views of reality. While separated for analytical reasons, the three of them are frequently embedded and intertwined in such a way that multiple framing layers can be found in a single instance of discourse. All of them together can trigger evaluative inferences about political action. Likewise, all of them can result in conflictual or consensual representations of relations between communities. Examples above have shown that in spite of being produced at a time of peace, underlying conflictual relations permeate the framing strategies of (at least) the two most extremist political parties analysed. Such conflictual relations show that the vagueness in the 1998 Agreement and subsequent framing of the document by at least some NI politicians can be linked to the idea of 'negative peace', defined as the containment of war and the lack of physical violence (Schäffner and Wenden, 1995, p. xix).

Case study 6.2: Conflict in the urban landscape

In previous case studies, I have mostly focused on the textual dimension of how politicians have responded to sociopolitical events. This case study, whose emphasis is on public discourses in the streets of NI cities, serves a double function: first, acknowledging that discourse is multimodal and that construal operations shall be considered and analysed in different semiotic modes (Van Leeuwen, 2012; Machin and van Leeuwen, 2016; Hart, 2025). Second, emphasizing that conflict can be related to the way in which cultural practices permeate public discourses, and that the public sphere is constituted by more than just statements by public figures. As such, in the 1998 Agreement, a clear reference is made to this role of culture in conflict resolution: 'An essential aspect of the reconciliation process is the promotion of a culture of tolerance at every level of society' (NIO, 1998). This reference to culture in the public sphere also aligns with previous studies, which have argued that the way in which semiotic resources are used in war monuments convey particular discourses and identities which mediate those artistic representations (Abousnnouga and Machin, 2010).

Conflict and division in NI is not only related to political positions, but it is also manifested in the configuration of space in the cities, which have been traditionally characterized by inter-communal division (see Abdelmonem and McWhinney, 2015, for a description of attempts at stitching division in Belfast). A key aspect in this division is murals and plaques. These do not only delimit the boundaries of spaces inhabited by members of each community, but they also recall and memorize history and serve an internal and external propagandistic function by reminding members of the NI communities of their ideological allegiance and showing to visitors a partial vision of the conflict (Roe et al., 1999; Rolston, 2010; Rapp and Rhomberg, 2012; Simone-Charteris, 2017).

A mechanism for signalling core values of a given community is by activating particular frames. These can be either figuratively or non-figuratively related to human experience, and hence more generic, or to intertextual (cultural and community-related) knowledge such as historical events, thus being issue-specific (de Vreese, 2005; Van Dijk, 2005). Being aware that both types of frames interact in political murals is important. It can be argued that some issue-specific frames (such as those related to the historical myths described in Chapter 3) are more prone to strengthening conflictual relations between communities, particularly if they are related to given events at the time of The Troubles and/or if they appeal to the Unionist siege mentality or the Nationalist victimhood one. It is not the aim of this case study to reflect about how framing is processed in each semiotic mode. However, previous studies on framing in the news have noted that there is a relation between visuals and emotions, and that emotionally charged images are powerful when framing political messages (Powell et al., 2015; Alonso Belmonte and Porto, 2020). Given the inextricable link between memory, identity and the configuration of physical spaces in NI, and the key role of murals in this divided place (Filardo-Llamas, 2012; Filardo-Llamas and González-Cascos Jiménez, 2014; Goulding and McCroy, 2021), I believe that it is important to explore how such murals construct (or silence) conflictual relations between the communities. The analysis below is based on a number of photographs taken by myself in the streets of Belfast in 2008 and 2010 and on photographs collected in public repositories (Crowley, 2022; McCormick, 2023).[21] It seeks to reflect on the multimodal activation of frames in murals. Thus, it shall not be treated as an exhaustive description of identities as reflected in murals (for overviews of this, see Goulding and McCroy, 2021; Rolston, 2010; Simone-Charteris, 2017), but as a discussion of the role that language and visuals play in the configuration of public spaces. As such, I claim that the linguistic landscape is a more than apt object for the analysis of framing mechanisms and that construals in such pictorial representations are morally justified by the activation of culture- and issue-specific frames.

One of the most frequently identified feature of such murals, particularly in Loyalist (Unionist) ones, is the activation of knowledge related to the WAR frame (Rolston, 2010). An example can be seen in all the pictures included under Figure 6.4, which shows photographs taken in what is known as the 'Ulster's freedom corner' in Newtownards Road, East Belfast. By explicitly stressing the name of this place – 'Ulster's Freedom Corner' (Figure 6.4b) – further inferential reasoning is activated, thus linking back to the 'siege mentality' of the Unionist community (McKittrick and McVea, 2000; see also Chapter 3) and their perception of being under threat (from which they need to defend themselves). This siege mentality is closely linked to their conceptualization of space (as discussed in the textual analysis of categorization above). It is the province of Ulster that is to be defended because it is legitimately one of the four nations in the UK (see Figure 6.4c): Northern Ireland, England, Scotland and Wales. The link between the four nations in the UK is not only visually represented by the flags in the murals but also textually in the use of the verb 'separate'. As explained in Chapter 4, this links to the Unionist conceptualization of British identity, which is based on a unity gestalt whereby the UK is presented as the CONTAINER in which all four nations are included.

As seen in Figure 6.4a, the WAR frame is not only textual but is also visually activated by the image of a person wearing a balaclava, military clothing and a weapon, and it is intertextually linked to past historical times (in the clothing of the other person depicted in the murals with which a symmetric relation is established). The historical link is not only based on them being similarly shaped but also in the left-right sequencing of the images, which reflect our

Figure 6.4a 'Ulster's present day defenders', Newtownards Road, East Belfast.

Figure 6.4b 'Ulster's freedom corner', Newtownards Road, East Belfast.

Figure 6.4c 'Who shall separate us', Newtownards Road, East Belfast.

Figure 6.4d 'Ulster's past defenders', Newtownards Road, East Belfast.

Western conceptualization of time going from the left (as identified with the past) to the right (i.e. the present or the future). These visuals categorize loyalist paramilitaries as an army, hence endowing them with legitimacy as they are not only organized but their existence is justified because they serve a specific purpose (OED, 2024). This legitimacy is textually reinforced through the categorizing noun 'defenders', which entails the existence of an enemy posing a threat to the self. Likewise, the idea that paramilitary groups are organized can also be seen in the noun 'brigade'. The historical legitimacy of contemporary paramilitary groups ('present day defenders' in Figure 6.4a) is traced back to the formation time (in 1972), hence establishing a link between two distinct times in history. This link with history – and historical legitimacy – can also be observed in another painting that forms part of this group of murals (see Figure 6.4d) where a similar structure can be found. History functions as an intertextual frame with which a comparison is established: present defenders are similar to those in the past. Such use also has evaluative potential and stresses the moral legitimacy of contemporary paramilitary groups which – like those in the past – defend the existence of Ulster from unmentioned external threats.

The activation of the WAR frame in these murals works on the three levels of framing identified throughout this chapter, hence resulting in multi-layered judgement of the commemorated sociopolitical events. First, members of paramilitary groups are categorized as an 'army' (and not as a violent gang, for example). This legitimizes their existence by endowing them with a 'valid' reason for carrying out violent action – the need to defend themselves from an existing threat – and by stressing their being organized. Second, at a time of, at least, legal peace, it figuratively frames the political situation in NI and stresses the existence of opposition between two communities which have different goals. Such goals, particularly when related to nationality, are also visually evoked. For example, the territorial claim about NI remaining a part of the UK can be inferred from the colours dominating the mural – red, white and blue – as the ones of the British flag, and also from the accompanying visuals as mentioned above (in Figure 6.4c). This aligns with previous studies, which have already noted the prominent role of flags in claiming territorial spaces as belonging to a given NI community (Storey, 2001, p. 158). Finally, categorization and metaphorical framing are inextricably related in these pictorial commemorations: a close relation is established between the time when the murals are visited/seen and the events which are being commemorated/understood. Thus, this activation of intertextual frames (mostly historical knowledge which evokes particular feelings) has a judgement function as it is through historical images that contemporary political statements are made (Storey, 2001, p. 158).

A similar activation of war intertextual knowledge can be seen in other (more recent examples), such as the mural erected in Castlereagh (East Belfast) in 2022 to commemorate the death of Queen Elizabeth (Crowley, 2022, mni03029), where a person dressed with army clothing is kneeling in front of a portrait of Queen Elizabeth I. In that case, a Union Jack is reproduced as the background of both figures.[22] Likewise, a clear relation between literal and metaphorical conceptualizations of war can be seen in another mural which was painted in 2022 in East Belfast (Crowley, 2022, mni08986) where two paramilitary Ulster Volunteer Force (UVF) figures are depicted. The metaphorical understanding is textually activated in the text accompanying that visual representation, with an explicit correspondence being established between war and politics, which are presented as comparable scenarios (Musolff, 2006).[23]

> [14] **In war** you can only be killed once. **In politics**, many times. Our British identity is non-negotiable! (Crowley, 2022, p. mni08986; my emphasis)

Republican murals have been mostly characterized by the activation of cultural frames, frequently related to historical knowledge. Several types of murals have been identified in republican areas. A clear example of the multiplicity of themes depicted in republican murals can be seen in Figure 6.5, which shows photographs taken at what is known as the 'International Wall'. This set of murals are painted in a peace line (i.e. a wall that divided Protestant and Catholic neighbourhoods) in Divis Street, at the Lower Falls area in West Belfast. While these photos were taken in 2008, they still reflect how mural painting is understood by the republican community: as a means of constructing their identity and making political statements addressed both at the members of the community and at (inter)national visitors. The murals below show a multiplicity of themes, as it has also been explained in previous studies: historical events, cultural attributes associated with what it means to be Irish and connection with international events (Storey, 2001, p. 158; Rolston, 2010).

The Irish cultural identity features in these murals both in its textual and visual format. The clearest example can be seen in Figure 6.5g. The green colour in the background together with the fonts used in the text clearly evoke Irish traits. Such identity is further reinforced by the visual reference to hurling, one of Ireland's native sports games. This can be seen in the two men playing with the ash stick, in the trophy which has the shape of the Irish mether (a drinking vessel in the Celtic tradition), and in the Irish cross with the name of the

Gaelic Athletic Association (GAA) written in Irish (Cumann Luthchleas). This link with Ireland is also stressed textually in the categorization of Councillor Liam MacCarthy as a 'Gael patriot', hence profiling that the island of Ireland as a whole is to be taken as the space to be defended and the one to which the republican community belongs. The link to political action can also be observed in the activation of intertextual frames: Liam MacCarthy, born in London but with Irish roots, was elected as chairman of the GAA in London and he was the person that commissioned the trophy in its current shape. Such trophy is still used in the All-Ireland Hurling competition organized annually by the GAA. The activation of such frames does not only have a commemorating function but also provides the foundation upon which contemporary politics can be judged and stresses the historical legitimacy of republican demands for a united Ireland.

The commemoration of prior events in history can also be observed in other murals. These include the 1981 Hunger Strikes, with a depiction of one of the men involved in it (Brendan Hughes) together with their demands (Figure 6.5a). As explained in Chapter 3, the Hunger Strikes have acquired an almost mythical trait for the republican community and they have contributed to building the victim and martyrdom mentality that characterizes this community (Bew and Gillespie, 1999; Fierke, 2013, p. 131). Such depiction can also be observed in other historical events that are pictorially represented and textually explained, for example, in the reference to the Manchester Martyrs (Figure 6.5e), recalling the history of three Irish nationalists that were executed in London in 1867 (as also explained in the text accompanying the painting). The categorization of these figures as 'martyrs' provides a frame upon which their actions are to be judged: their belief on Irish nationalism took them to high suffering and eventually to death (OED, 2024). A similar perception is visually activated by the representation of the posters which claimed their conviction. Posters also feature in the visual portrayal of the Hunger Strikes in Figure 6.5a. In those posters we have a textual reference to the actions done by the other (the British government in this case) to representative figures of the Irish republican community: 'conviction' and 'smash'. As such, the historical actions of the others – presented as the supposedly authorial figures – are delegitimized while the victimhood trait of the (unfairly accused) self is stressed.

While other historical events could have been mentioned, these two events activate an imprisonment frame which functions as the intertextual frame upon which contemporary political actions can be judged (also in Figure 6.5c). The prison frame is in this case visually reinforced in the depiction of the bars

Figure 6.5a Historical events: H-Block Hunger strikes, Divis Street, West Belfast.

Figure 6.5b International link: Free Palestine, Divis Street, West Belfast.

Figure 6.5c Contemporary politics: republican prisoners, Divis Street, West Belfast.

Figure 6.5d Historical events and international link: Frederick Douglass, Divis Street, West Belfast.

Figure 6.5e Historical events: The Manchester martyrs, Divis Street, West Belfast.

Figure 6.5f International link: Askatasuna, Divis Street, West Belfast.

Figure 6.5g Irish cultural identity: Gaelic, Divis Street, West Belfast.

behind which an unidentifiable figure can be seen. This generic prison frame is textually anchored and specified via the textual reference to Maghaberry, a high-security prison in NI where paramilitaries belonging to both sides of the social divide were interned. It shall be noted that the photograph in Figure 6.5c was taken in December 2008, at a time of protests demanding better treatment for prisoners (*The Belfast Telegraph*, 26 April 2010). Thus, the Hunger Strikes and protests by republican prisoners in the H-Blocks at the Maze prison stand as the historical frame upon which the contemporary protest was to be judged. The phrase 'end internment by remand' stresses the intertextual link with protests at the time of the Hunger Strikes, which originated among demands for better treatment in prisons and the end of 'internment without trial' (Alonso, 2007). Internment is thus not only a means of categorizing the act of confining someone to prison (OED, 2024), it also activates cultural knowledge about prior events in NI and triggers evaluative inferences which evoke shared emotions held by the republican community. The importance of internment can still be observed in contemporary NI politics, with the redefinition of the process in this news piece taken from an article published in the *Irish Republican News*, a periodical publication which is explicitly related to the 'Irish struggle for national self-determination':

[15] The **definition of 'internment'** is the act of putting someone in prison for political reasons without legal due process. This is what is happening to Republicans in the Occupied Six Counties today. ... **Remand** is <u>the new form of British internment</u> and this is consistently used to imprison Irish Republicans today. Republicans will be locked up on spurious charges and held on remand for a number of years before charges are dropped or the case falls apart. (*Irish Republican News*, 13 July 2023)

A final theme which is prevalent in republican murals is the attempt to compare the conflict in NI to other international conflicts (Storey, 2001; Rolston, 2010). As shown in Figures 6.5b and 6.5f, the conflicts in Palestine and the Basque Country feature as part of the collection of murals analysed here. It shall be noted that this international link is also stressed in the name given to the area – the 'International Wall'. The importance of this particular wall in making political statements, not only aimed at the domestic but also at a worldwide audience, can be observed in the changing status of these murals. In March 2024, the wall was covered with murals by local artists and Gazan artists to show support to the population in Palestine (*Breaking News Ireland*, 3 March 2024).

In the case under analysis, a visual mechanism of framing can be seen in Figure 6.5b, where a wall separating people in Palestine serves as a strategy of comparison with people living in the republican community in Belfast. The idea of division between two communities in a space is foregrounded for both conflicts, and the ingroup is presented (both visually and physically) as being confined inside the CONTAINER which is delimited by the wall, which acts as a border. As such a conceptual interaction can be observed between image schemas and framing mechanisms, exemplified both by categorization and intertextuality. Categorization also features in the textual component of the mural, with the situation in Palestine being presented as 'Nakba', an Arabic word standing for catastrophe and which is used to designate the de-Arabization of Palestine resulting from the 1948 Palestine War. The term is used by Palestinians with an extended meaning to refer to their ongoing persecution by Israel, and it has become a key term in the configuration of Palestinian historical memory (Masalha, 2012). Such intertextual frames allow for analogical correspondences to be established between the Palestinian Nakba and historical events in NI, such as Partition. These correspondences trigger evaluative inferences about the cause of the sense of displacement suffered by both communities and legitimizes their national(ist) claims. Likewise, such framing mechanisms evoke emotions which can be shared by members of both communities, as they can both feel aligned with a victimhood sense.

Similar correspondences can be observed in Figure 6.5f with the Basque demand for 'self-determination'. As in the examples analysed above, the role of flags as a means of constructing identity shall be emphasized. Likewise, the correspondence and parallelism between claims by Basque nationalists and the republican community can be seen in the text component of the mural, via reference to the existence of 'political prisoners', 'political parties [being] banned', 'incidents of torture' and 'civil rights [being] abused'.

How intertextual frames function as a means of comparison and judgement becomes clear in the text included in Figure 6.5d. By quoting the words of Frederik Douglass, not only cultural knowledge about the African American civil rights movement of the nineteenth century is activated, but a world view about the situation in NI is also promoted. As in previous cases, an analogy is established between republican claims and those made by representative figures of other international and historical movements. The republican movement is thus legitimized by being judged along the parameters of other movements. Murals included in West Belfast's International Wall rely on two types of intertextual comparison: (1) with past historical events which are of significance for the republican community and (2) with other international conflicts. In the case of the latter, all of them are constructed as an opposition between a powerful abusing entity and a victim. It is the latter role that functions as a prototypical and intertextual category for framing the role of the republican community in the NI conflict.

> [16] Perhaps no class has carried prejudice against colour to a point more dangerous than have the Irish and yet no people have been more relentlessly oppressed on account of race and religion.

The analysis of the examples above has shown the importance that intertextual frames have in commemoration and the maintenance of memory in the public landscape (Storey, 2001), and also how this works in promoting particular views about reality. In the analysis of loyalist murals categorization and metaphors played a more prominent role in the evaluation of the contemporary conflict, with intertextual frames being activated mainly as a means of providing historical legitimacy for the claims of the unionist community. Thus, framing strategies in loyalist murals are more widely related to the legitimization strategies of authorization – by appealing to the authority of tradition – and rationalization – by emphasizing the goals of this community (Van Leeuwen, 2007). While authorization is still prevalent in republican murals, mostly when contemporary politics is framed as being related to historical events, these seem to rely more on mythopoesis, that is, legitimization 'conveyed through narratives whose outcomes reward legitimate actions and punish non-legitimate actions' (Van Leeuwen, 2007, p. 92). Such mythopoesis is closely related to framing resulting from the activation of knowledge about other conflicts, mostly international, in which suffering individuals are implicitly presented as being similar to the ones in the republican community. Framing strategies in both loyalist and republican murals also evoke shared emotions which arise from the negative evaluation of others (while implicitly emphasizing the positive evaluation of the self) (Reyes, 2011). Framing strategies are thus of importance for analysing how conflict is commemorated in public spaces as it can shed light on whether conflictual relations are still explicitly (or implicitly) present in such public manifestations.

Summary: Comparison and judgement in conflict discourses

This chapter has focused on the role of comparison and judgement in the creation of conflictual construals of reality in public discourse. As shown in the case studies, via linguistic choices politicians and society construct the sociopolitical situation in such a way that they emphasize or minimize conflictual relations between groups. In the case of framing strategies, this is done via the activation of prefab chunks of knowledge called 'frames'. As shown in the analysis, such frames tend to be rich and multi-layered. Thus, they can trigger multiple inferences, which can eventually lead to (positive and/or negative) evaluation and subsequent emotions being evoked.

Framing strategies are related to what we could call inferential evaluation, that is, they do not necessarily convey an explicit use of positive or negative terms (Thompson and Hunston, 1999), but they allow discourse participants to judge a sociopolitical event in terms of positive social esteem and negative social sanction (see Hart, 2014, p. 49 for a discussion of these terms in CDS; see Martin and White, 2005 for an explanation of how judgement works in Appraisal Theory). Such activation of frames, as shown in the analysis, is not neutral and can stress the existence of conflictual relations in society (as seen in the activation of the WAR frame in murals or the use of words such as 'partition' or 'veto' when politicians discussed the contents of the 1998 Agreement). These conflictual relations are inextricably linked to our binary conceptualization of politics (Flusberg, Matlock and Thibodeau, 2018), which is even more prevalent in places characterized by ethnonationalist conflict and division between communities.

Previous studies on framing strategies have focused extensively on figurative language, and most notably metaphor. However, other accounts of the judgement construal operation in CL (Croft and Cruse, 2004) also consider categorization (understood as non-figurative framing). Besides these two mechanisms, in this chapter I have advocated for the analysis of intertextuality as part of framing strategies, as this is a key aspect in CDS (Reisigl and Wodak, 2002; Wodak et al., 2009). This is justified by three premises, as shown in the case studies above: first, a wide understanding of what is political discourse (Van Dijk, 1997), which is not only the one uttered by politicians (as analysed in case study 6.1 when politicians talk about the 1998 Agreement) but also the one about political actions and/or with political effects (as shown in case study 6.2 with the study of political murals and the configuration of the urban landscape). Second, one of the functions of political discourse is to legitimize the actions of the self (and their community) (Chilton and Schäffner, 2002; Van Leeuwen, 2007; Reyes, 2011). Third, legitimization can be achieved via mythopoesis, that is, the discursive configuration of narratives (similar to myths) which trigger evaluation (Van Leeuwen, 2007; Kelsey, 2017) and appeal to emotions (Reyes, 2011).

The examples in the case studies have explored these three framing mechanisms – categorization, metaphor and intertextual frames – in two semiotic modes: textual (in politicians' statements about the 1998 Agreement) and visual (in the analysis of murals). Such analysis has shown how these three types of strategies allow for reality to be judged and inferentially compared with different types of knowledge. Findings in the analysis section show how conflictual relations in the source frame – that is, the one which is textually or visually activated – can be mapped onto the discursive construal of contemporary politics. As such a multi-layered analysis of framing strategies is a necessary tool for understanding how cognition plays a mediating role in the relation between discourse and conflict.

7

Positioning and perspective

What do we mean by positioning and perspective?

As noted in Chapter 2, perspective is the cognitive ability associated with positioning strategies, and it is a direct consequence of our being in the world. Because we live in the here and now, 'we perceive the world from a certain vantage point in space and time' (Tenbrink, 2020, p. 103). Any construal of the world is thus dependent on the speaker's – and audience's – relative position (Croft and Cruse, 2004, p. 58). The analysis of how discourse is construed from a particular perspective is inextricably linked to the notion of situatedness, understood not only as a spatio-temporal location but also as relative to epistemic and cultural context. This attempt at explaining discourse as being situated at the intersection of multiple dimensions is what underlies Chilton's (2005) proposal for a model that would capture not only the spatial anchorage of discourse but also the semantic configurations which can be 'derived' from such spatial concepts. This geometric and three-dimensional model, which is based on a set of coordinate systems, lies at the core of Discourse Space Theory (DST) (Chilton, 2004, 2005, 2014).[1] While further detail on this theory will be provided below, this can be broadly summarized as an attempt to explain how the speakers' viewpoint is construed and 'understood in terms of space, time and epistemological stance' (Chilton, 2005, p. 86). DST has not only been widely applied in CDS (cf. Filardo-Llamas, Hart and Kaal, 2016 for an overview), but it is also the theoretical premise guiding 'proximization' (Cap, 2010, 2013a, 2017b), or the explanation of how political actors linguistically bring closer to the self some aspects of reality.

The description of perspective and positioning strategies included in this chapter requires a terminological clarification. Previous studies on 'ideology' in CDS have defined this slippery concept as related to the 'perspective' or 'world view' that a text presents, usually by trying to maintain power (Hart, 2025). While, generally speaking, similarities and overlaps can be established between these three words, they are conceptually different. Given the focus on the notion of conflict, neither ideologies nor world views feature prominently as theoretical concepts in this book (and hence have not been defined in Chapter 2). Still, their importance in CL-CDS cannot be neglected, particularly in those studies grounded on social cognition (e.g. Hart, 2014, 2025; Kaal, 2024; Koller, 2014). For clarification purposes, I include a brief description of how I understand each of these terms. Ideologies are the networks of social, or socio-cognitive, representations which provide the motivation and support for particular ways of acting and being in the world (Hart, 2025; Koller, 2014; Van Dijk, 1998). As such, in my view, ideology stresses the existence of a 'social mind' that has to be analysed in a social, political and cultural context (Van Dijk, 1998, p. 6). Closely related to this definition is the idea of world view, understood as the 'subjective realities' which are discursively constructed and negotiated via repeated patterns of instantiation which are contextually determined (Hart, 2025; Kaal, 2024). Some of such world views may be dominant, even naturalized and perceived as objective (or at least so by members of a community), and this lays the ground for the discursive construction of 'alternative' realities (which could be equated to world views). In my view, such (discursively induced) world views are, at least partially, shaped by (shared) beliefs or ideologies.

The notion of world view is inextricably linked to perspectivization (Kaal, 2024) and to how speakers position themselves. For clarification purposes, perspective is understood in this book as a construal operation which is discursively manifested via positioning strategies (Hart, 2014, 2025) and which is concerned with where speakers situate themselves within their conceptualization of the world and where other actors and actions are located relative to the speaker's position. Perspective can be metaphorically explained as the viewing arrangement of a scene, that is, how reality is viewed from the position of the utterer (and interpreter) (Langacker, 2008, p. 73). The term 'position' can be 'understood as a spatial metaphor conceptualizing the speaker's and/or hearer's relationship to their interlocutor(s), to their physical location, to the point in time of the ongoing utterance, and to where they are in the ongoing discourse' (Chilton, 2004, p. 56). Such positioning assumes the centrality of the self, which is the presupposed vantage point from which the scene is viewed. Entities in the discourse world – that is, the discursively activated mental representation of such scene – are thus construed at different distances relative to the self. Such distance, which can be proximal or distant, is not only physical but representative of discourse relations (metaphorical and abstract) between the different entities, actions and events in the discourse world (Chilton, 2005).

Positioning and perspective in political discourse

Previous studies on political discourse have already focused on the construal operation perspective, and particularly on the construction of 'discourse worlds' (Hart, 2017, pp. 80–1; see, for example, Filardo-Llamas, 2010, 2013; Filardo-Llamas, Hart and Kaal, 2016). The notion of discourse world and its relevance for the analysis of political discourse is initially proposed by Paul Chilton (2004, pp. 52–5), who defines such worlds as the mental spaces entertained by an utterer and which are presented as real. Two notions shall be stressed in this theoretical proposal, as they are the grounds upon which its main ideas are developed. First, Chilton's notion of 'discourse world' is largely based on Fauconnier's (1994) Mental Space Theory, a proposal within Cognitive Semantics whose main aim is to explain how meaning is based on an individual's understanding of experience, and how such mental spaces provide a medium for reasoning using cognitive models (Lakoff, 2018). As such, mental spaces provide a cognitive explanation for the conceptual structures that underlie meaning. These are dynamically constructed in interaction. Its elements are structured by image schemas, cognitive models and frames (as explained in Chapters 4, 5 and 6) and different kinds of relations are established between them. Second, Chilton's notion of 'discourse world' is also closely related to Werth's (1999, p. 20) concept of 'text world', understood as 'a deictic space, defined initially by the discourse itself, and specifically by the deictic and referential elements in it'. Besides the importance given to discourse as a key element in the configuration of conceptual structures, Werth (1999) stresses that text representations are not objective but rather biased, and that these reflect a 'human viewpoint'.

Multiple viewpoints can be provided for a single event, and these reflect different perspectivized construals. Such viewpoints have to meet a number of properties, which can be summarized under the acronym PACKAGED: (1) Pragmatic (i.e. arising of human purposes), (2) Attitudinal (related to human emotions and beliefs), (3) Cognitive (mediated by mental processes), (4) fed by Knowledge and memory, (5) Artistic (and resulting from human creativity), (6) Grounded (to human situations), (7) Experiential and (8) driven by Discourse (Werth, 1999, p. 21). These properties are necessary for understanding how discourse worlds function in political discourse as these do not only reflect a politician's (and community's) beliefs and attitudes, but they are also aimed at pragmatically legitimizing their particular view. They are mediated by their knowledge of the world and previous experiences and inextricably linked to the situations in which discourse is uttered. DST, as explained above, is a methodological attempt at analysing such discourse worlds (Chilton, 2004).

Discourse worlds are conceptual structures which are constituted of multiple elements, including entities (i.e. people or places), actions/events and propositions. These elements are positioned in the text along three axes – space, time and evaluation/axiology (or modality in Chilton's (2004) initial description) – relative to a deictic centre (Hart, 2017, p. 81). The notion of position is linked to perspective as a construal operation, and it functions as a 'spatial metaphor conceptualizing the speaker's and/or hearer's relationship to their interlocutor(s), to their physical location, to the point in time of the ongoing utterance, and to where they are in the ongoing discourse' (Chilton, 2004, p. 56). Spatial cognition, thus, features prominently as a key aspect of DST, in their argument that discourse involves the '(re-)construction of a mental space which functions as a cohesive conceptual frame for the representation of geographically and culturally bounded (social) realities' (Cap, 2017a, p. 92). When triggered by discourse, this mental space is a discourse world, which is, in fact, a subjective representation (viewpoint) in which ideas are anchored relative to the self.

DST has been successfully applied to the study of political discourse, and it has been of use for explaining how intersubjective world views are constructed (Cap, 2017b; Chilton, 2004; Filardo-Llamas, 2013; Filardo-Llamas, Hart and Kaal, 2016; Kaal, 2024; Kopytowska, 2015). Such world views reflect given ideologies and, following DST's principles, they may at least partially result from perspective-taking, not only in space but also in time and evaluation, and the positioning of actors and actions relative to those three axes (Chilton, 2004; Filardo-Llamas, Hart and Kaal, 2016). Those world views are not objective but reflect the position of the speaker in space and time as constructed in the mind of that speaker (Chilton, 2005). As shown in Figure 2.2 (in Chapter 2), the space axis (s-axis) captures the position of the speaker and other entities in geographical or territorial locations; the time axis (t-axis) reflects anchorage relative not only to the utterance time but also to other historical times whose significance in politics is stressed. Finally, evaluation (modality (m-axis) in Chilton (2004) or axiology (a-axis) in Cap (2013)) is proposed as an abstract umbrella term encompassing not only epistemic and deontic modality but also the broader notion of axiology and inferential affordances about positive entities being (at least ideally) located close to the deictic centre (compared to the negative ones) (see also Filardo-Llamas, Hart and Kaal, 2016). The relevance of discourse worlds in political discourse analysis can be observed in their being proposed as an analytic category which could help in processes of conflict resolution (Ramsbotham, 2010). Because vantage points (i.e. the position from which a scene is viewed) are subjective, they can be discursively adapted so as to match the one of other participants involved in a communicative situation. Aligned vantage points are more likely to result in consensual views about sociopolitical events, hence reducing the likelihood of conflictual interpretations.

There are two core elements which help explain why discourse worlds are intersubjective and construe reality from a particular perspective. First, viewpoint and positioning are bound up with the concept of deixis, as will also be explained below (Werth, 1999, p. 10). Deixis can be understood as the process of pointing at entities while simultaneously specifying their location (spatial, temporal or of any other kind) relative to the speaker and hearer (Chilton, 2003, p. 108). Such locations reflect a relation to the deictic centre, that is, the egocentric vantage point from which reality is viewed. Because locations are relative to a central physical or abstract point, a proximal-distant relationship is thus conceptualized between entities present in the discourse space.

Second, the CENTRE-PERIPHERY image schema is necessary for explaining affective responses to entities conceptualized in a discourse space (see also Chapter 4) (Chilton, 2004, p. 153; Chilton and Schäffner, 2002, p. 31). Positions in the three axes in the DST model can be understood as part of a remoteness SCALE, in which they can be placed as being closer or more distant to the centre. If the close-remote scale is mapped onto a morality (evaluative) scale, what is good (or morally right) tends to be conceptually presented as closer to the self than that which is negatively perceived. Such conceptualization ties in with the pervasiveness of image schemas in construals of the world and with the importance of orientational metaphors (UP-DOWN; CENTRE-PERIPHERY) in our understanding and evaluation of relations between entities (see Chapter 4; Chilton, 1996, pp. 50–5; Lakoff and Johnson, 1980). Placing entities in these three axes can thus help us explain how discourses construe events as being ego-aligned – that is, affiliated to the self's spatio-temporal and axiological positioning – or ego-opposed – or confronted to the self (Hart, 2014, p. 128). These proximal-distant relations in the discourse space contribute to (de) legitimizing the existence and performance of particular sociopolitical actors and may have an effect in the maintenance or resolution of conflict.

Both deixis and the CENTRE-PERIPHERY schema feature prominently in proximization (Cap, 2013a), a theoretical model derived from DST that has been successfully applied to the study of political discourse. This theory seeks to explain discursive constructions of crisis and threat as a means of legitimizing political decisions. As noted by Cap (2013b, p. 295), the concept of proximization can be 'defined as a force construal operation meant to evoke closeness of the external threat, to solicit legitimization of preventive measures'. Proximization provides, in my view, a detailed description of lexico-grammatical cues which can be analysed in an instance of discourse, and it offers two analytic concepts which can shed light on how we discursively conceptualize antagonistic relations between entities: these can either be IDCs (inside-the-deictic centre) or ODCs (outside-the-deictic centre). Besides entities occupying two distinct spaces which are conceptually embedded within the broader discourse space, different elements in the structural configuration of such entities can be placed in different positions in the spatio-temporal and axiological remoteness scale. As such, entities may clash in space, time and/or values, thus increasing or narrowing the symbolic distance between such entities. Since the deictic centre can be discursively shifted (Chilton, 2005), so can the relative position of those entities. If we consider that the discourse space is structured along a three-dimensional vector space, it is relative to each of the axes (space, time, evaluation) that distance is to be constructed. As will be proved in the analysis (see also Filardo-Llamas, 2010, 2013), shifts in the vantage point in only one of the axes can be of use for legitimizing political actions in conflict situations.

Analysing perspective: Deixis

As mentioned above, DST is a deictic theory of language (Chilton, 2005; Hart, 2017; Werth, 1999). As such, DST tries to explain how instances of discourse are grounded to a particular context, that is, how the activated mental representations relate to the utterer's conception of reality (Langacker, 2008, p. 259). To understand such grounding, we need to identify two types of strategies. First, conceptualizing strategies, that is, those seeking to explain how entities and actions are portrayed in an instance of discourse (as explained in Chapters 4, 5 and 6); second, deictic strategies, or those aimed at explaining how the conceptual referent (i.e. any idealized entity in the world) relates to the discourse context – understood both as situational and cognitive. Explaining both strategies implies not only describing actors, actions and events but also identifying them relative to such discourse context (Langacker, 2008, pp. 276–7). The importance of deixis for the analysis of perspective as a construal operation has been widely attested (Croft and Cruse, 2004, p. 46; Hart, 2014), and it is also related to the indexical function of language. This indexical function has, in my view, two interrelated layers: first, indexicality underlies the use of some linguistic expressions, whose meaning depends on the interpretation prompted by the relation between those expressions and situational features (Chilton, 2004, p. 56). Second, political discourse operates indexically, as choices of language 'can implicitly signal political distinction' (Chilton, 2004, p. 201), that is, opposition to or affiliation with particular sociopolitical views. This second layer has been implicitly covered in Chapters 5 and 6, in the analysis of NPs as referential expressions. It is the aim of this section to explore indexicality – or deixis – as related to construal.

Studies on deixis in pragmatics have been mainly concerned with how language encodes features of the context of utterance, or speech events, and how the interpretation of any utterance also depends on the analysis of such context of utterance (Levinson, 1983, p. 54; Verschueren, 1999, pp. 18–19). Deixis thus functions as an 'anchor' of language to the real world which is achieved by pointing at entities that can be placed along different dimensions. For CL, this anchorage is not only relative to the situational (physical) context of utterance, but it reflects that perception is embodied (Stockwell, 2020, p. 49). As such, deictic expressions are both verified with reference to an actual world and create a perspectivized view of such world while also orientating the utterer and audience within it.

The most basic – and traditional – division of deixis involves looking at three types: person deixis, spatial deixis and temporal deixis (Levinson, 1983; Verschueren, 1999). Person deixis concerns the encoding of participants, and it is most commonly analysed via personal pronouns. Person deixis shall be considered a type of social deixis (Chilton, 2004, p. 56; Verschueren, 1999, pp. 20–1), as this term does not only encompass the perceived indexing of participants but also the attitude towards them (presented as personal distance) and how this relates to knowledge about the social structure and power relations between those participants. Previous studies on political discourse have stressed the importance of analysing (personal) pronouns (Chilton, 2003, 2004; De Fina, 1995; Filardo-Llamas and Boyd, 2017; Wilson, 1990) not only because they show the politicians' solidarity towards entities, actions and events but also because it is easy to shift their indexed referents when used in context. The notion of solidarity is important for explaining why it is important to analyse social/person deixis in political discourse. Following Brown and Gilman's (1972) distinction of power and solidarity pronouns and how this relates to the notion of sympathy, two types of involvement can be identified: one which I have called 'ideological solidarity', related to the speaker's position towards different

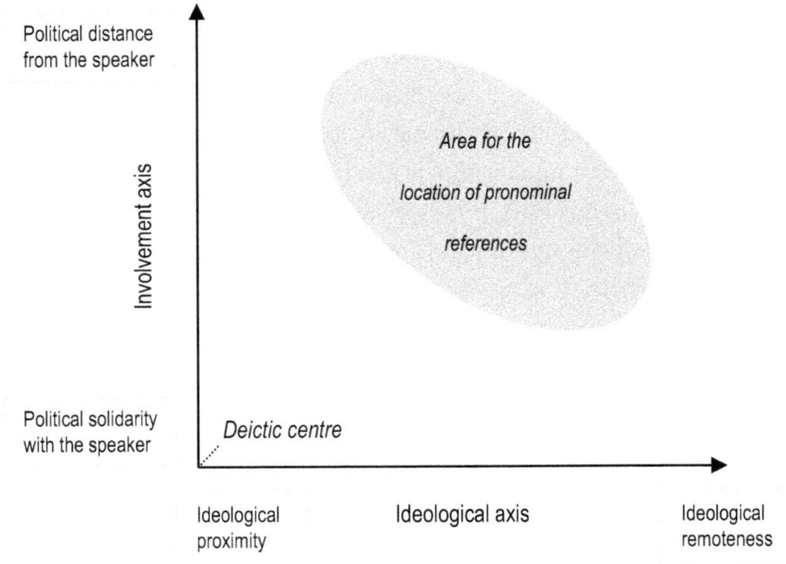

Figure 7.1 Social deixis in political discourse.

sociopolitical communities, and another called 'political solidarity', related to the participants' physical or metaphorical involvement in a particular action or event. Both types of solidarity/distance relations, as indexed by pronominal choices, are summarized in Figure 7.1. While this explanation is mostly related to the use of personal pronouns, a similar positioning effect can be achieved by other nominal grounding cues, such as the use of demonstratives or definite articles (Stockwell, 2020, p. 54).

Space deixis is related to the 'encoding of spatial locations relative to the location of the participants in the speech event' (Levinson, 1983, p. 62) and relative to the utterer's perception of such locations. In cases of conflict, the analysis of space deixis becomes even more relevant as entities, actions and events can be explicitly related to political or geopolitical spaces (Chilton, 2004, p. 56; see also Chapter 4). Such geopolitical anchorage is linked to the concept of 'territoriality', that is, 'the process whereby individuals or groups lay claim to territory' (Storey, 2001, p. 1). Given that people form bonds with particular places, how an utterer positions themselves in relation to territory is important for understanding how they discursively construct their identity (see also Billig, 1995, p. 174). As with social/person deixis, solidarity relations can be established with particular geopolitical locations, mostly by discursively placing them in the referential scope of the deictic centre. Space deixis is encoded in locatives, spatial adverbs, distal demonstratives, and verbs of motion (Stockwell, 2020,

p. 54). Given the prominence of spatial cognition in this chapter (and thus the metaphorical understanding of social and time deixis in terms of space), it shall be noted that space deixis is understood here in a physical and literal sense as referring mostly to the anchorage of discourse to identifiable territories, defined as bounded areas of geographic space which are occupied by a person, a group of persons or an institution (Chilton, 2004, p. 58; Storey, 2001, p. 1).

Most accounts of deixis have focused on 'pure' forms which are only meaningful in context, such as the adverb 'here' whose referent clearly varies depending on the context of utterance. However, given the importance of territoriality for understanding positioning in geopolitical conflicts, I believe that the names of geographical territories shall also be considered in the analysis. In my view, such names do not only function as indexical of a speaker's categorization of reality (as explained in Chapter 6), but they also reflect how the utterers position themselves relative to those locations. Geographical names function as 'long-term cognitive frames and current discourse cues – of mental maps, rather than of geographical measurement' (Chilton, 2003, p. 198). Thus, by exploring how politicians refer to specific locations, and where they anchor their discourse world, we shall be able to obtain how they imagine the map in which the political reality is circumscribed. As such, the analysis of names is crucial for explaining relations between entities and territories: not only are spaces viewed from a particular vantage point, but these are also constructed as being associated with (members of) the ingroup and the outgroup. Although related to different construal operations, a similar view underlies the relation between naming practices and image schemas as explained in Chapter 4.

Time deixis – which is usually expressed via temporal locatives, temporal adverbs and verbal tense and aspect (Levinson, 2003, pp. 74–5; Stockwell, 2020, p. 54) – is related to the encoding of temporal points and spans relative to the three possible temporal deictic centres: time of utterance (or where the speaker is at the time of speaking), event time and reference time (Levinson, 1983; Verschueren, 1999, p. 96; Stockwell, 2020, p. 54). The temporal deictic shifts which allow for this multiplicity of deictic centres to be discursively constructed are important for political discourse, as it lets speakers establish a proximal-distant relationship not only with the time of utterance but also with a reference time which utterers may feel affectively aligned with. Thus, not only a situational 'now' is important but also the relation between that now and past and future events. As noted throughout this book, perceived 'remoteness' of those events is related to construal operations and it is a 'function of discourse representation' (Chilton, 2003, p. 109). Perceptions about history are of particular importance as the profiled historical events do not only constitute the intertextual frames upon which contemporary events are judged (see Chapter 6), but they are also discursively positioned as being 'close' to the speaker in time. This allows for affective ties to be established between different event times. This role of history is central to national ideologies and is important in understanding how future policies may be discursively legitimized (Chilton, 2004). Thus, its relevance in NI political discourse cannot be overseen. By establishing relations between different points in time, politicians may heighten the emotional impact of their utterances.

Analysing deictics can help explain how the conceptual elements that form part of a discourse world are mapped onto the three-dimensional space proposed by DST. Deictics are the grammatical realizations that can assist analysts in uncovering the relative position of those conceptual elements in the discourse space. Deictics function as space builders (Fauconnier, 1994; Hart, 2014) along multiple dimensions which eventually form part of the rich discourse space: the time-space, the space-space or the domain-space (equivalent, in my view, to framing strategies as explained in Chapter 6).[2] Following Werth's (1999, p. 187) proposal, deictics can help us access the discourse world and identify its constitutive elements (which we call 'world builders'). Such builders can be of four different types: times (as in time deixis), place (as in space deixis), entities (as in social deixis) and relations (by indicating their position in the discourse space relative to the utterer). Identifying space builders, in my view, is important for identifying which spaces – and subsequent relations between entities in those spaces – are dynamically constructed as discourse unfolds.

Multiple mental spaces can be activated by a single instance of discourse with different kinds of relations being established between them. There is a parent mental space (usually equivalent to the speaker's entertained reality) and derived spaces with which such parent space is connected (Fauconnier, 1994; Werth, 1999). Deictic expressions (as explained in this chapter) and referential expressions (as covered in Chapters 5 and 6) are the key world-building elements. Most authors foreground the importance of deictics in analysing perspective and world view. However, in this book I align with Stockwell's (2020, p. 55) theory of reference being made to a mental representation, thus justifying the inclusion of all person pronouns, names and nouns in the analysis because they all inferentially index some kind of position. While both deictics and referential expressions index a position relative to the speaker, the latter also foregrounds attributes of the entities – something which can also be done by verbs signalling possession and attributes (Werth, 1999; Hart, 2014, p. 167). Location world-builders index physical or abstract location in time and space, which is in turn indicative of the speaker's perspective (Werth, 1999, p. 188). Shifts in the anchorage point via space and time deixis result in a deictic sub-world and an explicit proximal-distant relation being established between such sub-world (mental space) and the parent one. Because of those explicit connections between multiple spaces, affective relations between multiple times and spaces are established. This renders deixis as a useful strategy 'used to build and sustain a sense of involvement through the use of deictic expressions' (Johnson, 1994, p. 228). Indexicality thus contributes to the coherence of the text while at the same time supporting the persuasive role of speeches. This is done by building social and political relationships which are also based on the existence of shared cognitive frames upon which the deictic centre is anchored (Chilton and Schäffner, 2002, pp. 30–1).

The importance of looking at spatial anchorage via deixis and how this relates to construals of the world is inextricably linked to our identity being determined by our bond with a territory (regardless of whether that is public or private) and by an explicit or implicit opposition with another group (Storey, 2001). While further examples showing the importance of spatial anchorage in ethnonationalist contexts will be provided in the case studies, it shall be mentioned that such anchorage is also useful to explain other kinds of conflicts. Examples [1] and [2], for instance, try to show how conflictual relations emerge when looking at gender identity. These extracts, taken from different discussions on Reddit reflecting on women-only spaces, show different perspectives on the existence of such spaces, and they are useful to explain how spatial cognition dominates the semantic construction of abstract worlds.[3]

[1] *A:* First time posting. I recently attended ... a conference known for promoting women in technology. This year, they <u>expanded</u> their focus to <u>include</u> non-binary individuals, which led to an <u>influx</u> of male attendees.
B: I'm angry about this. **We are losing space** and I have no idea how to fix it. The word woman is being replaced with BS terms and **our spaces** are being completely **<u>overtaken</u>** by men.

[2] All of sudden I'm being spoken **over** and even told I have no voice in the matter because I'm a male and I need to let the 'women' speak. No joke, some have even reverted to <u>excluding</u> trans women <u>from the word</u> woman now and while I've always had difficulty with being gendered correctly ..., I've been referred to and called a male and a man more times in the last couple weeks than ever before.

> ... because I have no idea what it's like as a woman with the reproductive anatomy of a full-fledged female, I **should stop trying to infiltrate these spaces** and stop demanding things of their spaces.
> ... How are **we** supposed to respond or even be able to have **a voice in places** where we're now being invalidated?

The use of first-person plural pronouns and its deictic value in both examples can help us explain how physical (conference-led) and abstract (political, word-meaning) spaces are conceptualized. In both cases, a bond is deictically established between a space and members of a community occupying such space (we = biological women; we = women), both of them being placed at the deictic centre. This deictic centre (and its associated identity) is under threat from external FORCES which are invading and dominating it (see also Chapter 4). The use of the preposition 'over' shall be noticed in both examples, as it physically or figuratively indicates that (at least a part of) the space is being covered (OED, 2024). A distance relation with other groups is established not only through this preposition but also via lexical choices indicating movement (e.g. 'influx' in [1]; 'infiltrate' or 'exclude' in [2]) and the use of general gender-free terms, such as 'individuals'. This opposition also co-textually relates to the use of a third-person pronoun 'they', whose referent is unknown. All these signal the existing distance between two social groups. The word 'women' (in both examples) activates a cognitive frame (see Chapter 6) whose interpretation varies depending on the individuals' (self-proclaimed) identity. As such, conflict does result not only from opposed interpretations of such terms but also from the spatial relations that are established between groups occupying the different spaces that are discursively constructed. These examples also showcase how multiple construal operations function at the same time, as meaning in them results from the schematic activation of a space and the relation with other FORCES, the contested categorization of entities, and the position which is conceptually occupied by members of the ingroup and the outgroup. Figure 7.2 visually presents how the relation between the two communities is discursively constructed in example [1] and how such relations can be explained by means of spatial cognition. As shown in it, conflict between two communities results from the perceived occupation of the ingroup's space (women) as a result of the (FORCE) threat posed by the outgroup (men). Similar representations underlie the conceptualization of abstract spaces seen in example 2.

As shown in this section, the analysis of person, space and time deictics can help us explain which communities and political groups a speaker constructs

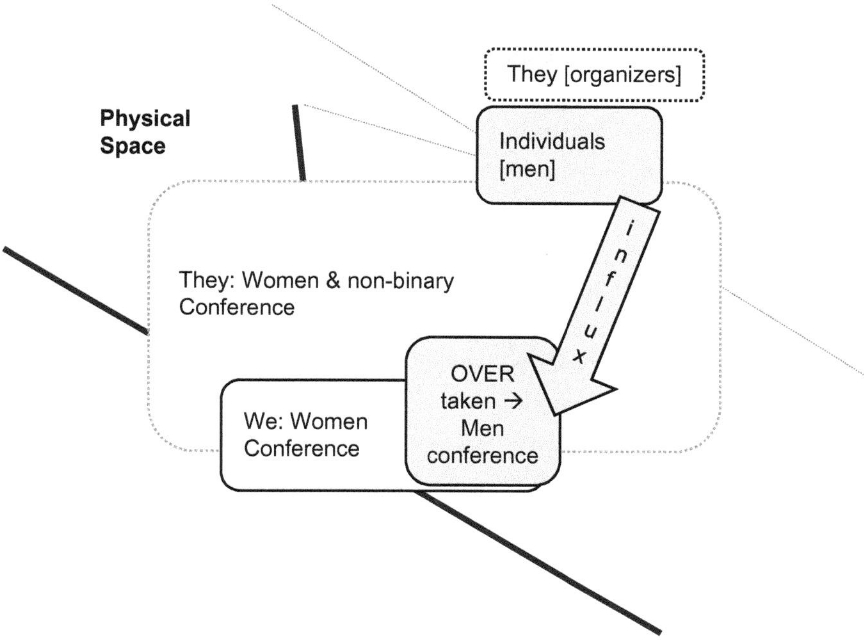

Figure 7.2 Spatial cognition and the occupation of space by different social groups.

as occupying the centre, that is, what they align with. The existence of this IDC community is not only legitimized but it also needs to be defended. Deictics can also help us uncover which other communities are discursively presented and the distant-proximal relationships that are spatially established between them. Such spatial configuration is not only to be understood as physical but also as being figuratively related to abstract notions. Conflictual relations can thus be explained as a result of the relations established between such groups. Given the dynamic nature of discourse, such relations can be shifting and may be discursively adapted, hence amplifying or minimizing the opposition or similarities between communities (see Filardo-Llamas and Boyd, 2017 for an example on the use of the pronoun 'we').

Analysing perspective: Modality and stance

As mentioned throughout this chapter, the notion of perspective inextricably relates to the idea that when communicating we construct mental spaces which are deictic in nature. Such mental spaces are discursively constructed from a particular viewpoint which may shift as discourse unfolds and which can guide participants in a discourse situation throughout the 'maze of connected mental spaces' which form part of the actual discourse world (Fauconnier, 1994, p. xli). Previous references to the study of perspective or viewpoint in CL stress that this encompasses not only sensory spatial viewpoint (i.e. physically embodied) (Tenbrink, 2020, pp. 103–10) but also abstract ones (Fauconnier, 1994). This multifaceted nature of viewpoint can be seen in its definition as 'as a discourse participant's alignment with an aspect of a frame or situation' (Dancygier and Vandelanotte, 2016, p. 14). The idea of viewpoint, thus, clearly captures that the speaker (conceptualizer) adopts a position towards an element (i.e. an entity or action) in the described situation or knowledge structure. This position can be spatio-temporal (as explained above when referring to deixis) but also 'likelihood and knowledge, attitude and feeling, or solidarity/power dynamics' (Vandelanotte, 2017, p. 158). As such, viewpoint can and shall be understood as being multifaceted and construed along a cognitive-deictic divide which may shift as discourse unfolds (Vandelanotte, 2017, p. 171). The multiple layers that conform viewpoint eventually form a network in the overall construction of the discourse space, as also explained in Chilton's DST model (2004, 2005, 2014) and the Space-Time-Axiology (STA) dimensions of proximization theory (2010, 2013a, 2017b). While the section above focused on the study of deixis as a means of explaining spatio-temporal (intersubjective) positioning, in this section the focus lies on this epistemic and attitudinal dimension of viewpoint.

In DST, this abstract positioning is explained by focusing on the analysis of modality, understood as 'the speaker's assessment of, or attitude towards, the potentiality of a state of affairs' (Radden and Dirven, 2007, p. 233). Such assessment, which reflects the interaction between the speaker and the text, can be related to knowledge and truth value (epistemic modality) and to (moral) attitudes (deontic modality). Thus, assessment is based on the proximal-distant relations established on an abstract space between the assessed entity and the deictic centre (i.e. point of reference upon which such evaluation is anchored) (Chilton, 2004, pp. 58–9; Hart, 2014, p. 165). The analysis of modality in political discourse is linked to the notion of (political) control, as (symbolic) domination can result from the way information is presented (Chilton and Schäffner, 1997, p. 212). As mentioned in Chapter 4, the idea of 'control' relates to force dynamics inasmuch as the speaker's conception of reality and the desirability of processes is extrapolated to the current reality (Langacker, 2008, p. 306). Because of this, reality is construed from the speaker's point of view, which is projected as the only (objective) one. Depending on the type of modality used, epistemic control (i.e. control over conceptions/representations of reality) or effective control (control over relations between participants in reality) may be exercised (Hart, 2025). As noted by Marín-Arrese (2021, p. 290), epistemic control will result in the hearer's acceptance of information while effective control is aimed at 'the legitimization of actions ... by discursively constructing them as necessary, desirable, righteous, or feasible'.

The analysis of viewpoint and modality has been frequently included as part of 'stance', particularly when understood as a public and relational act (Englebretson, 2007, p. 14). The notion of positioning features prominently in the definition of stance as 'a public act by a social actor, achieved dialogically through overt communicative means, of simultaneously evaluating objects, positioning subjects (self and others), and aligning with other subjects, with respect to any salient dimension of the sociocultural field' (Du Bois, 2007, p. 163). These three dimensions in the description of stance are of particular interest as they can help us explain how alignment and misalignment are produced as a result of (shared) evaluation and positioning towards given entities. Du Bois' definition of stance also stresses that three bipolar assessment SCALES can be considered as part of stance-taking: evaluative (along a good-bad scale), epistemic (along a true-not true scale) and effective (along a right-wrong scale). While in all of them we can find an underlying scale upon which proximal-distant relations can be traced between a speaker and the assessed entity, I consider that the evaluative dimension is rather to be analysed as part of the construal operation of judgement (as was explained in Chapter 6).

Given their abstract nature, epistemic and effective modality are also inextricably linked to the notion of 'axiological proximization', understood as a 'forced construal of a gathering ideological conflict between the "home values"' of the entities occupying the CENTRE of the discourse space and those alien and antagonistic to them which occupy the conceptual PERIPHERY (Cap, 2013a, p. 94). This definition of axiological values in such abstract terms relates to explanations of how alignment works in political discourse: 'Concomitant to positioning themselves, stance takers define alignment with each other, whether the alignment is convergent or divergent' (Du Bois, 2007, p. 164). Alignment may result not only from sharing a position in the physical space but also from the one occupied in more abstract spaces. Epistemic and effective modalities do not capture the whole complexity of such positioning, as further inferential knowledge may be required for explaining how the assessment of both reality and relations within it functions discursively, particularly in conflictual contexts. In the same way that intertextual frames may be discursively activated when judging a particular situation as being good or bad (see Chapter 6), abstract positioning may be described as being close or distant from the core values shared by sociopolitical communities. Incorporating these multiple dimensions is of particular importance for the analysis of conflict (as will be shown below), which can be explained as the effect of misalignment processes resulting from shifting positions along scales which differ in their degree of abstraction (see also Cap, 2010; Filardo-Llamas, 2013).

Theoretical and methodological proposals for the study of both modality (Chilton, 2004; Hart, 2025; Marín-Arrese, 2011, 2021) and proximization (Cap, 2013a) are thoroughly based on the analysis of lexico-grammatical categories which are indicative of a position in the epistemic, effective or axiological scale. As such, the analysis of modality shall depart from the identification of modal verbs and adverbs, conditional structures, evidentials and markers of cognitive attitude (Werth, 1999, pp. 274–7; Radden and Dirven, 2007, pp. 233–63). An example of the inextricable link between spatial anchorage and axiological positioning (including epistemic, effective and emotional alignment) can be observed if we analyse the speech uttered by US President Donald Trump on 6 January 2021. In it, he urged his supporters to march to the Capitol and occupy it so as to prevent the formalization of Joe Biden's victory in the 2020 November elections.

> [3] **All of us here** today <u>do not want</u> to see **our** election victory stolen by emboldened radical-left Democrats, which is what **they**'re doing. And stolen by the fake news media. That's what **they**'ve done and what they're doing. **We** <u>will never</u> give up, **we** <u>will never</u> concede. It doesn't happen. You don't concede when there's theft involved.
>
> ...
>
> **Many of you** have travelled from all across the nation to be here, and I <u>want</u> to thank you for the extraordinary love. That's what it is. There's <u>never</u> been a movement like this, ever, ever. For the extraordinary love for **this** amazing country, and **this** amazing movement, thank you. (Trump, 2021)[4]

A close analysis of this extract shows how reality is presented from the speaker's point of view, and how this results in a clear alignment between members of the ingroup (deictically constructed mostly through pronominal references ('all of us' and 'we')) and misalignment with members of the outgroup (not only constructed via pronominal references to 'they' but also categorized as belonging to the 'radical-left Democrats' or 'the fake news media'). The deictic construction of both groups is of interest and shows how personal pronouns can be discursively manipulated so as to construe perspectivized event spaces (see also Dancygier and Vandelanotte, 2016, p. 27): the discourse space of the ingroup is built around an inclusive use of the pronoun 'we', representing those who are physically 'here' (i.e. at the Capitol) and those who share 'love for this amazing country'. It is the 'country' (and inferentially its defence from the outgroup) that is presented as the core value of the ingroup. Through the use of an inclusive first-person plural pronoun ('we'), a relationship is established between the speaker and the audience. This relation is based on shared positive emotions ('thank' and 'love') which contribute to bonding them all as occupying the physical and abstract deictic centre.

The discourse space of the outgroup is built around the pronoun 'they' which functions as a discourse builder and whose sociopolitical referent is specified in the co-text via categorizing NPs ('Democrats' and 'news media'). Particular attributes are made salient about such groups via premodification, and Democrats are presented as belonging to the 'radical-left' while the 'news media' are characterized as 'fake'. The actions of the outgroup are framed as a theft, thus delegitimizing their electoral success. The use of the verb 'want' in the negative form has a double effect: first, it epistemically foregrounds the importance of the future in political discourse and construes a desirable potential reality which is inferentially opposed to the undesirable existent one. Second, it exercises effective control on the audience – notably Trump's supporters – and legitimizes their behaviour, that is, the occupation of the Capitol.

The analysis of this extract has two implications. First, it shows how the adoption of a specific point of view may result in alignment between members of a community (we) and misalignment with members of another (they). Stance plays a key role in this, as the speaker's position is not only physically constructed but is also linked to the speaker's representations of reality and actions within it. Such representations may stress the existence of threats by others, whose actions can be epistemically presented as posing a real (future) threat to the existence of the self. Given the performative function of language, actions (also violent ones) can be legitimized as a response to that existing threat (Cap, 2013a). Second, it shows that discourse spaces are constructed through interrelated networks of discursive representations of event spaces. Given the dynamic nature of discourse, the perspective from which such events are presented may shift not only in terms of physical anchorage but also of stance and, as explained in the next section, intersubjective relations between members of a community.

Analysing perspective: Viewpoint and intersubjectivity

The analysis of deixis and stance explained above implies looking at the pragmatic (and three-dimensional) positioning of the speaker which is anchored to physical and abstract mental spaces. However, studies on political discourse have noted that point of view is not an objective conceptualization of reality but a matter of (intersubjective) construal in which particular relations are held between participants in the communicative situation (i.e. conceptualizers) and the referents of discourse (Hart, 2025). Such positioning can be explained by exploring certain grammatical constructions (Hart, 2014, p. 112), including transitivity and voice (as also explored in the analysis of image schemas in Chapter 4), tense and aspect, and the distinction between objective and subjective construals (see chapter five in Hart, 2025 for a detailed discussion of these grammatical realizations of viewpoint).

Viewpoint seeks to explain how scenes are conceptualized and presented as being seen from a particular 'vantage point', that is, the point where the speaker (observer) is positioned (Radden and Dirven, 2007, p. 24). While it is assumed that the prototypical vantage point is the one of the speaker, this can be fictively adapted so as to describe the situation from the hearer's or other individual's perspective (Langacker, 2008, pp. 76–7). Examples of this would be conditional sentences or reported speech and evidentiality (Vanderbiesen, 2016). Closely related to the notion of 'vantage point' is the distinction between 'subjectivity' and 'objectivity', which can also be considered an attempt to describe the engagement of the hearer and speaker in how scenes are conceptualized (Langacker, 2008, p. 77). This distinction between objectivity and subjectivity stresses the type of relationship that is established between the conceptualizer (subject) and the object of conceptualization. As explained by Verhagen (2007), the configuration of construal operations functions on two dimensions: first, a horizontal dimension whereby the structure of the scene is imposed, for example, by shifting the scope of attention and profiling different elements within the scene (as mentioned, for example, in Chapter 5). Second, a vertical dimension whereby a relation is established between the object of conceptualization and the viewer. This vertical relation can be explained as based on distance (as noted in the two sections above) or on involvement. It is, in my view, the latter that allows us to understand how discourses construe events as being a person's subjective view or an objective factual observation.

Looking at communication in the political arena requires not only considering how a single individual construes reality but also how such construals discursively configure a relation with other participants – that is, with the (multiple intended) audiences (Filardo-Llamas and Boyd, 2017). As noted by Verhagen (2007, p. 6), 'any linguistic usage event comprises two conceptualizers, the first performing the role of being responsible for the utterance, the second that of interpreting it in a particular way'. Thus, when exploring political discourse, intersubjectivity becomes of particular importance, especially when looking at epistemic stance and at the conceptualization of who is responsible for (political) actions (Marín-Arrese, 2015). As such, an objective construal is one that is presented as being detached from the speaker, and it resembles a factual observation. A subjective construal is one in which the speaker is involved in any way (Radden and Dirven, 2007, p. 40). An intersubjective construal is one in which not only the speaker is involved but the hearer's perspective is also acknowledged, thus creating some kind of shared relation between the two conceptualizers involved in the communicative situation (Marín-Arrese, 2015). In my view, this shared perspective can be modulated along the three dimensions established in DST: time, space and stance, involving not only epistemic stance but also any kind of axiological proximity which could contribute to spreading a shared sense of identity. As can be seen in the following examples, all taken from Queen Elizabeth I's coronavirus speech, linguistic cues can help us identify whose position is adopted in the speech.[5]

[4] Many people of all faiths, and of none, are discovering that it [self-isolating] presents an opportunity to slow down, pause and reflect, in prayer or meditation.

[5] I hope in the years to come everyone will be able to take pride in how they responded to this challenge.

[6] That the attributes of self-discipline, of quiet good-humoured resolve and of fellow-feeling still characterize this country.

Example [4] shows a subjective construal through which the speaker reports what she sees without her and the audience necessarily being involved in it. This subjective construal is apparently more objective as the focus of attention is the object of conceptualization, that is, the event which is being discursively presented. The use of third-person grammatical constructions together with the present tense contribute to such representation. Following Langacker's (2008, pp. 77–8) explanation, the perceived maximal objectivity in the construal of the situation stems from the maximal asymmetry between what is viewed – presented as the onstage focus of attention – and the viewer – the subject of conceptualization – who is left offstage. In spite of perceptions of maximal objectivity resulting from such grammatical choices, when explained from the conceptualizer's perspective, we can observe there is a maximal subjectivity, as the scene is presented from the speaker's vantage point.

This apparently maximal objectivity contrasts with how the speaker is conceptualized in [5], where the Queen's position as speaker is profiled. This can be seen in the use of the pronoun 'I' as the subject whose desire is accounted for. An intersubjective relation is arguably established with the audience through the use of the pronoun 'everyone', which allows for both utterer and audience to be involved in the process of taking 'pride'. By placing attention on them, the role of the speaker and audience as people emotionally involved in the future evaluation of reactions to the pandemic is emphasized. By profiling their existence as the object of conceptualization – and feelings –, it is the viewers' position that is emphasized while silencing the object (i.e. the content) to which they react. Example [6] is arguably more complicated as what apparently seems to have maximal viewing objectivity – in the use of present tense and abstract nominals – is rendered intersubjective through the demonstrative article 'this'. As explained by Cognitive Grammar (Radden and Dirven, 2007; Langacker, 2008), demonstrative particles do not only ground the scene to the current discourse frame – as the nation inhabited by speaker and audience – but also establish a proximal relation with it, which in this case is related to the values which all members of such nation share. As such, the speaker and audience are moved 'onstage', and their social role is at least partially profiled. By using the demonstrative, 'this country' becomes the shared vantage point from which the situation is viewed and the existence of the (positive) attributes present in the statement is not only profiled but also validated as the core values underpinning the identity shared between speaker and audience.

While for explanatory reasons a distinction has been established in this chapter between viewpoint, stance and deixis, all the examples show that they all interact and contribute to perspectivized construals of reality. All together they have an effect in the creation of a Discourse Viewpoint Space, understood as 'the "global" viewpoint that is construed by the network of lower-level viewpoints' (Dancygier and Vandelanotte, 2016, p. 20). Thus, similar linguistic cues to the ones mentioned in the two preceding sections shall be identified when uncovering intersubjectivity, including personal pronouns, determiners, verb tenses, modal verbs, evidential adverbs, conditional structures, verbs of perception or reporting verbs (see Dancygier and Vandelanotte, 2016; Hart,

2014, 2025; Marín-Arrese, 2015 for further details). As will be shown in the case studies, identifying objective-intersubjective-subjective construals proves to be useful for the study of conflict and political discourse. Exploring such viewing arrangements about a particular scene can shed light onto the reasons why it can be perceived as conflictual and/or consensual, depending not only on whether speaker and audiences share the physical (and abstract) vantage point from which a scene is construed but also on whether their role as the object of conceptualization is profiled and which processes these participants are involved in. All in all, it can be argued that conflict results from participants in the communicative situation not sharing the Discourse Viewpoint Space in the case of objective construals (i.e. when the subject and/or a community is profiled), or from participants viewing the scene from opposed vantage points when there is a subjective construal (i.e. when there is apparently maximal objectivity).

Case study 7.1: Devolution

As explained in Chapter 3, different types of government have been implemented in NI throughout its history. Two types are of particular interest because of what they mean for the exercise of state control: direct rule and devolution. Direct rule is equivalent to power being exercised from a central government. In NI this meant this area being governed directly from London, usually through the figure of a Secretary of State, and it was particularly relevant after 1972 (Eliott and Flackes, 1999; Storey, 2001). Opposite to it is the idea of devolution, which is based on political theories of decentralization and is a mechanism 'for facilitating the resolution of conflicting views at a local scale' (Storey, 2001, p. 135). As noted in the literature, different attempts have been made in NI at implementing devolution with different arrangements on the type of roles – consultative, legislative – that would be granted to the NI Assembly (Eliott and Flackes, 1999). Devolution featured prominently in the 1998 Agreement, where the defining features and powers of the NI Assembly were described (NIO, 1998, Strand 1). Such type of 'regional autonomy with parliament' does not only characterize the way in which the UK is currently organized, but the existence (and well-functioning) of such regional elected assembly is part of an 'overall "peace strategy" designed to end years of militant political conflict' (Storey, 2001, p. 136). As such, it can be argued that devolution can be understood as a strategy for eliminating or reducing secessionist pressures within a state, and that its success (in governance) allows different parties to constructively interpret it in such a way that it reflects consensus (as lack of conflict) by relying on a shared local identity in comparison to the desired (and opposed) national identities associated with the political parties representative of both the nationalist and unionist communities (Storey, 2001; Cochrane, 2021). This idea is summarized in Figure 7.3 where the local spatial anchorage and identity are shown in relation to (opposed) national ones. A clear relation can be established between the

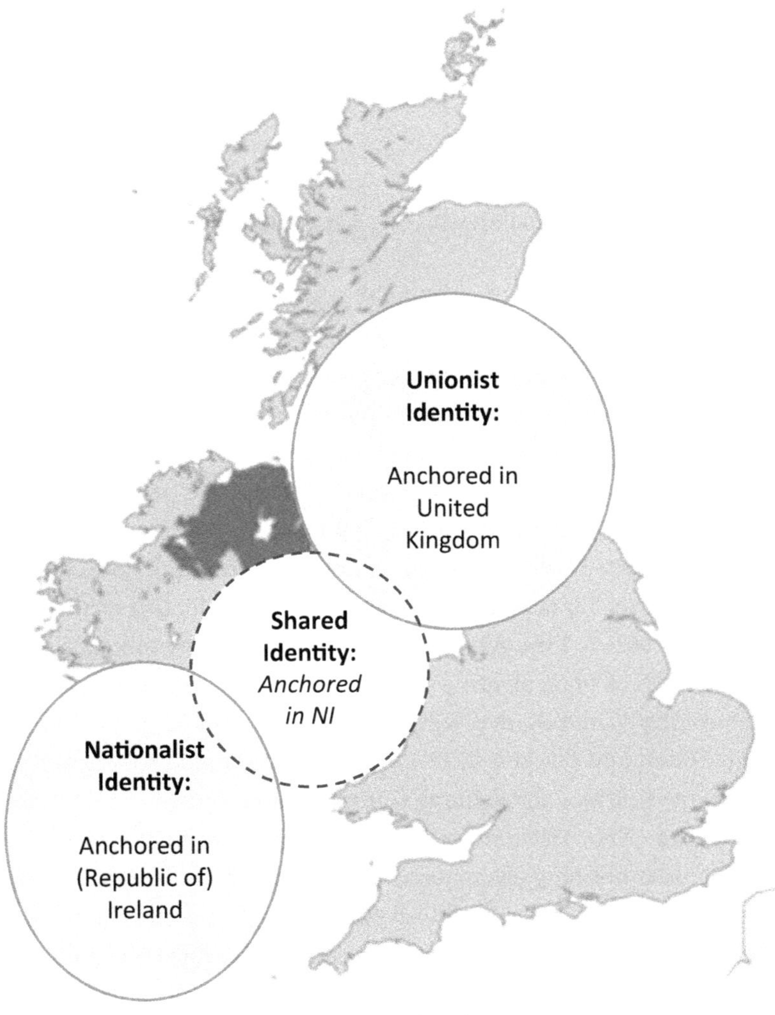

Figure 7.3 Shared identities in NI and spatial anchorage points.

idea of anchorage and the structural configuration of geopolitical entities as CONTAINERS which was explained in Chapter 4.

The importance of devolution as a mechanism for solving broader conflicts in a more local level underlies the chronology of political events in NI (see Chapter 3 and the appendix). In spite of new devolved democratic institutions being set out by the 1998 Agreement and regulated by the 1998 Northern Ireland Act, subsequent crises have taken place in NI. Many of these have resulted in a suspension of devolved government, and hence a return to Direct Rule (see Melaugh, 2024 for a chronology). Given the importance of spatial anchorage in the construction of identities and the need to legitimize measures related to government procedures by politicians representing different (and opposed) communities, in this case study I analyse both a suspension and a restoration of devolved powers. This aims at showing shifts in perspective-related strategies and how they can result in more or less conflictual relations being established. As such, I will analyse examples taken from statements reacting to the first suspension of the NI Assembly after the 1998 Agreement, on 11 February 2000,[6] and statements on the Agreement on the devolution of policing and justice powers, signed on 5 February 2010.[7] Tracing a clear evolution of discourses throughout time lies outside the scope of this book and its interest on construal operations. The analysis is thus presented as an example of perspective-related discourse strategies and their effect on the maintenance and/or resolution of conflictual relations.

Variation in spatial anchorage and the discursive construction of the (spatial) deictic centre can help us understand how this can increase conflictual positions and/or favour reaching consensus. As shown in examples [7] to [10], a difference can be observed in what unionist and republican politicians place at the centre of political life in NI at the time when the NI Assembly was suspended: the devolved institutions (the NI Assembly and Executive) by the UUP (in [7] and [8]) and the peace process by republicanism (in [9] and [10]). In both cases, it is this political deictic centre that is threatened by the actions of political actors belonging to the outgroup. As such, the 'Stormont Institutions' are threatened by Sinn Féin (SF) and the Irish Republican Army (IRA) (in [7]) and the Irish peace process is at risk by the demands of Unionism (in [10]). Presenting such members of the outgroup as approaching the (political) deictic centre, and thus being a threat to it (Cap, 2013a), results in a delegitimization of their political actions. In contrast, a clear legitimization of the self (the UUP and the IRA/the republican community) can be observed in how their actions contribute to the existence and maintenance of what they present as the core political entity, regardless of whether that is the Executive (in [8]) or the (peace) discussions (in [9]).

[7] The Ulster Unionist Party Assembly team is unanimously of the view that the threat that is now posed **to the new Stormont institutions** is entirely the fault of Sinn Féin and the IRA. (UUP, 2000)

[8] I can see no way in which my party can be expected to **re-enter** the Executive solely on the basis of understandings. Try to put the institutions **back in place** I will do. (Trimble, 2000)

[9] The IRA were persuaded to **enter into discussions** with the Independent International Commission on Decommissioning to help **move** the situation **out of the political vacuum** in which it had been stuck for the previous 18 months. (IRA, 2000a)

[10] To the casual observer or even those who should know better the current difficulties **in the Irish peace process** appear simple enough. It is all down to why the IRA has not decommissioned by now. … There will be no winners and the only losers will be the plain people of Ireland and *our* friends and supporters *throughout the world*. I say there will be no winners. That's wrong. Because … the reactionary bigots will have succeeded in **dragging unionism back to their agenda**. (Adams, 2000b)

As seen in these examples, differences in the political anchorage of actions can result in a legitimization of the self's political actions – usually in relation to their own identity, which is co-textually activated – and a delegitimization of the actions of the others. Such clear opposition between groups which occupy different political positions in the discourse space construes them as involved in a conflictual relation. Space prepositions and adverbs ('in', 'to', 'back') together with verbs of movement ('enter', 'move') metaphorically anchor the actions of the two main political groups (and communities) to different political entities and spaces. The relations between both groups are thus determined by their inability to share the political space (regardless of whether this is the NI institutions or the peace process). It shall be noted that this explicit positioning of political actions at the centre of discourse contrasts with a lack of temporal anchorage beyond scattered references to the actual time of events (e.g. 'tomorrow' (Mandelson, 2000b) for the release of the bill suspending institutions, or 'within the next 24 hours' (Adams, 2000b)/ 'in the last 24 hours' (Adams, 2000d)). Such use of time deictics does not only ground discourse to the event and utterance time but also foregrounds the importance of political action at the moment of speaking. Because they are relative to the situational context, time deixis is not prevalent in the construction of political identities. Not profiling such temporal dimension is at the expense of the prominence given to the other ones, as is the case of the spatial dimension explained above (see Cap, 2010, 2013a for more detailed discussions).

The metaphorical placement of different political actions in the deictic centre when reacting to political failure contrasts with the construction of discourse spaces in 2010 after politicians agreed on the devolution of policing and justice to NI. In this case, spatial anchorage features less prominently, and a clear contrast is established by politicians on both sides of the political spectrum between the 2010 events and the past, from which they attempt to distance themselves. Because 'the past' activates knowledge about violence and opposition when referring to the NI context, this allows for inferences to be made about a new time – equated to the now/present deictic centre (Verschueren, 1999). Thus, the contrast with the past does not only construe two discourse spaces anchored in different event times, but it also activates a shared cognitive frame upon which the time deictic centre is anchored (Chilton and Schäffner, 2002, pp. 30–1). Such references to the past can be seen in statements made by both DUP and SF politicians (examples [11] and [13]). In both cases they are also co-textually combined with a shared spatial anchorage, for example, in references to the 'people of Northern Ireland' (example [11]) or to 'the local people' (in [12]). Such lexical use is of interest as it allows for the inferential configuration of a shared local identity based on the geographical territory they occupy (Storey, 2001). An intersubjective view is presented in example [11] by making salient a specific aspect of the shared unionist identity – their being Northern Irish – and by discursively creating a subjective construal with maximal objectivity: it is the content which is profiled through sentences in the third person, and this content is seen from a point of view which the DUP and all the people of NI can share. SF, on the contrary, presents an objective construal whereby the intersubjective mention of 'all our people' (example [13]) is profiled. No spatial anchorage is provided as there is no shared national feature with which the intersubjective group – 'all our people' or 'everyone' – could feel aligned. The lack of explicit spatial anchorage allows SF to also address audiences who might not feel aligned but would rather profile their Irish one. In this case, it is the role of the political uttering subject (Martin McGuiness) and members of the community he stands for that are the object of conceptualization. This objective construal rather focuses on the comparison between two times: the past and the present.

[11] No future generation would forgive us for squandering the peace that has been so long fought for. **Today's** agreement is the surest sign that there

will be **no going back to the past** ... It **is almost forty years** since *the people of Northern Ireland* had responsibility for *our* own policing and justice powers. This agreement provides the potential that **in just a few months time** we will once again take responsibility for these key powers. This agreement ensures that as a society we continue to **move forward to a better future**. (Robinson, 2010)

[12] I also believe that it [the agreement] is stronger because it has been made **in Ulster**. While we have had assistance **from outside** it is *local people* that made this agreement and will make it work. (Robinson, 2010)

[13] With determined and courageous leadership we must continue to lead that shrinking minority **out of the trenches of the past**. In this I am confident we can be assured of the support of *the vast majority of our people*. We need to make life better for *all our children and grandchildren*. (McGuinness, 2010)

A similar attempt to accommodate multiple audiences can be seen in [12]. In spite of a constant appeal to the people of NI as beneficiaries from devolution, the local nature of the negotiations is emphasized through a reference to 'Ulster' (a term mostly used by the Unionist community to refer to NI). This does not only appeal to the core beliefs of the unionist community – hence stressing the political significance and validity of this new agreement –, but it also stresses the local nature of this success and explicitly minimizes the link with either the UK or the Republic of Ireland, thus separating this political event from nationalist claims by either of the communities. The likely controversial effect of such spatial anchorage 'in Ulster' is presented as the cognitive attitude of the speaker, that is, it indicates the speaker's partial epistemic support for such spatial anchorage (Marín-Arrese, 2021b, p. 295). The use of 'I believe' allows for an objective viewpoint to be adopted while profiling Peter Robinson's epistemic positioning (Hart, 2025). This can be compared with the subjective construal of the contrast between local and external politics in achieving the agreement, in which the (political) role of the speaker is downplayed: 'we had assistance from outside'. The future success of the agreement – and thus the maintenance of peace – is discursively presented through an effective stance strategy. By using the modal of volition 'will', it is the intentionality of the local people of NI that is highlighted (Marín-Arrese, 2021b, p. 296). The example shows that both deontic FORCE – volition – and the local anchorage of politics contribute to a perspectivized representation of reality with which a wider realm of society could align.

In the three examples ([11], [12] and [13]), inclusive uses of the first-person plural pronoun 'we' were found. A shared identity with which members of both groups can feel identified is thus constructed via lexical and inferential references to the geographical territory they occupy (Storey, 2001), a shared temporal deictic anchorage at the time of utterance (Levinson, 1983, p. 54; Verschueren, 1999, pp. 18–19) and an activation of shared cognitive frames. Consensus is discursively possible because multiple speakers and audiences can feel intersubjectively aligned with their viewpoint about a single situation: the devolution of policing and justice to NI. This is achieved by either presenting a subjective construal of factual political actions (usually showing epistemic certainty about the benefits of policies or document), by subordinating possibly contested views to the epistemic authority of the speaker and by profiling the role of the speaker and their represented community in objective construals of their political role.

Statements reacting to devolution of police and justice in 2010 are characterized by a prominent use of 'we' as a person deictic. Politicians belonging to both parties frequently use it combined with modal verbs indicating effective, and notably deontic, stance (as in [13] and [14]) – that is, that which compels discourse participants to participate in an action or state of affairs (Marín-Arrese, 2011a, 2021b). Such combination of deontic modality with an explicit appeal to intersubjective positions profiles the need for politicians and members belonging to both sides of the community to be involved in the desired course of action. Viewing the desirability of this action from an intersubjective perspective can be explained as a strategic use of stance expressions which could help multiple audiences to align with the desired action (i.e. lead the minority out of the violent past). Alignment is justified by also referring to the potential benefit resulting from that desired action (i.e. improving the lives of others) (Marín-Arrese, 2021; see also Langacker, 2008, pp. 484–485 for an explanation of cause and effective stance).

[14] In the next few weeks **we will take** this agreement to the people of Northern Ireland. **We will ask** the *[sic]* to endorse the agreement that has been reached today and to take a considerable step forward. … This agreement provides for the completion of devolution and a new start for parading. *It will mean* a new start for Executive business and a refocusing on the issues that matter to the people of Northern Ireland. And i*t will mean that the police will have* the resources to deal with the challenges that they face. … Today is the *[sic]* not just the end of one phase but the beginning of another where we must work to deliver for the people of Northern Ireland. (Robinson, 2010)

While intersubjective actions feature prominently in Peter Robinson's statement on the devolution of policing and justice to NI, these are often combined with a subjective use of deontic modality in Gerry Adams's statement at the time (in [15]). The use of the semi-modal 'need' allows him to stress the call for action by an external participant (Marín-Arrese, 2021b, pp. 295–6), and it emphasizes SF's objective viewpoint about the role of the government. This appears in the immediate co-text of another instance of effective stance: 'we are also agreed'. The structure is repeated throughout the statement and it shows an explicit intersubjective directive (Marín-Arrese, 2011a, p. 205), whereby the consensual intersubjective nature of the process of decision-making is emphasized (Marín-Arrese, 2021a).[8] Assessing reality through effective stance shows the speaker's perspective on political actions – understood as occurrences in Langacker's (2008, p. 484) terminology – and stresses the role of multiple political actors in 'determining and influencing the course of reality' (Marín-Arrese, 2021a, p. 195). Such viewpoint foregrounds the shared nature of the active role that political actors play in solving sociopolitical conflicts.

> [15] We are also agreed on the **need** to deliver for our community, it is what they expect. There are families and children living in poverty; elderly people feeling vulnerable and in fear. ... **Our government needs to** reach out to these people. **It needs to** deliver. (Adams, 2010)

Statements uttered in 2010 also make a frequent use of epistemic modality (as in [11] and [14]) – that is, expressions of the speaker's assessment of the likelihood or probability of an event occurring. A similar combination of subjective (in [11]) and intersubjective construals (in [14]) can be observed, with the former stressing the speaker's perspective about the future of NI. As in previous examples, epistemic stance markers show the speaker's position on the future of this area, and they are discursively intertwined with deontic uses of the same modal verb ('will') that stress the active role of the speaker's political party.

Intersubjective effective stance is prominent in statements reacting to devolution of powers being returned to NI. However, different stance strategies can be observed when speakers react to the collapse of the NI institutions in 2000. For example, a wide array of markers of epistemic cognitive attitude ('I am sure', 'I know', 'I believe', 'I have no doubt') were found in the statements by David Trimble (as leader of the UUP) and Peter Mandelson (as Secretary of State) when referring to the lack of decommissioning by the IRA (see example [16]). The use of these verbs together with the first-person pronoun shows reality as viewed through the authorial voice of the uttering politician whose commitment to the validity of such information is stressed (Marín-Arrese, 2021b, 2021a). Such subjective view of reality legitimizes their political action – that is, the suspension of institutions – because it responds to their knowledge about the (threatening) action of members of the outgroup (i.e. the IRA). Similar subjective positions can be found in statements by Gerry Adams and the IRA although such subjective viewing is more opaque because it is textually presented as impersonal (and seldom intersubjective) cognitive factives (in [17]) and impersonal factive predicates (in [18]). Epistemic stance strategies thus allow speakers to legitimize their actions and delegitimize the actions of other political actors by relying on their knowledge about reality. Adopting such strategies provides a perspective about reality, and these utterances are imbued with 'evidence, authority and truth' (Chilton, 2004, p. 23). As noted by Marín-Arrese (2021a, p. 138), epistemic stance acts are an 'indirect legitimization strategy' which provides 'epistemic justificatory support of knowledge and information'.

[16] **I am sure** that many nationalists and republicans will feel as cheated as most unionists do that the IRA has vetoed, for the moment, a new future based on participation and partnership. (Trimble, 2000)

[17] As **everyone knows** in a review of the process ... certain agreements were made which led to an unprecedented move by the IRA to engage with the Independent International Commission on Decommissioning and the Ulster Unionist Party participating in institutions which they had boycotted since the Good Friday agreement in May 1998. (Adams, 2000b)

Conflict may arise when beliefs held (and promoted) by different communities are of a contradictory nature. Authorial messages, opaque subjectivity and intersubjective or impersonal epistemicity in the construal of such messages may help speakers in overcoming the epistemic vigilance of an ingroup audience. Still, lack of shared knowledge and opposed positions by members of the audience (i.e. those belonging to the outgroup) with respect to the perspectivized view of reality may result in an emotional distancing from such discourses, thus increasing the perceived conflict between political and social actors. This is even more prominent when members of the outgroup are discursively presented as the spotlight of primary focal prominence (Langacker, 2008, p. 451) because they are the subject (actor) of the proposition whose reality is evaluated. Examples of this can be seen in [16] and [18], where members of the outgroup ('nationalist and republicans' or 'David Trimble') are the subject of the subordinated clause. As such, knowledge about the outgroup is foregrounded, thus paving the path for a conflictual interaction in which different positions about reality can be transmitted and contested.

[18] **The truth** is David Trimble never put such a proposition because his tactical approach to the agreement, unlike the rejectionists, was to constantly renegotiate it, to whittle it down, to minimize and to protract the process. (Adams, 2000b)

Of particular interest for showing how different epistemic stances may trigger conflictual views of reality is the study of negation and counterfactuality. Negation shall be understood both as a stance marker (i.e. it shows the speaker's viewpoint) and a marker of alternativity which evokes a cognitively accessible positive scenario (Dancygier, 2012). As a function of discourse, negation makes sense because it relates to propositions asserted elsewhere (Chilton, 2004, p. 59) or which can be inferred from the context. By using negation speakers evoke 'the positive conception of what is being denied' (Langacker, 2008, p. 59). Such positive conception is discursively construed as a possibility by making it cognitively accessible. Because it involves counterfactuality, by using negation speakers can place such proposition on a remote space, distant from the factual (real) deictic centre. The use of negation, together with other counterfactual and epistemic indicators such as the use of conditional structures, was of particular importance in statements uttered at the time when NI institutions were suspended because of the lack of IRA decommissioning. Examples [19] to [22] reflect the chronological unfolding of events and are of use for explaining conflictual views about the actions of the IRA.

[19] Further our contact has very recently emphasized that **there is no threat** to the peace process from the IRA. ... **If it becomes clear to us that decommissioning is not to happen**, the Commission will recommend to the governments that it be disbanded. (IICD, 2000)

[20] The Ulster Unionist Party Assembly team is unanimously of the view that **the threat that is now posed** to the new Stormont institutions is entirely the fault of Sinn Féin and the IRA. (UUP, 2000)

[21] Today's report that the IRA **<u>has said</u> that they pose no threat** to the peace process ... These reports **are further evidence of** the IRA's ongoing positive contribution to the peace process. **It is clear that the IRA have been engaged** positively with the IICD. (Adams, 2000a)

[22] The assurance, repeated this week, **that there is no threat** to the peace process from the IRA is important and will be welcomed. However, the report also stated that **there has not yet been any decommissioning**

of arms by a major paramilitary group. This is totally unacceptable. (Mandelson, 2000a)

Two counterfactual markers can be observed in the report issued by the International Independent Commission on Decommissioning (IICD) (in [19]): negation ('no threat') and negation subordinated to an indirect inferential evidential ('it becomes clear … that … is not to happen') as part of a conditional structure. As mentioned above, the use of negation activates the cognitive possibility of the existence of a threat. The UUP relies on this strategy to construe the existence of such threat as the positive alternative ('the threat that is now' in [20]) as a means of delegitimizing the actions of SF and the IRA. Interestingly, the viewing position is made explicit in the co-text as being the one of the UUP, and by relying on the maximal scope of the object of conceptualization, the authority of the UUP is highlighted in this subjective construal. The existing threat is not only presented as being close to the deictic centre but also as having an effect on those political institutions in NI, which are also discursively presented as being part of the deictic centre. As shown in Figure 7.4, conflictual views may arise because the positive cognitively accessible scenario is construed as being real by explicitly relating it to a different political entity from the one activated in the original negated proposition.

Similar conflictual viewpoints can be triggered by the use of the conditional sentence in the IICD report (in [19]). The structure 'if it becomes clear' encompasses two stance markers. On the one hand, the use of the conditional structure 'if' creates a counterfactual space and endows it with causal meaning (Chilton, 2004, p. 149; Radden and Dirven, 2007, p. 31). As such, decommissioning is construed as belonging to the irrealis space, thus allowing for politicians to claim that it has not happened (as shown in Peter Mandelson's

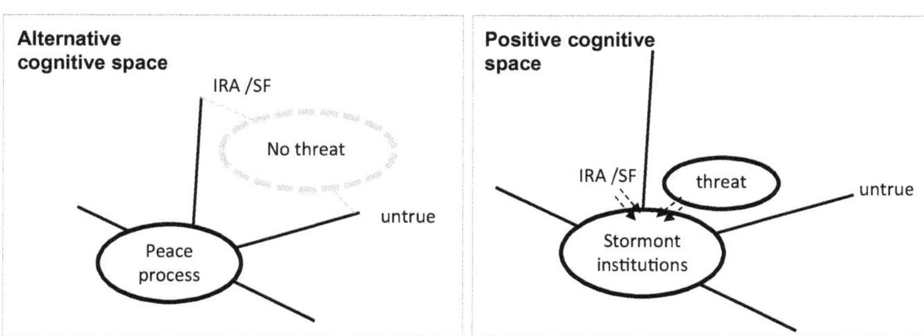

Figure 7.4 Negation and alternative spaces.

statement in [22]). The causal meaning of the conditional can also be relied upon to eventually justify the future suspension of the IICD (and of local political institutions). On the other hand, the use of the epistemic marker 'clear' with the verb 'become' also stresses the lack of political action. The adjective 'clear' is an indirect inferential evidential which stresses the need for 'observable results' and evidence supporting those claims (Marín-Arrese, 2011a, 2021a), that is, proof for decommissioning (in [19]). Because this observation is closely related to the speaker's viewpoint (as also made explicit in the phrase 'to us' following 'clear'), it can be contested. Similar epistemic markers are used by politicians representing the republican community, whose actions were contested. In his reaction to the events, Gerry Adams emphasizes the existence of such results – 'are further evidence' and 'it is clear' in [21] – when referring to the actions of the IRA and their commitment to the peace process. As in the case of negation, political speakers show and claim to have knowledge about different actions (decommissioning vs involvement in the peace process and engagement with the IICD) in the broader political event.

Case study 7.2: Decommissioning and weapons. Statements by paramilitary groups

All throughout this book, paramilitary groups – and their actions – have featured prominently in the development of the peace process in NI, mostly because of the controversial status of weapons. While in previous case studies I have mostly focused on how politicians react to (the lack of) decommissioning, in this section I analyse the actual voice of paramilitary groups and how they legitimize their own actions. As shown in previous research (Filardo-Llamas, 2013), statements by paramilitary groups are adapted to their different social and political audiences (i.e. supporters and members of the ingroup and politicians belonging to the same or the opposed community). This multiplicity of audiences can be observed in discourses being anchored to a specific geopolitical space which is discursively constructed as an imagined homeland (see also Anderson, 1991) and their desired goals being placed at the deictic centre. In contrast, members of the outgroup are often presented as having a threatening role towards those entities that occupy the deictic centre (see Filardo-Llamas, 2013 for a more detailed description).

The need to focus on paramilitary discourse relates to the key role of such groups in NI sociopolitical life. While the opposition (and consensus) between

SF and the DUP has featured prominently in prior case studies, we cannot forget that communal division in NI is closely related to paramilitary violence. In spite of a peace agreement being signed in 1998, paramilitary violence in NI still continued, not only with major attacks committed by dissident factions of main groups (e.g. the Omagh bomb in 1998, or the killing of journalist Lyra McKee in 2019) but also with punishment attacks or a high number of politically motivated deaths (see Cochrane, 2021, pp. 261–82; Edwards and McGrattan, 2010, pp. 146–7; Melaugh, 2023). A complete description and analysis of paramilitary discourse lies beyond the scope of this book (but see, for example, Goulding, 2021 for a study of the discursive changes in Irish republicanism). Following previous descriptions of communal division in NI (see Chapter 3), paramilitary groups are associated with either the loyalist (Unionist, Protestant) or republican (Nationalist, Catholic) community.[9] Two main loyalist paramilitary groups shall be mentioned: the Ulster Defence Association (UDA) and the Ulster Volunteer Force (UVF),[10] and both of these groups have been linked to minor political parties (the former to the Ulster Democratic Party (UDP) and the latter to the Progressive Unionist Party (PUP)). Both paramilitary groups initially supported the 1998 Agreement. Both of them have also engaged with the IICD, have decommissioned weapons and have asked their members to stand down from violent action.

The most widely known republican paramilitary organization is the IRA, which is frequently associated with SF. The IRA initially supported the 1998 Agreement, and has also engaged with the IICD on decommissioning, and it officially ended its armed campaign in 2005. While other minor republican paramilitary groups could be mentioned, these were frequently formed as dissident factions from existing organizations. An overview of the peace-related actions[11] of the three main paramilitary organizations whose statements have been analysed in this case study is included in Table 7.1. It is these actions that have been considered as the events along which statements have been selected for the analysis. All the analysed texts can be found in Melaugh (2023).

The analysis of the speeches included in the table shows how paramilitary organizations adapt their discourse when legitimizing their (lack of) actions towards peace. Such actions involve mostly engagement with the IICD and acts of decommissioning. Speeches and statements are presumably addressed at two different audiences: members of their own community and the broad spectrum of political actors.

Legitimizations of the self (i.e. the ingroup) are in this case study of particular importance as they do justify not only their historical existence but

Table 7.1 Involvement of Paramilitary Organizations in Peace-related Events

Organization	Community	Decommissioning	End of activity	Statements for analysis
UDA	Loyalism	2007 (11 November 11): arms put beyond use 2010 (6 January): decommissioned	1994 (13 October): ceasefire 1998 (23 January): renewed 2001 (12 October): specified[12] 2003 (22 February): renewed 2004 (12 November): despecified 2007 (11 November): stood down	1998. 23 January. UDA/UFF. Statement on the maintenance of ceasefire (23 January) 2007. 11 November. Remembrance Day Statement. 2018. 9 April. Loyalist declaration of transformation
UVF	Loyalism	2007 (3 May): arms put 'beyond reach' 2009 (27 June): decommissioned	1994 (13 October): ceasefire 2001 (12 October): specified 2005 (14 September): specified 2007 (4 A pril): renounced violence 2008 (14 May): despecified	2007. 3 May. Statement by UVF 2009. 27 June. Statement on decommissioning 2018 (see above)

Organization	Community	Decommissioning	End of activity	Statements for analysis
IRA	Republicanism	4 acts: *2001* (23 October) *2003* (8 April) *2003* (21 October) *2005* (26 September): final act	*1994* (31 August): ceasefire *1997* (20 July): renewed *2005* (28 July): ended armed campaign	*1998*. 30 April. Statement on decommissioning. *2000a. 1* February. First statement on decommissioning. 2000b. 5 February. Second statement on decommissioning. 2000c. 15 February. End of engagement with IICD. *2001a. 20* September. Statement on decommissioning. 2001b. 23 October. Statement on decommissioning. *2003a and b. 13* April. public and private statements on developments in peace process. 2003c and d. 21 October. First and second statements on weapons. *2005a. 23* March. Easter statement. 2005b. 28 July. Ending of the armed campaign. 2005c. 26 September. Statement on putting arms beyond use. *2006*. 13 April. Easter statement. *2007. 5* April. Easter statement.

also the actions done by members of the paramilitary organization uttering the statement. The analysis of person deixis (combined with the indexical function of referential expressions, as explained in Chapters 5 and 6) is of particular relevance for this. In the case of republican paramilitaries (i.e. the IRA), it is worth mentioning the combination between third-person referential expressions with names in English ('the IRA leadership') and in Irish ('Óglaigh na hÉireann') with the use of the first-person plural pronoun 'we', as seen in [22], [23] and [24]. Multiple perspectivizing strategies can be observed in those examples. All the sentences present a combination of subjective and objective construals in which there seems to be an apparently maximal objective cope (Langacker, 2008, pp. 77–8, 468–70). This combination of viewing arrangements usually follows the structure subjective construal + objective construal. In the three examples, we first find a third-person sentence in which the uttering political actor is objectively introduced through a referential expression in which the name of the organization is mentioned (e.g. 'the IRA'). This is followed by a profiling of the subjective role of the members of the organization, who are presented as being involved in the situation through the pronoun 'we'. This results in a different representation of reality, with IRA actions aimed at solving the peace process being usually introduced by third-person noun phrases so as to maximize the perceived factuality and objectivity.

[22] As an earnest of **our** willingness to resolve the issue of arms, **the IRA leadership** wish to *confirm* that **our** representative will intensify the engagement with the IICD. (IRA, 2001a)

[23] **Óglaigh na hÉireann** supports the peace process. **We** want it to work. **We** affirm that our cessation is intact. (IRA, 2003b)

[24] **The IRA** is fully committed to the goals of Irish unity and independence and to building the Republic outlined in the 1916 Proclamation. **We** call for maximum unity and effort by *Irish republicans everywhere*. **We** are confident that by working *together* Irish republicans can achieve **our** objectives. (IRA, 2005b)

An implicit perspectivizing strategy can be found in the use of Irish in [23]. Lexical choices also index belonging to a particular community, and the use of Irish has been traditionally associated with nationalist-republican claims in NI (Mac Coinnigh, Ervine and Deeds, 2019, pp. 557–60). As such, the Irish language functions as a cultural anchorage point and symbolically places Ireland as the deictic centre. By appealing to shared knowledge an intersubjective relation can be established between members of the paramilitary organization and the broader republican community.

Self-referential noun phrases are frequently combined with an exclusive use of the first-person plural pronoun 'we' (or 'our') (as in [22] and [23]) (Wodak et al., 2009) which indexes the members of the leadership. A slight diachronic difference can be observed in the examples, with earlier statements foregrounding the political role of the IRA via exclusive uses of 'we'. As such, the IRA is self-legitimized as an actor whose role is significant in the advancement of the peace process. When the IRA confirms the end of their armed campaign, uses of 'we' shift and there is co-textual variation, with both exclusive and inclusive uses combined. As can be seen in [24], not only the political role of the IRA is legitimized but this is presented as being inextricably linked to the broader republican community which they represent. The explicit widening of this referential scope is stressed through the use of the space deictic 'everywhere' and the historical anchorage of republican goals and beliefs in the 1916 Proclamation. Likewise, actions of the community (i.e. inclusive uses) are subordinated to an effective stance marker – 'are confident' – which stresses the potentiality of the intersubjective action of working together (Marín-Arrese, 2021b, p. 297). By using the word 'confident' not only the internal ability of the members of the IRA is emphasized but also the external role of the other members of the community is invoked for succeeding in the action of shared work.

Historical anchorage (i.e. the discursive proximization of historical events so that they are part of the deictic centre) is more prominent in latter statements, which are produced with a commemorative function (Achugar, 2008; Filardo-Llamas, 2013). In earlier ones, aimed at advancing the peace process, time deictics usually shift between very specific references to past events combined with a past simple tense (usually referring to the actions undertaken by the IRA, as in [25]). Likewise, while historical actions by the self are presented as part of a subjective construal which is distant in time, the effect of the negative actions done by the others is proximized and presented as still being felt in the present. As can be seen in [26], the repeated use of the present perfect stresses the consequences of actions done by the British government and unionist politicians, thus delegitimizing the role of the latter in the peace process.

[25] **In August 1994** … the leadership of the IRA **called** a complete cessation of military operations in order to create the dynamic for a peace process. 'Decommissioning' **was no** part of that. There **was** no ambiguity about this. (IRA, 2001b)

[26] Much hurt **has been inflicted** by British Government policy, by successive British Governments and by the old unionist regime. Great pain **has**

> **been caused** by the British army, the RUC and loyalist paramilitaries. (IRA, 2003b)

Similar strategies of self-representation can be observed in statements by loyalist paramilitary groups, with third-person NPs, present perfect and the verb 'confirm' being used when referring to the decommissioning of loyalist weapons (in [27]). Both the use of 'confirm' in [27] and 'affirm' in [23] function as epistemic stance markers and stress knowledge by the leadership of both paramilitary groups about the occurrence of a particular action (Langacker, 2008, pp. 484–5). The use of a verbal clause followed by a proposition stresses the commitment of the leadership of both paramilitary groups to the validity and certainty of that which is recalled (i.e. the completion of decommissioning, in [27], and the cessation being intact, in [23]) (Halliday and Matthiessen, 2014, pp. 302–5; Marín-Arrese, 2021a, p. 138). As noted in previous studies, this type of stance-taking strategy does not only stress authorial voices in discourse and the factuality of the propositional content but also serves a legitimizing function (Chilton, 2004; Hart, 2011b; Marín-Arrese, 2021a).

> [27] **The leadership of the Ulster Volunteer Force and Red Hand Commando** today confirms it has completed the process of rendering ordnance totally, and irreversibly, beyond use. (UVF, 2009)

Not only is stance relevant for legitimizing actions done by paramilitary groups, but it is equally significant for explaining how such groups construct their (political) relationships with the others via interaction. As such, deontic modality is prevalent in the analysed statements, and it is effective in showing the speaker's moral rightness in their demand for particular actions to be done (Chilton, 2004; Marín-Arrese, 2021a). Following Marín-Arrese (2021a), deonticity is considered a particular sub-type of effective stance whereby the utterer is conceived as the subjective source of moral rightness that judges an action to be not only necessary but also beneficial for the self (and others). The outgroup responsible for performing the required action changes throughout time in IRA statements and adapts to changing circumstances. For example, the use of the person deictic 'everyone', which has a wide referential scope, together with the existential verb to 'be' and the deontic noun 'responsibility' in [28] foreground the role of all social and political actors (not only the IRA) in achieving a sustainable peace in 2001, in the midst of calls for IRA decommissioning and doubts about this paramilitary group's commitment to peace. The impersonal construction of the clause results in a subjective construal of reality with maximal objectivity in the representation of the scene. This type of clause also stresses the strong intrinsic nature of the necessity of committing to peace (Radden and Dirven, 2007, pp. 248–50). The choice of the noun 'responsibility' inferentially evokes the moral values upon which the actions of those unnamed other sociopolitical actors are to be judged. The use of another compelling deontic modal – 'should' – together with the negative subject – 'no one' – and the epistemic verb 'doubt' in [29] shall also be mentioned, as they appear in the near co-text. Negation together with the epistemic verb ('no one should doubt') has a double function: on the one hand, it foregrounds the difficulties of the actions done by the IRA (thus legitimizing its role in the peace process); on the other, it inferentially lays the moral context for judging the behaviour of those political actors that deny the IRA's active involvement in the peace process. Similar objective construals underlie the use of compelling modality (mostly in the noun 'responsibility') when discussing the actions to be done by unionist politicians or the two governments.

[28] **There is a responsibility** upon <u>everyone</u> seriously committed to a just peace to do our best to avoid this. (IRA, 2001b)

[29] <u>No one</u> **should doubt** the difficulties these initiatives cause for us, our volunteers and our support base. (IRA, 2001b)

In latter statements, released after decommissioning, both republican and loyalist paramilitary groups address dissident members and place violent, criminal actions done by former members of the groups in a distant mental space. Such distancing is achieved via the negation of an obligation attribute ('no responsibility' in [30], 'unacceptable' in [31]) together with a relational verb (Halliday and Matthiessen, 2014, p. 273). Thus, a distinction is established between those members of the paramilitary group that are committed to peace and that occupy the person ('we' vs 'those'), space ('within' vs 'outside' in [31]) and axiological deictic centre. As such, the actions of core (peaceful) members of the group are self-legitimized. A subjective viewing arrangement in both examples maximizes the perceived objectivity and the authorial validity of such claims.

[30] The IRA **has no responsibility** for the tiny number of former republicans who have embraced criminal activity. They do so for self-gain. We <u>repudiate</u> this activity and denounce those involved. (IRA, 2006)

[31] **We** reject and <u>repudiate</u> as **unacceptable** and contrary to loyalist principles any criminal action claimed to have been undertaken in **our** name or attributed to any individual claiming membership of one of **our** organizations. **We** further declare that any engagement in criminal acts by any individuals *within* our organizations will be regarded as placing *those* persons *outside* the memberships. (UDA/UVF, 2018)

As seen in the examples above, discursive constructions of the outgroup are important because they show how relations between social actors are construed. Variation in who is profiled as the recipient of the demand or who is placed on a distant mental space can contribute to more or less consensual, collective (and eventually peaceful) representations of societies characterized by inter-communal division. Likewise, actions of paramilitary groups are self-legitimized by relying on the intentionality category of effective stance (Marín-Arrese, 2021a). This foregrounds the willingness of their members to perform particular actions which could have a positive impact in the peace process (as could be seen in 'willingness' in [22], 'want' or 'wish' in [23]). Such uses do not only self-legitimize the actions of paramilitary groups but stress the moral rightness of their actions. As such, volition-related strategies maximize the moral commitment of paramilitary groups to peace and their (at least apparent) involvement in achieving such peace while seeking to gain the audience's acceptance of the said actions.

Summary: Positioning and perspective in conflict discourses

This chapter has focused on how sociopolitical actors construe perspectivized views of reality in political discourse. As shown in the case studies, via linguistic choices politicians and paramilitary groups build proximal or distant connection and engagement with other communities, hence emphasizing or minimizing conflictual relations between members of those groups. Two main conceptual operations shall be mentioned for understanding how the cognitive ability of perspective works in discourse: positioning strategies and proximization.

Positioning strategies are based on our ability to see the world from a particular perspective. As explained throughout this chapter, this involves taking a particular point of view (Hart, 2014) in the discursive configuration of a mental space. Such space is anchored to a person, space and time deictic centre (Chilton, 2004, 2014). As noted throughout this book, mental and discourse spaces can shift from physical to abstract, thus foregrounding, for example, geographical spaces (which are prevalent in the configuration of national identity (Anderson, 1991; Storey, 2001)) at different moments in time. Likewise, the axiological values shared by the 'we' can also function as an anchorage point from which reality is viewed (Cap, 2010). Ingroup and outgroup relations tend to be more conflictual when the referential (and anchorage) scope of the deictic centre is narrower (i.e. when there is a narrow viewing arrangement) because this makes it more difficult for multiple audiences to align with a shared deictic space. On the contrary, it is easier to reach consensus when the referential scope of reality is widened. Positioning strategies which tend to render more consensual views include, for example, inclusive uses of 'we', wide geographical spaces being placed at the deictic centre, or unquestionable values being presented as those to be shared by the multiple audiences of a political statement (see also Filardo-Llamas, 2013). As such, uncovering the physical and moral position from which mental spaces are constructed is a useful strategy for understanding the role of perspective as a construal operation in conflictual discourse.

While positioning mostly refers to the point of view from which discourse is construed, proximization is useful for explaining relations between sociopolitical actors. This strategy results from a combination of deictics with particular uses of force dynamics (as also shown in Chapter 4). Of particular interest is how political actors linguistically bring closer to the self, or distance themselves from, some aspects of reality (Cap, 2013a, 2017a). The analysis of the case studies has shown that proximization is useful for understanding how opposition to particular groups can be constructed by presenting them as a (proximal) threat to the self, as was the case when discussing the decommissioning of paramilitary groups. Closely related to proximization is the construal of epistemic mental spaces, whereby the certainty (and truthfulness) of particular actions and events is foregrounded. As such, those actions and events are legitimized because utterer and audience are assumed to align with those world views (Marín-Arrese, 2021a). The role of negation has proved to be of particular interest because it allows for the construction of two alternative mental spaces which are discursively opposed while stressing that it is only possible for one of those mental spaces to exist (Dancygier and Sweetser, 2005, pp. 28–55; Chilton, 2014, pp. 157–77). Negation, as shown in the case studies, can help us explain not only how conflictual relations are discursively created but also how perceptions of the ingroup can be recontextualized so as to self-legitimize the existence of given political actors. Negation is thus a useful strategy to challenge the discursive proximization of the outgroup as a threat.

Perspective as a cognitive ability does not only relate to the physical position of the utterer but also to a perceived moral authority. This can be discursively realized through effective stance, and particularly through deonticity. The adoption of a particular deontic stance involves a conceptual anchorage in the moral position of the utterer, which is symbolically construed as the deictic centre (Hart, 2011b; Marín-Arrese, 2021a, p. 136). As shown in case study 7.2, the analysis of effective stance can help us identify how the relation between the 'real' mental space occupied by the utterer relates to another mental space in which the other is required to do something. Representations of that other (which can be pronominally placed as being more or less distant from the self) together with the strength with which action is compelled (i.e. high or low) can shed light on who is to be blamed if situations are not peacefully solved. Likewise, how deontic modality is linguistically realized can also allow for more or less intersubjective alignment, thus resulting in more or less consensual configurations of the moral mental space.

While not aimed at providing an exhaustive analysis of political discourse in NI, the examples in the case studies have been useful to understand how utterers may position themselves with regard to other members of society. As such, it has been observed that the opposition between 'the we' and 'the other' can be minimized or maximized by adopting discursive positions with a more or less wide deictic scope. The case studies have also emphasized that positioning shall not only be understood as related to the physical circumstances but that it also includes more abstract dimensions such as epistemic or deontic stance. Likewise, via linguistic choices, objective or (inter)subjective views of reality may be construed. All such choices may result in smaller or bigger sections of society aligning (or not) with the mental representation of reality, depending on whether it is possible for one or more members of the multiple audiences to position themselves in a shared discourse viewing space. Perspectivized mental spaces may thus contribute to the self-legitimization of political parties or other groups, such as paramilitary ones, whose actions may be contested.

8

Conclusion: Managing conflict via discourse

Several ideas have permeated and been repeated throughout this book, written with the aim of contributing to discourse-based approaches to the study of conflict. As explained in the introduction, I wanted to reflect on how cognition mediates communicative behaviour in conflict situations, particularly as exhibited by public figures representing opposed communities. To do so, I selected a conflictual context which could provide analytic material for exemplifying both theoretical claims and methodological decisions in the qualitative analysis of discourse. The book has sought to address two embedded dimensions: first, gain insight into how discourse has been managed in NI at different conflictual moments in time. Second, contribute to the theoretical discussion about the role of cognition when mediating the relationship between discourse and conflict while stressing the methodological validity of CL as a tool for the qualitative analysis. This chapter summarizes the main conclusions of the book along these two dimensions.

Paradoxical and compatible realities in NI politics

Chapter 3 proved how the history of NI can be described as being characterized by trouble and division between two communities. While such division has taken the form of overt violence at some moments in history, it can be argued that more covert forms of opposition can also be found in NI, and also in other places which are socially shaped by ethnonationalist conflict between two communities. Two continuums can be used to explain how such social relations are established in these contexts: one whereby the existence or absence of conflict is measured, that is, relations between communities being described as members of such groups being involved in literal or metaphorical war or as being in peace; another which ranges from overt physical violence to covert sociocultural opposition, thus described along a physical-abstract characteristic of the communal divide. This description of social division along these two continuums is based on findings in previous descriptions of conflict resolution, which can be explained as the achievement of a 'negative peace' because violence is contained. For conflicts to be completely solved, that peace is not to be negative but positive in the sense that just and equitable social structures are to be developed (Schäffner and Wenden, 1995). The role of cognition is thus to be acknowledged in studies on conflict resolution, particularly when the objective is aimed at minimizing perceived oppositions between communities. As such, I would argue that political discourse can be defined by its construal of paradoxical or compatible realities, depending on whether it reflects more conflictual or consensual views. As explained in the case studies included in this book, the perceived incompatibility between the discourse worlds which are created by sociopolitical actors can be adjusted by relying on the use of different linguistic strategies.

The opposition between NI communities could be explained as being related, among other things, to three different dimensions of reality: politics, that is, divergent policies being proposed by representatives of political parties; society, because members of the communities construct their identity along social parameters which are mostly determined by their national affiliation with the UK or the Republic of Ireland; and cultural, as they rely on a variety of cultural symbols and historical myths which contribute to the shaping of different and opposed mentalities. These dimensions have guided the analyses included in each chapter: controversial policies or political actions in post-Agreement NI have been selected as the ones which have determined the events to be considered. These have included, for example, the signing of the 1998 Agreement, the role of devolved NI institutions or the configuration of geopolitical relations after the UK withdrawal from the EU. Likewise, controversial aspects such as reactions to weapon decommissioning or the reforms of the police service have also been explored. Social configurations of identity and their relation to the desired constitutional status of NI have also featured prominently in the explanation of how and why discourse can minimize or maximize perceived conflict between the two communities. Finally, in the book I have tried to emphasize the role of cultural cognition (Kahan and Braman, 2006) as this aspect could be of interest for exploring how discourses reflect and evoke positive or negative emotions, which can eventually result in the legitimization of political action (Reyes, 2011). This has been particularly relevant when observing pictorial representations of the conflict in NI streets.

All these aspects have been of use for explaining the discursive construal of conceptual variation in political communication in NI. As noted by Ramsbotham (2021) radical disagreement between communities results from the construction of opposed discourse worlds. This idea can be further developed by arguing that sociopolitical consensus can be achieved via the construction of compatible discourse worlds. Clear examples of this have been given in the case studies, which have explored how politicians have managed discourse after the signing of the 1998 Agreement. Higher opposition was found in the early stages of post-agreement NI, with the representatives of the two most extreme parties (SF and the DUP) construing the same reality in opposed discursive terms. As such, when discussing the 1998 Agreement or decommissioning, SF's discourse worlds are mostly based on the centrality of the republican imagined community (Anderson, 1991, p. 7). The identity of Republicans is frequently anchored to an Irish imagined homeland, with the role of the island of Ireland as the key national CONTAINER. Because it is national identity that configures the central identity of the community, political life is presented as being conflictual because of the involvement of the British government in NI affairs. The role of Unionists is often presented in relation to the one of Britain. Such social opposition is justified by appealing to a cultural mentality shared by members of the republican community: the idea of victimhood. Historical events or relations with other international contexts are discursively activated when legitimizing the perceived status of the republican community as victims suffering from the actions of the others (which could be the British government, the unionist community or the RUC, as the former police force).

A similar focus on national identity and shared cultural knowledge could be found in the analysis of the DUP's discourse, whose identity is constructed as Ulster British. This identity is linguistically enacted through the construction of two embedded national CONTAINERS: one standing for NI, as the key anchorage point; the other being the UK, to which NI belongs. Negative political actions are discursively constructed when referring to those political forces that could threaten the future existence of NI. That threat determines who occupies the outgroup: other members of the unionist community at the time of negotiation of the 1998 Agreement, the IRA and other republican paramilitary groups when discussing decommissioning and policing, or the EU and the Republic of Ireland at the time of Brexit. Such construals are clearly influenced and shaped by the cultural siege mentality shared by at least some members of the Unionist community and which has motivated their description as 'the community of fear' (Patterson, 2002, p. 326) because of their constant claims of republican and nationalist attacks and of possible British betrayal. Variation can also be found in discourses within the unionist community, as was exemplified in the use of religious language which characterizes the DUP (compared to the UUP). This shows that cultural cognition is multi-layered and that different members of a community might align with one or more of the dimensions of sociocultural and historical knowledge (or frames) activated in an instance of discourse.

Radical disagreement in the analysed statements seems to be a consequence of the discourse worlds of NI political parties being anchored on national identity and/or core historical or symbolic values which appeal to the communities' victimhood and fear mentalities. Both aspects are clearly embedded and shaped by the ideological beliefs that characterize sociopolitical positions – that is, communities – in NI. Foregrounding such constitutive elements results in a delegitimization of political actors (i.e. members of the outgroup), political actions (e.g. the role performed by politicians in the negotiations) and policies (such as the 1998 Agreement or reforms in the status of the police). Thus, opposed discourse worlds in NI are characterized by the existence of conceptual alternativity in the construction of political reality. Because it is not possible for representatives and members of each community to align with the alternative views, this results in radical disagreement about sociopolitical events. As explained throughout the case studies, such disagreement may be based not only on different construals being presented (e.g. in the configuration of the border of NI after the UK's withdrawal from the agreement) but also on different interpretations being triggered by an instance of discourse (as it was the case in reference to the (lack of) existence of a threat when discussing decommissioning).

The case studies have also shown that sociopolitical consensus could be reached if construals resulted in what could be termed 'compatible discourse worlds'. These elicit a representation of society with which all members of society could feel aligned. To achieve this, politicians in NI follow two main strategies: they either silence those aspects of reality that could be prone to conflictual interpretations or they foreground properties of policies and events which could be more easily accepted. Examples of this could be seen in some of the discussions about the constitutional status of NI after Brexit. While conflictual interpretations were mostly related to the role of the border (and subsequent associated actions such as movement of people and goods), consensus could be achieved if the focus was placed on the space shared by both sides of the communal divide – that is, anchoring discourses to a 'dual' NI – or on an economic CONTAINER within which both communities could feel included. This is possible by backgrounding the discursive salience of elements related to national identity or which could activate each community's sociocultural background knowledge. Further examples of this were found in commemorative speeches uttered twenty years after the 1998 Agreement was signed. In them, policies which could have a potential benefit for all of society are placed as the central element, and discourses are constructed in such a way that those actions or documents are presented as occupying the centre of NI political life. This was the case in the construal of the 1998 Agreement by most political parties as occupying the centre of NI political life. Likewise, most extreme parties did not only legitimize such policies, but they also placed them as having an effect in constructing peace. This means that they trigger a configuration of society with which multiple audiences could feel aligned. To do so, a key temporal comparison is also of discursive importance, as compatible discourse worlds in the analysed statements are frequently characterized by the contrast between the violent past and the not-so-violent present.

The analysis of NI political discourse in this book shall not be understood, however, as exhaustive. That has been the focus of other types of studies, mostly done from the social and political sciences (e.g. but not only Mac Ginty, Muldoon and Ferguson, 2007; O'Donnel and Hayward, 2010; Cochrane, 2021; Keating, 2021; Hayward, 2023). The case studies in this book shed light on changes and shifts in NI political discourse and how these could help in achieving peace. However, it is important to bear in mind that it was beyond the scope of this book to explore such changes from a diachronic perspective (i.e. as reflecting modifications in discourse throughout time and how these contributed to achieving overarching peace) or from a political one (i.e. exploring how each political party has evolved so as to adapt to the changing circumstances). Still, the analysis of NI political discourse does offer some insight onto how ethnonationalist conflict is maintained: first, it has helped comprehend how space can be constructed as a bounded entity and the role that this has in the configuration of multiple identities. Second, it has shown that identity is a key aspect for the (de)legitimization of policies which could impact on understandings of the constitutional status of a place. Finally, it has advocated for acknowledging the role of cultural cognition in the analysis of how discourse is managed in conflict situations. As such, NI shall be understood as a case study exemplifying how discursive construals of geopolitical spaces are mediated by beliefs related to the configuration of a community national identity and its historical and symbolic evolution throughout time. As shown in the examples, cognition does influence how political discourse has been managed in the NI conflict.

Conflict, discourse and cognition: Final insights

As explained in the introduction, this book is the result of a personal interest in understanding the relationship between discourse and cognition. My need to reflect on the relation between language, knowledge and mental representations has influenced the structure of the book. It was organized along construal operations which could guide the analysis of linguistic cues so that findings and claims could be extrapolated to other contexts. This has also determined the role of NI political discourse as an analytic case study combined with the inclusion of examples taken from other contexts in the theoretical descriptions provided in each analytic chapter. This final section seeks to summarize the main theoretical premises which lie beneath this book while trying to explain how and why I believe that cognition has a mediating role in the dialogic relation that is established between discourse – understood as the communicative products – and conflict, which in my view could be the cause of opposed representations of society and/or the effect of particular instances of communication. Cognition, in my view, shall be understood as encompassing two elements: the knowledge shared by participants involved in any communicative situation and the mental representations (or discourse worlds (Chilton, 2004)) which are triggered by linguistic choices. Conflict and discourse can be thus considered equivalent to the broader sociopolitical and immediate situational context in which communication is produced; cognition is also contextual inasmuch as it reflects what is in the participants' minds.

This book has adopted an experiential and variational approach to the study of language. Experiential because linguistic meaning is not understood as an objective reflection of the world, but rather as constructing the needs and experiences of different individuals and cultures. Such experiential approach aligns with claims in CL that emphasize that language reflects embodied cognition, that is, when we communicate we echo our relation with the (physical) world (Geeraerts and Cuyckens, 2007; Hart, 2017; Stockwell, 2020). Variational because it aligns with the principle of conceptual alternativity (Talmy, 2000b) and with the non-essentialist view of CL, which claims that meaning is not resident in words and bigger chunks of language but assigned to such linguistic cues by human beings (Janicki, 2006). The notion of construal, as the key theoretical notion aimed at explaining alternative discursive representations, has proved to be of use in exploring how conflict may be discursively managed.

To explain the relation between conflict and construal, it is necessary to recall the three main features which characterize the existence of conflict. First, conflict is bipolar in nature, that is, it is based on the existence of a binary opposition between two entities – usually described as us vs them (Van Dijk, 1998). This binary opposition can be presented as being physical or symbolic. Second, conflict is conducted and constructed through language. This means that linguistic choices can maximize or minimize the prevalence of opposition between entities. Finally, conflict is based on previous beliefs. Knowledge (or cognition) thus plays a key role in conflict management and resolution, as it is such knowledge that determines how language is to be understood, the inferential processes which may be linguistically activated and the emotions which can be discursively evoked (see also Janicki, 2015). These three key elements in the definition of conflict – as bipolar, linguistic and related to previous beliefs – also feature in the definition of construal, which is not only alternative in nature but also dependent on linguistic choices whose meaning is situated, that is, context-dependent.

The bipolar nature of language has been noted in each of the construal operations. The structural configuration of reality is based on schematicity, which allows for the creation of stative entities vs dynamic processes and for a construction of reality as an event or an action. Because image schemas are bipolar – that is, organized along continuums which foreground different types of conceptualizations –, they can be tweaked so as to construe conflictual or consensual configurations of society. Different examples were provided in the case studies, such as the discursive placement of different entities in the centre (vs the periphery), the construal of un/bounded containers, the representation of events vs caused actions or the different levels of attachment that could be experienced between entities. Linguistic choices, such as prepositions, transitivity or voice, can result in different gestalts. Such conceptualizations can (re)produce or challenge communal division, and they can be adapted to the (political) needs of different contexts. Depending on where the self and the others are placed in those structural configurations would certainly have an effect on the creation of paradoxical or compatible discourse worlds.

Attention and salience can also be explained as related to what could be called a continuum of prominence. Via linguistic choices, speakers can focus on given aspects of society which are moved to the figure position, that is, they are made salient. Prominence is useful for explaining how conflictual relations are construed as, for example, responsibility could be explicitly assigned to the others – thus delegitimizing their existence – or it could also be backgrounded.

Likewise, by focusing on concrete aspects of an event, partial (and partisan) views could be spread, thus highlighting the positive/negative role of different sociopolitical actors. Different linguistic choices have been mentioned in the case studies, including the use (or not) of premodification so as to emphasize or silence controversial attributes or sociopolitical responsibility, picking reified nominalization to silence the role of actors and/or foreground the existence of negative situations, or the lexical choice of metonymic references which may make specific aspects of reality salient. Depending on the nature of the partial world view, this could result in radical disagreement between participants in a communicative situation. If the elements which are foregrounded align with the audience's beliefs, consensus might be reached; if there is a clash between such mental representation and beliefs, conflict will be maintained.

Attention-triggering strategies are arguably related to another continuum, whose validity has been previously explored in conflict studies: specific vs abstract terms. If specificity may be conflictual because the mental representation is partial, abstraction may be conflictual because it is more prone to divergent interpretations (Janicki, 2015, pp. 82–106). A clear example of the double function of abstraction has been provided in the analysis. The 1998 Agreement, as a conflict resolution document, was based on ambiguous uses of language which frequently reflected some degree of abstraction. However, this also resulted in conflictual interpretations and opposed discourse worlds being constructed by NI politicians. This specific vs abstract continuum can clearly be related to applications of the 'ladder of abstraction' (Hayakawa, 1965, pp. 167–70) as a mechanism for exploring how inferential processes based on users' cognition mediate the relation between discourse and conflict. This notion, which has seldom been applied in discourse studies (except in previous work by Janicki (2006)), has already been proposed by political scientists as a solution for exploring how mass media shapes beliefs, opinions, attitudes and behaviour of audiences (Schmitt-Beck, 1998).

Inferential processes are equally important for understanding how framing strategies influence the creation of conflictual construals of reality. The role of cognition is of particular importance here as it is previous beliefs (understood in its broadest sense) that determine the type of frames that are activated by lexical choices. Such frames are related to the cognitive mechanism of comparison, whereby participants in a communicative situation lay the ground upon which reality is to be judged. As the other construal operations, framing strategies are also related to a continuum which is organized along a good-bad scale. As such, the analysis of frames is related to evaluation: The more the shared evaluation between different members of the social divide, the more compatible it is for users to align with the discourse world constructed by a political representative. Framing strategies tend to be associated with lexical choices, which can activate multiple layers of knowledge, either figuratively or non-figuratively. As such, when generic knowledge – that is not culture specific – is activated, it is easier to reach compatible mental representations. On the contrary, if frames are issue or culture specific (or also community specific), these could result in conflictual representations of society.

The analysis of perspectivization can shed light on how relations between communities are construed, as discourse worlds may either reflect a subjective – and more likely conflictual – or intersubjective view of reality. As such, discourse worlds are presented from a particular position with which other users interact. Such interaction is constructed along a proximal-distant continuum which reflects three types of anchorage dimensions: space, time and values. Entities, actors and actions are mentally represented as occupying a position in a space where other entities, actors and actions can also be found. Because discourse is situated, such position is not only occupied by elements indexed via discourse but also by members of the communities involved in conflict. Maximizing or minimizing the referential scope of the position from which discourse is construed could result in disagreement or consensus, as it could encompass (or not) the speakers' position in the world, and also those of the members of the community they stand for or of those belonging to other communities. Several linguistic cues can help in anchoring the world to different perspectives, and most notably those that have an indexical function such as personal pronouns, adverbs of place and time, verbs of movement, verb tenses or modality indicators.

This book was conceived with three key words in mind: 'discourse', 'cognition' and 'conflict'. The three of them are, for me, equally important, and the three of them have shaped how this book has been written. I have explicitly advocated for a qualitative analysis of language that is based on CL and which could help explain how sociopolitical conflict is produced, reproduced, sustained and solved. I claim that discourse-based conflict studies could benefit from exploring how different construal operations can result in opposed or compatible discourse worlds. First, because this shows that discourse is dynamic (i.e. constructed in interaction) and situated (i.e. influenced by contexts of production and reception). And second, because understanding how discourse worlds are linguistically created can help in finding novel communicative avenues in the search for conflict resolution. Indeed, language, as the most important tool in achieving successful communication, needs to be analysed for understanding how conflict is created and maintained. But language is meaningless on its own because, when used in context, it reflects and is influenced by the human mind.

The Irish rock band The Cranberries have summarized some of these ideas in their album *No need to argue* (1994). In it they explore their personal and cultural struggles, and probably without being aware of this, they explicitly acknowledge the role of cultural cognition. I started this book with a quote taken from a novel about the Troubles. In the same spirit, I would like to finish it quoting Dolores O'Riordan in 'Zombie', probably one of the best-known songs ever written about the NI conflict:

> When the violence causes silence,
> we must be mistaken.
> It's the same old theme since 1916.
> In your head, in your head,
> they're still fighting

Let's just be aware of what is in our head so that we do not behave like dehumanized zombies involved in conflict, but as human beings involved in consensual communication.

Appendix: A short chronology of events in post-Agreement NI

1998
- 10 April, a peace agreement is signed.→ (*Chapters 4 and 6*)
- 25 June, elections for the new NI Assembly.
- 15 August, the RIRA explodes a car bomb in Omagh killing twenty-nine people.
- 18 August, the RIRA declares the suspension of all its military actions.

1999
- 2 July, launch of document entitled 'The Way Forward', proposing the formation of an Executive which would be bound to IRA decommissioning.
- September-November, review of the agreement.
- 9 September, the Patten Report on Policing is released. → (*Chapter 5*)

2000
- 1 February, the IICD's report on IRA decommissioning. → (*Chapter 7*)
- 3–5 February, statements by UUP and IRA on decommissioning.
- 11 February, suspension of devolved government. → (*Chapter 7*)
- 15 February, IRA ends engagement with IICD. → (*Chapter 7*)
- 30 May, restoration of devolution. → (*Chapter 7*)

2001
- January and February, ongoing events of paramilitary violence.
- April and June, political talks (NI parties and the two governments).
- 1 July, David Trimble resigns as first minister.
- 10 August, NI Assembly suspended for one day.
- 14 August, IRA statement on their withdrawing decommissioning proposals. → (*Chapter 7*)
- 17 August, Policing implementation plan is published.
- 21 September, NI Assembly suspended for one day.
- 18 October, Unionist ministers resign from the NI Executive.
- 23 October, the IRA begins decommissioning after Gerry Adams' request. → (*Chapter 7*)
- 6 November, First and deputy first minister elected.

2002
- 8 April, IRA carries out a second act of decommissioning.
- 14 October, Assembly suspended after accusation of SF spying at Stormont.

2003
- 22 February, UDA/UFF announce a twelve-month ceasefire. → (*Chapter 7*)
- April and May, IRA statements on decommissioning and the peace process. → (*Chapter 7*)
- 26 October, IRA act of decommissioning. → (*Chapter 7*)
- 26 November, elections to the NI Assembly. SF and DUP as largest political parties. Political deadlock over appointment of first minister.

2004	• January–November. Political talks with several crises. • December. Failure of talks over lack of transparency of IRA decommissioning.
2005	• 5 May, UK general election. There is a Labour majority. In NI, the DUP becomes the most voted unionist party and SF the most voted nationalist one. • 28 July, IRA statement announcing the end of its armed campaign. • 26 September, the IICD announces that all IRA weapons have been put beyond use.
2006	• 15 May, NI politicians take their seats at the NI Assembly for the first time since 2002. • 13 October, St Andrews Agreement is unveiled as roadmap to restore devolution. • 24 November, a transitional NI Assembly comes into effect after elections for it are called.
2007	• 7 March, elections held in NI. • 8 May, devolution day. SF and the DUP have agreed to power-sharing in the NI Executive. → (*Chapter 5*) • 27 June, Tony Blair resigns as British prime minister.
2008	• 4 March, Ian Paisley stands down as NI first minister. He is substituted by Peter Robinson.
2010	• 12 January, SF and the DUP meet to talk about disagreement on devolution of policing powers. • 5 February, Hillsborough Agreement. It allowed the devolution of policing and justice powers. → (*Chapter 7*) • 12 April, justice and policing powers are devolved to the NI Assembly. • 6 May, UK general election. There is a Conservative majority.
2014	• 23 December, Stormont House Agreement aimed at solving identity issues. It sought to deal with the legacy of the Conflict.
2016	• 26 January, SF withdraws from regional government over a crisis with the DUP. NI Executive is dissolved. • 23 June, referendum on the withdrawal of the UK from the European Union. The majority voted to leave.
2017	• 29 March, UK prime minister triggers Article 50. This begins the two-year countdown to the UK formally leaving the EU.
2020	• 11 January, restoration of NI Executive after the signing of the New Decade, New Approach Agreement two days before. • 31 January, the UK leaves the EU and enters a one-year transition period.
2022	• 5 May, elections to NI Assembly. The DUP refuses to form a new executive in protest over the 'Northern Ireland Protocol' of the Brexit Agreement. • 13 June, British government introduces the Northern Ireland Protocol Bill seeking to fix problems with the protocol. → (*Chapter 4*)
2023	• 27 February, Windsor Framework is agreed. It seeks to regulate NI relations with the UK and the EU.

Notes

1 Introduction

1 Some of the terms used to refer to 'shared knowledge' are 'member resources', defined by Fairclough (1989, pp. 11, 24) as prototypes about a diverse collection of things ranging from the knowledge of language to representations of the social and natural worlds, values, beliefs and assumptions; 'K-device' (standing for knowledge-device) (Van Dijk, 2008), explained as psychological, sociocultural phenomena which are subjectively acquired by different individuals. When these mental constructs are shared between participants in a communicative event, we can talk about 'common ground'.

2 These two broad roles of languages are closely related to Halliday and Matthiessen's (2014) identification of three metafunctions in communication: textual, interpersonal and ideational. The relationship between them and different perspectives in the analysis of political discourse is more widely explained in Chilton and Schäffner (2002), Filardo-Llamas and Boyd (2017), Filardo-Llamas and Morales-López (2021).

3 Northern Ireland Statutory Rules, 2016. No. 8. *Change of Council Name (Derry and Strabane City Council) Regulations*. Available at https://www.legislation.gov.uk/nisr/2016/8/contents/made.

2 What can cognitive linguistics offer for conflict studies?

1 Studies on how misinformation spreads have also found this to be the case and have identified familiarity with content coming from the in-group or elite sources or aligning with personal views as some of the cognitive and socio-cognitive drivers of false beliefs (Ecker et al., 2022).

2 Chilton (1996) and Suurmond (2005) explore the philosophical schools which have influenced contemporary understandings of the relationship between discourse and conflict. Both authors argue that such link exists, and they emphasize the key role of the domination exercised by one discourse in people's mind in creating and maintaining conflict. Hence, they propose directing attention to the relation between the realities that people live in and the discourses found in those locations when trying to explain conflict.

3 Other studies have also stressed the need to look at the multiple functions performed by political discourse and hence the need to consider all these aspects in the analysis. These reflect the representational and evaluative perspectives to the study of political discourse (Chilton and Schäffner, 2002; Filardo-Llamas and Boyd, 2017; Filardo-Llamas and Morales-López, 2021). In this book, however, I am advocating not only for the adoption of different perspectives in the analysis. Rather, I claim that meaning is not only representational – that is, showing a particular world view – but that such representation can be discursively negotiated.

4 See Lavietes (2023) for a news piece on the topic, among other online references. Similar uproars took place in Spain over an interview with the minister of equality and her (lack of) definition of woman. Likewise, in a televised political debate before the July 2023 general election in Spain, candidates refused to define that term so as to avoid different groups of people being offended by their definition.

5 It is not possible to list all the scholars working on interface between cognitive linguistics and Critical Discourse Studies (CL-CDS). CL-CDS can be defined as the branch within CDA that explores 'the cognitive-semiotic processes involved in understanding discourse and the fundamental role that these processes play in the construction of knowledge and the legitimation of action' (Hart, 2017, p. 77). An overview of theories, analytic tools and case studies can be found in Filardo-Llamas, Hart and Kaal (2016) and Hart (2017).

6 Given the focus of this book on the relation between conflict and discourse, no specific reference is made to the theoretical foundation of CDA/CDS, which could be found in multiple sources (Van Dijk, 1998; Fairclough, 2010; Wodak and Meyer, 2016; Flowerdew and Richardson, 2017). Still, the influence of CDA scholars in the line of thought followed in this book needs to be minimally acknowledged. Given that my main focus is on public and political discourse, and that sometimes the boundary between CDA and Political Discourse Analysis is fuzzy (Filardo-Llamas and Boyd, 2017), I have decided to refer mostly to political discourse as the main area of analysis. Political discourse is understood in this book as not being only the one uttered by politicians but as any kind of public discourse which could have political relation – either because it has an effect on the development of policies or because it reflects or reacts to political acts (see Van Dijk, 1997 for a discussion on what is included in the scope of political discourse). Because it lies outside the scope of this book, no terminological distinction is made in this book between Critical Discourse Studies (CDS) and Critical Discourse Analysis (CDA). For a discussion on the difference between the two, see Flowerdew and Richardson (2017).

7 While this study refers to consumer decision-making, parallelisms can be established between marketing and political discourses inasmuch as they both try to persuade the audience to behave in a particular way (be that buying a product or performing a political action, for example). Thus, the authors' distinction between low-level

construals – including very detailed and contextualized representations – and high-level construals – having a higher degree of schematicity and abstraction – is of interest for this work. Likewise, their explanation of the relation between construal and (psychological) distance seems to align with studies on political discourse focusing on the role of spatial cognition (Chilton, 2004, 2005b; Dunmire, 2012; Cap, 2013; Filardo-Llamas, Hart and Kaal, 2016; Kaal, 2024).

8 No explicit reference is provided in this description to metonymy – which is based on a correlated analogy being established between an entity A and an entity B. While metonymy features frequently on descriptions of figurative language (Dancygier and Sweetser, 2014) and CL (Croft and Cruse, 2004), its role in political discourse analysis is sometimes overshadowed by the prominence given to metaphor (Cienki, 2013, p. 299). In this book, references to metonymy will be made in Chapter 5, as part of the analysis of attention and salience.

9 While this idea could be further expanded, I take a loose view on the concept of cognitive model referring to the mental representations that are conceptualized through language. Accounting for different levels of specificity allows us to acknowledge not only the physical and experiential basis of cognitive models but also the cultural dimension. In this way, the different types of encyclopaedic knowledge which may be activated when uttering or processing discourse can be considered. For a more detailed discussion of the relation between image schemas, metaphors and idealized cognitive models, see Cienki (2007).

10 The complete remarks can be found in the following page: https://www.gov.il/en/departments/news/excerpt-from-pm-netanyahu-s-remarks-at-the-opening-of-the-knesset-s-winter-assembly-16-oct-2023. Last accessed: 23 October 2023.

11 More information about this can be found in the *Business Insider India* (https://www.businessinsider.in/politics/world/news/netanyahu-deleted-a-post-on-x-about-a-struggle-against-children-of-darkness-around-the-time-of-a-tragic-hospital-explosion-in-gaza/articleshow/104509726.cms) and in *The Washington Examiner* (https://www.washingtonexaminer.com/policy/defense-national-security/netanyahu-hamas-iran-axis-evil). Both pages were last accessed on 23 October 2023.

12 Contrasting categories have been explained by Lakoff (1987, pp. 79–81) as being related to stereotypes, that is, social expectations we have about particular categories and the associated judgements we make through them. The need to consider the influence of culture when reflecting about the evaluative power of metaphors has been also stressed by Charteris-Black (2005, p. 51) in his discussion of light/dark metaphors.

13 It could be argued that the distinction between nomination and predication strategies is blurry. However, for the sake of clarity, a description of each of them is provided here. Nomination strategies are related to those discursive choices that imply some kind of discursive construction of social actors, entities or process through, for

example, processes related to membership categorization, nouns or verbs denoting those entities or processes, metaphor or other tropes. Predication strategies involve the discursive qualification of those social actors, entities or processes. They can also be realized via metaphors, nouns or adjectives although in this case they also involve a clear positive/negative evaluation of the said actors or processes.

14 The concept of discourse world has been suggested by Ramsbotham (2010) as a possibility for exploring discourse-based approaches to the study of radical disagreement.

15 A conscious choice has been made when writing, and the acronym DST has been selected as it does not only reflect the original name of the proposal, 'Discourse Space Theory' (Chilton, 2005b; Cap, 2017), but also its subsequent development as 'Deictic Space Theory' (Chilton, 2014, 2017). In my view, both aspects – deicticity and discourse – are equally important and shall be equally represented so as to stress the existence of an abstract conceptual notion which is meaningful in context.

16 Alignment can be understood as metaphorical closeness in terms of (ideological) values. An analogy is established between physical proximity in space (and sometimes in time) and abstract proximity in values.

17 Cap (2010, 2013) provides an overview of the different lexico-grammatical realizations that can be analysed in the study of proximization. They include not only deictic markers but also lexical choices and grammatical categories. Other studies have also focused on the proximizing potential of inference-based categories such as the activation of historical parallelisms (see Berrocal, 2017).

18 Langacker (2019, pp. 140–1) explains the analogies that can be established between the language needed for describing aspects of construal and the basic aspects of visual perception.

19 I have decided to use the term construal operations, following Croft and Cruse (2004). In their latter description of such operations, Talmy (2000a) refers to them as 'schematic systems' and Langacker (2019) as 'construal dimensions'. Christopher Hart (2014, pp. 110–12) sometimes refers to them as 'conceptual operations'. A more detailed discussion of the different attempts at systematizing the study of construal operations can be seen in Croft and Cruse (2004, pp. 43–5) and Verhagen (2007).

20 I have chosen to refer throughout the book to 'linguistic choices' for the sake of consistency with the examples that will feature prominently in the analysis chapters. Still, it is important to bear in mind that discourse is multimodal and that other semiotic modes, such as visuals or gestures (among others), are equally important in creating alternative construals of reality. Examples of multimodal analysis of political discourse can be seen in Hart (2025), Cienki (2004) or Machin and van Leeuwen (2016). The multimodal nature of political communication will feature, however, in Chapter 6.

3 The choreography of Northern Ireland: Historical and political background

1 Dixon (2002) explains the political use of this term: The process of 'political choreography' is 'an attempt to manage public and party perceptions by choreographing politics', that is, by staging and scripting events in such a way that it seems that the interests of each of the groups are protected.

2 An updated account of the NI conflict can be found in Cochrane (2021). Other relevant sources are also cited throughout this chapter.

3 Nowadays, Unionists frequently still feel under threat, and Republicans claim that they are still inhabiting a 'British colony'. These two groups often live in differentiated areas in the cities or villages, and they do not only identify with the territorial differences related to nationality but also to other cultural and religious traits.

4 The size of NI and the inclusion of only six of the nine counties that formed part of the traditional province of Ulster were determined by numerical reasons and by the desire to maintain the unionist majority in the area.

5 The police force – the Royal Ulster Constabulary (RUC) – was created in 1922 under the Government of Ireland Act, and it was exclusively Protestant. Thus, it was perceived by Nationalists as the armed wing of Unionism, as we will also see in the analysis chapters.

6 The Orange Order is an organization celebrating the Battle of the Boyne, fought in 1690, and which resulted in the defeat of Catholic King James II by the Protestant William of Orange.

7 Nearly six months after the introduction of internment, a civil rights march was organized in (London)Derry to protest against it. The march had been previously banned by the British authorities, and it ended with the death of thirteen unarmed men and the wounding of other seventeen by the Parachute Regiment of the British Army. The army claimed that someone had fired on them first, but the official enquiry conducted by Lord Widgery could not prove these allegations (Buckland, 1992, p. 156).

8 The ceasefire did not necessarily mean abandoning the struggle for the republican community, as they set out in the 'ten strategic objectives' included in an internal document entitled 'TUAS' (Hennessey, 1997, p. 289). Such title – TUAS – has been interpreted in two different ways: 'Totally Unarmed Struggle' and 'Tactical Use of Armed Struggle'. Once again, this shows the importance of language in NI, where the 'real' meaning of an utterance depends on who is to interpret the message and on the objectives to be achieved through it.

9 Since both terms have political connotations and are used differently by each of the communities, in this book I refer to this document as the '1998 Agreement' or merely 'the Agreement'.

10 This can be seen in some of the chronologies gathered in the website *CAIN* (Melaugh, 2023). Going through them, one can observe the high number of sectarian attacks, pipe bombs or even killings that were produced during the years following the signing of the 1998 Agreement. The only difference between these attacks and the ones during the Troubles lies on the post-Agreement ones being 'neglected' and ascribed to sectarian violence rather than paramilitary groups. This arguably seeks to keep the peace process moving, but at the same time it endows violence with a 'covert' nature.

11 These terms were frequently used by the media to describe the likely scenarios that could be encountered in the process of the UK exiting the EU. 'Hard Brexit' refers to the UK leaving the EU with only a very basic trade agreement or, in the likelihood of a very hard Brexit, a restoration of World Trade Organization (WTO) rules with no agreement with the EU. 'Soft Brexit' is understood as the UK leaving the EU but negotiating 'continued membership on the European Economic Area (EEA) or staying in the single market and customs union while giving up influence over single market rules' (Gadd, 2019, p. 9). A list of terms describing other possible negotiations of Brexit can be found in Gadd (2019).

12 The name IRA is used here to refer to the main paramilitary group in the republican community. However, dissent within the group has frequently led to the formation of new groups, examples of which include the Official IRA, the Continuity IRA or the Real IRA. A very brief overview of those republican groups which (have) opposed the peace process can be found in Cochrane (2021, p. 272). More information on the motivations of the IRA can be read in Alonso (2001, 2007).

13 The perception is that most loyalist and republican paramilitarism does not have political energy anymore. Still, there is one exception to this: the New IRA. This group, together with its political counterpart, Saoradh, seeks 'to destabilize the political process through violence' (Cochrane, 2021, p. 279). However, their capacity to sustain such an activity is doubted.

14 Cochrane (2021, pp. 216–17) explains that dissident violence has followed different ways in Republicanism and Loyalism. While a few republican dissident groups can be found, this is not so much the case in Loyalism. Such difference can be explained by two reasons: (1) the disappearance of the Provisional IRA, and hence the lack of a target at which violence could be addressed, and (2) the perception by the Protestant community that they had benefited from the 1998 Agreement without the constitutional status of NI being at risk.

15 While ethnic explanations of the conflict are the most common ones among scholars, they are not the only ones. Edwards and McGrattan (2010, pp. 127–38) also acknowledge other possibilities, including Marxist explanations, religious differences, irreconcilable ideologies and even a gender dimension. Still, it is the ethnic explanations that is most closely related to the Us vs Them ideological square

(Van Dijk, 1998) which has been traditionally used in (Critical) Discourse Analysis. This explains the explanatory prominence given to it in this chapter.

4 Gestalt and structural configuration

1 For a terminological distinction between schema, images and image schemas, see Johnson (1987, pp. 18–40) and Oakley (2007).

2 Bold type, underlining and italics are used in the examples to direct attention towards the linguistic cues where each construal operation is instantiated. Variation in format serves to emphasize multiple cues or contrasting choices.

3 The notions of figure and ground are of significance when explaining how attention, as a construal operation, is distributed in discourse. As such, they will also be relevant in Chapter 5. Likewise, MOTION may also involve the creation of a proximal-distant relation with SOURCES or GOALS, particularly when they are construed as CONTAINERS. Such proximal-distant perspective in the construal of events is covered in Chapter 7.

4 Only the basic configuration of the MOTION schema has been included here. How this schema is conceptualized is frequently culture specific (Chilton, 1996, pp. 52–53). Examples can be seen in Slobin's (1991) study of cross-linguistic variation between verbs of motion in English and Spanish. Because English is the language of study in this book, descriptions of MOTION events are based on those identified for English grammatical realizations (Radden and Dirven, 2007).

5 While in English it is MANNER that is conflated with MOTION, in other languages (such as Spanish), it is the PATH or the GOAL that are profiled, with MANNER being expressed by an adverbial (see Radden and Dirven, 2007, pp. 278–9; Slobin, 1991 for further details). This will not be discussed in further detail because it is not the aim of this book to explain such typological differences, but rather to reflect on how the structural configuration inherent to image schemas mediates the relation between discourse and conflict.

6 The speech can be accessed in the following link: https://ec.europa.eu/commission/presscorner/api/files/document/print/en/speech_24_5201/SPEECH_24_5201_EN.pdf (last accessed June 2025).

7 A more detailed chronology is available in the website of the Northern Ireland Assembly: https://www.niassembly.gov.uk/assembly-business/brexit-and-beyond/timeline-and-key-documents/ (last accessed November 2024).

8 These speeches are available on the website of the *UK Political Speech Archive*: https://www.ukpol.co.uk/ (last accessed November 2024).

9 A debate between one still-present SF MEP (standing for the Republic of Ireland) and one former SF MEP (standing for NI) has been analysed. The debate is available

on SF's YouTube Channel: https://www.youtube.com/watch?v=ry8JjOXPau4 (last accessed June 2025).

10 All the analysed statements were uttered on 10 April 2018. These include the following: Gerry Adams, 'The Good Friday Agreement remains bedrock for progress'; Karen Bradley, 'Reaffirmation of the commitment of the UK government to Belfast Agreement' and 'Building Peace'; Jeremy Corbin, 'We must cherish and learn from the Good Friday Agreement'; statements by Gregory Campbell, Colum Eastwood, Naomi Long, John Stewart and the Workers Party. They can be found in the *CAIN* website: https://cain.ulster.ac.uk/events/peace/soc.htm#2018 (last accessed November 2024).

5 Attention and salience

1 This description is based on traditional definitions within CL. They rely on Lakoff and Johnson's (1980) distinction between metaphor, involving cross-domain mapping, and metonymy, as mapping within a cognitive domain. A detailed account of other definitions can be found in Panther and Thornburg (2007).

2 Mostly resulting from variation in the definition of 'one domain', which can be understood as a conceptual domain or as a domain matrix (see sections three and four in Panther and Thornburg, 2007 for a discussion).

3 While not explicitly based on socio-cognitive analysis, Van Leeuwen (1996) also stresses the importance of analysing discourse strategies which are used for the categorization of social actors. Among them generalization is also mentioned. Socio-cognitive approaches in which social actor analysis has been applied can be found in Koller (2012).

4 The controversy in this case lies over an allegedly unnotified protest in (London)Derry on 25 August 2023. The Public Processions (Northern Ireland) Act (1998) requires such street demonstrations to be notified in advance to the Parades Commission. Conflict arises in this case over families walking together to the hearing of one of the soldiers involved in the 1972 Bloody Sunday. The SDLP leader was accused by a loyalist activist of taking part in an unnotified parade. Further information about the incident can be found in https://www.independent.co.uk/news/uk/colum-eastwood-sdlp-londonderry-salvation-army-police-service-of-northern-ireland-b2473201.html (last accessed December 2024).

5 News about this can be read in the article entitled 'Ryanair accused of greenwash over carbon emissions claim', published by *The Guardian*. It is available in https://www.theguardian.com/business/2020/feb/05/ryanair-accused-of-greenwash-over-carbon-emissions-claim (last accessed December 2024).

6 The justification by ASA can be found in their website: https://www.asa.org.uk/rulings/ryanair-ltd-cas-571089-p1w6b2.html (last accessed December 2024).

7 Both Langacker (2008) and Tenbrink (2020) include 'elaboration' as a means of foregrounding or backgrounding cognitive detail. Elaboration is, in Langacker's (2008, pp. 55–6) view, closely related to schematicity. A schematic characterization, that is, a book, is instantiated by a number of more specific, or elaborated, ones (i.e. a novel, a comic, a poetry book, an essay, etc.). As mentioned in Chapter 2, the distinction between construal operations guiding this book is determined by explanatory purposes even if they all co-occur. This is why schemas have been covered in Chapter 4 – when exploring how gestalts are constructed, and why they will be implicitly referred to again when looking at framing in Chapter 6. As can be apparent from a comparison of the linguistic cues covered in this chapter and those in Chapter 4, speakers construe more schematic – coarse-grained – or specific – fine-grained – views of reality, with different aspects of that reality being made salient. Manipulations along this schematicity-specificity continuum can result in more conflictual or consensual construals of reality.

8 Early studies on pragmatics and political discourse used the notion of implicit meaning to explain disagreement between political parties in NI. While not explicitly relying on the notion of scales, but rather on Relevance Theory, a clear connection can be drawn between the proposal for the study of scalar implicature and claims made in those studies (Wilson and Rose, 1997).

9 The analysed documents include the following: SF. 1999. *Statement in Response to the Patten Report.* 9 September; SDLP. 1999. *Statement Issued in Response to the Patten Commission Report.* 9 September; UUP. 1999. *Statement in Response to the Patten Report.* 9 September; DUP. 1999. *Statement by Ian Paisley on the Publication of the Patten Report.* 9 September.

10 'We are mindful of the service and sacrifice by all those brave RUC officers who have served the community' (UUP 1999).

11 'Over the years that RUC have seen themselves and have been seen as the armed guardians of the Union with Great Britain and the armed wing of unionism' (SF 1999).

12 In everyday conversations the police force was known as the RUC. In fact, the word 'Ulster' does not even appear in some of the references to such forces found in a glossary listing words related to the conflict (Dunn and Dawson, 2000).

13 A photograph of this mural, which no longer exists, can be found in the mural directory compiled by Dr Jonathan McCormick and hosted in the *CAIN* archive. Available at https://cain.ulster.ac.uk/mccormick/photos/no1681.htm#photo (last accessed December 2024).

14 A photograph of this graffiti can be found in McCormick's mural directory. Available at https://cain.ulster.ac.uk/mccormick/photos/no2667.htm#photo (last accessed December 2024).

15 This case study is based on the following statements. All were uttered in 2003: Gerry Adams, *Speech of Sinn Féin President at Balmoral Hotel Belfast*, 21 October; David Trimble, *Statement by the Leader of the UUP, on Decommissioning*, 21 October; Irish Republican Army (IRA), *'First' Statement on Weapons*, 12.15 pm 21 October; Irish Republican Army (IRA), *'Second' Statement on Weapons*. Responses by the SDLP and the DUP have not been considered because they were not directly involved in the agreed sequence of events. Likewise, following internal interpretations of the NI political conflict (Whyte, 1990, secs 194–205) as one taking place between the two dominant communities, statements by representatives of the British and Irish government, as well as the IICD statement, have also been discarded in this case study.
16 For reasons of space, construals related to the time scale have not been explained in detail, but a similar strategic use of scalar adjustment can be observed in the amount of detail that is provided about the time at which weapons have been decommissioned: 'at the earliest opportunity' or 'on previous occasions' should be understood as being points along a vaguely construed temporal open-ended scale.
17 A detailed list of statements and events can be found in the yearly list of source documents on the Irish Peace Process compiled as part of the *CAIN Archive: Conflict and Politics in Northern Ireland*. Available: at https://cain.ulster.ac.uk/events/peace/soc.htm (last accessed December 2024).
18 The analysed statements are the following: Gerry Adams, *Statement on the agreement with the DUP of a date for devolved government in Northern Ireland* (27 March 2007); Ian Paisley, *Statement on the agreement with SF of a date for devolved government in Northern Ireland* (27 March 2007(a)); Martin McGuinness, *Speech on the resumption of devolved government in Northern Ireland* (8 May 2007); Ian Paisley, *Speech on the resumption of devolved government in Northern Ireland* (8 May 2007(b)).
19 The terms 'figure' and 'ground' are used in CL to explain the construal operation of attention, that is, the cognitive process of foregrounding a particular entity in a representation of a scene. The term 'figure' signals the entity which receives prominent attention and around which the scene is organized (Divjak, Milin and Medimorec, 2020). Langacker (2008, pp. 58–60) explains this process as foregrounding and backgrounding.
20 Several studies have focused on the ideological implications of using the passive voice (e.g. Fowler et al., 1979; Hart, 2014, 2025).

6 Judgement and comparison

1 This aligns with Langacker's (2019) inclusion of salience and comparison under the name 'prominence' when discussing the dimensions of construal. Dancygier and Sweetser (2014, p. 17) also implicitly refer to both structural configuration and

comparison as being related to frames, which, in their view, invoke a particular 'gestalt structure' which 'gives conceptual access to an entire structure'. Likewise, a parallelism can be found between Hart's (2014) explanation of framing strategies as being richer in detail and specificity and Kövecses's (2017) proposal for the identification of different levels of metaphor, ranging from schematic and more basic conceptualizations to richer mental spaces. While certainly an overlap is observed between both cognitive operations, I believe that looking at them separately can help us explain how different types of shared knowledge influence discursive construals of reality in such a way that more or less conflictual representations can be transmitted.

2 Evaluation is conceived as a broad term showing the speaker's opinions or feelings along a good-bad scale. This notion of evaluation is an adaptation from more general understandings which would incorporate positioning and stance, which are studied in this book under the perspective construal operation (see Chapter 7). For detailed discussions on evaluation, see Thompson and Hunston (1999), Martin and White (2005) and Thompson and Alba-Juez (2014). Further references can be found in political discourse analysis, with moral evaluation featuring prominently as a legitimization strategy (Van Leeuwen, 2007, 2017). Likewise, a relation can be established between evaluation and the activation of emotions in political discourse (Reyes, 2011; Alcántara-Plá, 2024).

3 For a discussion on the difference between objectivist and experientialist understandings of categorization and meaning, see Lakoff (1987) and Janicki (2006).

4 'S' stands for speaker and 'P' for property.

5 Given the qualitative approach followed in this book, I will only focus on the effect of using different pre- and post-modifiers and how such choices may construe alternative representations of the same reality. However, it shall be noted that corpus-based approaches have similarly argued in favour of analysing the linguistic context within which particular nouns appear so as to identify their semantic preference. As noted by corpus linguists, studying collocations can shed light on patterns of use which reflect the attitudes of users (Mautner, 2016; Taylor, 2019).

6 This sentence shall be understood not only as referring to those studies in which 'categorization' features as the technical term used to describe the process but also as those studies referring to naming and nomination, with the latter featuring prominently in the Discourse Historical Approach within CDS (Reisigl and Wodak, 2002).

7 The article can be accessed in the following website: https://time.com/6334409/is-whats-happening-gaza-genocide-experts/ (last accessed December 2024).

8 Discussions about the differences in terminology between domains and frames can be seen in Cienki (2007), Dancygier and Sweetser (2014), Zoltan Kövecses (2020, pp. 50–92), Semino et al. (2018).

9 Langacker (2008) uses the term 'space' to emphasize a conceptualization which can be partitioned into semiautonomous regions. Such 'regions' in the conceptual structure would be equivalent to the definition of frame provided above. All of them together would belong to one conceptual domain. Since it is not the aim of this book to enter into the subtleties and nuances implicit in such terminology, the term 'frame' will be mostly employed, except when citing directly the authors. This has been done to ensure consistency throughout the chapter.

10 For simplification reasons, the arrows linking elements in the source, target and blended space have been omitted. Bold colour indicates the foregrounded properties, and subtle change in width of bold lines indicates variation in the degree of salience.

11 Some authors have explained this mapping process as a conceptual blend resulting from the correspondence between elements in the source domain with elements in the target one (Charteris-Black, 2004; Hart, 2014, pp. 137–61). A similar view can be observed in the explanation of metaphors provided by Text World Theory, in which metaphorically triggered mental representations are embedded within the speaker's discourse world (Werth, 1999; Gavins, 2007). What is relevant, in my view, is that the importance of metaphor as a reasoning cognitive mechanism underlies all such theoretical descriptions. Likewise, we cannot forget that, regardless of its apparently objective nature, metaphorical language is subjective as it results in a construal of reality within which given elements are not only selected but also made salient, and that such construal is based on the speaker's judgement.

12 See Semino et al. (2018) for an overview, Boeynaems et al. (2017) for a comparison between these approaches, and Hart (2023) for a discussion on how the reponse-elicitation approach can be integrated in CDA.

13 The complete speech can be watched in the following link: https://www.youtube.com/watch?v=XGJwCUHVgc0 (last accessed December 2024).

14 In a loose adaptation of Cameron's (2011, p. 16) explanation of metaphor systematicity, I consider that systematic metaphors are those which eventually create a metaphorical scenario (Musolff, 2006, 2017) by textual repetition of patterns in a single or multiple instances of discourse uttered by (representative) members of a given community. Such scenario results from the thematic relation of interconnected frames which allow for a network of correspondences between the source and target domains to be established. For example, discourses aimed at justifying the separation of the UK from the EU often lexically described it as the two entities being in a 'troubled' or 'rocky' relationship, hence legitimizing the subsequent 'divorce' (Đurović and Silaški, 2018). By repetition, this creates a conceptual scenario which lies at the core of the inferential process triggered by this figurative framing. Considering this a systematic metaphor allows, in my view, not only to incorporate the notion of repetition but also to reflect on the indexical value of metaphors as singling out members of a community (cf. Chilton, 2004).

15 Findings in experimental studies are not consistent, with some of them proving that there is a cognitive persuasive effect when metaphor is used (Thibodeau, 2016) and others claiming that no statistical relevance has been found supporting such claims (Brugman, Burgers and Vis, 2019).

16 Clear overlaps can be observed between Charteris-Black's (2004) explanation of the role of metaphor in the discursive effect of some conceptualizations which eventually present politicians as heroes and Kelsey's (2017) description of the affective dynamics and mythology underlying references to political heroic icons. While using different terminology to explain the mediating role of knowledge, such overlaps also justify the need to incorporate more nuanced layers in the analysis of framing strategies.

17 The *CAIN* website offers a more detailed summary of these political positions. The Campaign Leaflets that were used at the time of the referendum can also be consulted there. They are available in the following link https://cain.ulster.ac.uk/issues/politics/refparties.htm (last accessed December 2024).

18 The analysed speeches are the following: Gerry Adams, *Presidential Address to Sinn Féin Ard Fheis*, 18 April; John Hume, *Statement at the Launch of the SDLP 'Yes' Campaign*, 28 April; David Trimble, *Speech to the Northern Ireland Forum*, 17 April; Ian Paisley *Statement at the Launch of the DUP 'No' Campaign*, 15 April.

19 In the UUP Press release entitled *Trimble sets the record straight* and issued on 16 April 1998, an attempt is made at answering some of the charges made by the DUP about the 1998 Agreement. This document is organized following this structure: DUP CLAIM 'SOMETHING' – UUP ANSWERS.

20 Different sources were consulted in the analysis of responses to the 2006 Agreement (see Filardo-Llamas, 2008a for further details), the cited documents are the following: Adams, Gerry. *Speech on the Commemoration of the 30th Anniversary for IRA Volunteers Joey Surgeoner, Paul Marlowe and Francie Fitzsimmons*, Belfast, 16 October 2006; DUP. *St. Andrews Agreement/Devolution Consultation. Your Verdict – What Is It to Be?* DUP, 23 October 2006.

21 Mural painting in NI is undergoing constant changes. Thus, some of the murals referred to here or collected in those websites may have disappeared and/or may have been substituted by others. I believe, though, that the theoretical implications of considering murals for understanding the relation between cognition and discourse in public spaces remains valid regardless of the actual representations included in the analysis.

22 The mural can be seen in https://ccdl.claremont.edu/digital/collection/mni/id/23227/rec/15 (last accessed December 2024).

23 The mural can be seen in https://ccdl.claremont.edu/digital/collection/mni/id/23185/rec/8 (last accessed December 2024).

7 Positioning and perspective

1 In more contemporary descriptions of the theory, it has been 'renamed' to Deictic Space Theory. This stresses the model being an extended theory of deixis. While deixis is fundamental in explaining positioning (see also Croft and Cruse, 2004), I decided to profile that the meaning of such deictic uses is related to their use in context. The focus, in my view, shall thus be on 'discourse – that is situated, embodied and speaker-oriented linguistic performance, rather than on non-situated linguistic knowledge' (Chilton, 2005, p. 79). This decision also aligns with recent references to this within the CL-CDS approach (e.g. Cap, 2017; Hart, 2025).

2 Fauconnier (1994) also refers to hypothetical spaces and mood. However, these are, in my view, not explicitly related to deictics but to more abstract conceptualizations related to stance. As such, these will be explained in more detail in the next section.

3 For ethical reasons, the specific source for each example is not provided. Example [1], including a discussion between two speakers (A and B), is taken from a sub-Reddit for women who are disillusioned with mainstream feminism; example [2] is taken from a sub-Reddit on transgender male-to-female issues. Both examples were triggered with a broach search on Reddit including the words '(trans) women spaces'.

4 The complete transcript of the statement can be found in this website: https://apnews.com/article/election-2020-joe-biden-donald-trump-capitol-siege-media-e79eb5164613d6718e9f4502eb471f27 (last accessed December 2024).

5 The speech by Queen Elizabeth was broadcasted by the BBC on 5 April 2020. With the title 'We will meet again', it can be watched on https://www.youtube.com/watch?v=2klmuggOElE&ab_channel=BBC. The transcript of the speech can be found in https://www.bbc.com/news/uk-52176208. Both websites were last accessed in December 2024.

6 The analysed statements cover the sequence of events resulting in the suspension of devolved government and include the following, IICD (2000) *Report of the Independent International Commission on Decommissioning*, 31 January; UUP (2000) *Statement by the UUP Assembly Team*, 1 February; Gerry Adams (2000a), *Statement by SF President*, 1 February; IRA (2000a), *First Statement on Decommissioning*, 1 February; David Trimble (2000), *Article written for* The Belfast Telegraph, 2 February; Gerry Adams (2000b), *Article written for* The Irish News, 3 February; Peter Mandelson (2000a), *Statement by the Secretary of State to the House of Commons*, 3 February; Gerry Adams (2000c), *Statement in response to the statement by Peter Mandelson*, 3 February; IRA (2000b), *Second Statement on Decommissioning*, 5 February; John Hume (2000), 'Time to save the process', *The Irish News / The Irish Times*, 7 February; Gerry Adams (2000d), *Statement by SF President*, 11 February; Peter Mandelson (2000b), *Statement with decision to suspend the NI Assembly and*

Executive, 11 February; IICD (2000b), *Report on Decommissioning*, 11 February. All the analysed texts have been collected from Melaugh (2023).

7 The analysed sources include the following: NIO (2010) *Agreement between SF and the DUP on Devolution and Policing*, Hillsborough Castle, 5 February; Peter Robinson (2010) *Statement by the DUP*, 5 February; Martin McGuinness (2010) *Statement by SF*, 5 February; Reg Empey (2010) *Statement by the UUP*, 5 February. All the analysed texts can be found in Melaugh (2023).

8 Although it lies outside the scope of this book, some studies on political discourse have tried to identify a parallelism between the different stages in the effective and epistemic cycle and the use of stance (Marín-Arrese, 2021a). It remains to be tested whether subjective or intersubjective construals feature more prominently at different moments in the cycle and whether this could influence the discursive representation of conflictual relations.

9 As noted in Chapter 3, the adjectives used for describing each community are to be understood as generalizing. However, the reality is much more complex and more nuanced classifications can be found in detailed studies of paramilitary violence at both sides of the divide (see, for example, Simpson, 2013, pp. 8–30). Because it is the main aim of this book to explain how construal operations work, no reference is made to dissident voices, split sections or cover names of paramilitary groups. A very detailed and updated description of organizations, their ceasefires and their position on the 1998 Agreement can be found in the *CAIN archive* hosted by the University of Ulster: https://cain.ulster.ac.uk/issues/violence/paramilitary.htm (last accessed December 2024).

10 The UDA is also known as Ulster Freedom Fighters (UFF) and the UVF is also known as the Red Hand Commando (RHC). For simplicity reasons, these two names will not be used in the analysis.

11 I understand as peace-related actions those that are aimed at overcoming violence, including decommissioning of weapons and calling for an end of their 'military' activity. Actions included on the table are based on those mentioned in the *CAIN archive* (see footnote 9 for this chapter).

12 'Specified' indicates that the British government considered that the ceasefire called by the organization had ended. 'Despecified' means that members of the organizations are not committed to violence and are involved with the IICD, thus being eligible for early release from prison for offences committed before the 1998 Agreement.

References

Abdelmonem, M. G., and McWhinney, R. (2015) 'In Search of Common Grounds: Stitching the Divided Landscape of Urban Parks in Belfast', *Cities*, 44, pp. 40–9.

Abousnnouga, G., and Machin, D. (2010) 'Analysing the Language of War Monuments', *Visual Communication*, 9(2), pp. 131–49.

Achugar, M. (2008) *What We Remember: The Construction of Memory in Military Discourse*. Amsterdam: John Benjamins.

Albert, C. (2008) *The Peacebuilding Elements of the Belfast Agreement and the Transformation of the Northern Ireland Conflict*. Frankfurt: Peter Lang.

Alcántara-Plá, M. (2024) 'Understanding Emotions in Hate Speech: A Methodology for Discourse Analysis', *Discourse & Society*, 35(4), pp. 417–33.

Alonso Belmonte, I., and Porto, M. D. (2020) 'Multimodal Framing Devices in European Online News', *Language and Communication*, 71, pp. 55–71.

Alonso, R. (2001) *Irlanda del Norte. Una historia de guerra y la búsqueda de la paz*. Madrid: Editorial Complutense.

Alonso, R. (2007) *Matar por Irlanda*. Madrid: Alianza.

Anderson, B. (1991) *Imagined Communitites. Reflections on the Origins and Spread of Nationalism*. London: Verso.

Arthur, P. (1996) 'Political Parties: (1) Elections and Strategies', in A. Aughey and D. Morrow (eds) *Northern Ireland Politics*. New York: Longman, pp. 67–73.

Aughey, A. (1996) 'Unionism', in A. Aughey and D. Morrow (eds) *Northern Ireland Politics*. New York: Longman, pp. 31–8.

Aughey, A. (2002) 'The Art and Effect of Political Lying in Northern Ireland', *Irish Political Studies*, 17(2), pp. 1–16.

Bardon, J. (1993) *A History of Ulster*. Belfast: Blackstaff.

Barry, K. (2023) 'Lack of Power-Sharing in Northern Ireland Is Making Politics More Polarised', *University of Birmingham News*. Available at: https://www.birmingham.ac.uk/news/2023/lack-of-power-sharing-in-northern-ireland-is-making-politics-more-polarised. (last accessed June 2025).

Bateman, C. (1995) *Divorcing Jack*. London: HarperCollins.

Ben-Rafael, E., Shohamy, E., Hassan Amara, M. and Trumper-Hecht, N. (2006) 'Linguistic Landscape as Symbolic Construction of the Public Space: The Case of Israel', in D. Gorter (ed.) *Linguistic Landscape: A New Approach to Multilingualism*. Clevendon: Multilingual Matters, pp. 7–30.

Berrocal, M. (2017) 'Proximizing the Ukraine Conflict: The Case of the United States and the Czech Republic', *Lodz Papers in Pragmatics*, 13(2), pp. 327–46.

Bew, P., and Gillespie, G. (1999) *Northern Ireland. A Chronology of the Troubles. 1968–1999*. Dublin: Gill & Macmillan.

Billig, M. (1995) *Banal Nationalism*. London: Sage.

Billig, M. (2003) 'Preface: Language as Forms of Death', in M. N. Dédaic and D. N. Nelson (eds) *At War with Words*. Berlin: Mouton de Gruyter, pp. vii–xv.

Billig, M. (2008) 'The Language of Critical Discourse Analysis: The Case of Nominalization', *Discourse and Society*, 19(6), pp. 783–800.

Bloor, M. and Bloor, T. (2007) *The Practice of Critical Discourse Analysis: An Introduction*. London: Routledge.

Boeynaems, A., Burgers, C., Konijn, E. A. and Steen, G. J. (2017) 'The Effects of Metaphorical Framing on Political Persuasion: A Systematic Literature Review', *Metaphor and Symbol*, 32(2), pp. 118–34.

Brown, P. and Levinson, S. C. (1987). *Politeness: Some Universals in Language Usage*. Cambridge: Cambridge University Press.

Brown, R., and Gilman, A. (1972) 'The Pronouns of Power and Solidarity', in P. Giglioli (ed.) *Language as a Social Context*. Hardmonworth: Penguin, pp. 252–82.

Brugman, B. C., Burgers, C. and Vis, B. (2019) 'Metaphorical Framing in Political Discourse through Words vs Concepts: A Meta-Analysis', *Language and Cognition*, 11(1), pp. 41–65.

Bryan, D. (2000) *Orange Parades. The Politics of Ritual, Tradition and Control*. London: Pluto.

Bryan, D. (2003) 'Belfast: Urban Space, "Policing" and Sectarian Polarization', in J. Schneider and B. I. Susser (eds) *Wounded Cities: Destruction and Reconstruction in a Globalized World*. Oxford: Berg, pp. 251–70.

Buckland, P. (1992) *A History of Northern Ireland*. Dublin: Gill & Macmillan.

Burke, L. (2020) Lessons from Northern Ireland: Policing, Polarization, and Moving Forward, Policy Brief. *German Marshal Funds*, 10 August. Available at: https://www.gmfus.org/news/lessons-northern-ireland-policing-polarization-and-moving-forward (last accessed June 2025).

Cameron, L. (1999) 'Identifying and Describing Metaphor in Spoken Discourse Data', in L. Cameron and G. Low (eds) *Researching and Applying Metaphor*. Cambridge: Cambridge University Press, pp. 105–32.

Cameron, L. (2011) *Metaphor and Reconciliation: The Discourse Dynamics of Empathy in Post -Conflict Conversations*. London: Routledge.

Canavan, M., and Turkoglu, O. (2023) 'Effect of Group Status and Conflict on National Identity: Evidence from the Brexit Referendum in Northern Ireland', *Journal of Peace Research*, 60(6), pp. 921–34.

Cap, P. (2010) 'Proximizing Objects, Proximizing Values. Towards an Axiological Contribution to The Discourse of Legitimisation', in U. Okulska and P. Cap (eds) *Perspectives in Politics and Discourse*. Amsterdam: John Benjamins, pp. 119–42.

Cap, P. (2013a) *Proximization. The Pragmatics of Symbolic Distance Crossing*. Amsterdam: John Benjamins.

Cap, P. (2013b) 'Proximization Theory and Critical Discourse Studies: A Promising Connection?', *International Review of Pragmatics*, 5, pp. 293–317.

Cap, P. (2017a) 'Spatial Cognition', in J. Flowerdew and J. E. Richardson (eds) *The Routledge Handbook of Critical Discourse Studies*. London: Routledge, pp. 92–119.

Cap, P. (2017b) 'Studying Ideological Worldviews in Political Discourse Space: Critical-Cognitive Advances in the Analysis of Conflict and Coercion', *Journal of Pragmatics*, 108, pp. 17–27.

Cap, P. (2018a) 'From "Cultural Unbelonging" to "Terrorist Risk": Communicating Threat in the Polish Anti-immigration Discourse', *Critical Discourse Studies*, 15(3), pp. 285–302.

Cap, P. (2018b) '"We don't Want any Immigrants or Terrorists Here": The Linguistic Manufacturing of Xenophobia in the post-2015 Poland', *Discourse and Society*, 29(4), pp. 380–98.

Catalano, T., and Waugh, L. R. (2013) 'The Ideologies behind Newspaper Crime Reports of Latinos and Wall Street/CEOs: A Critical Analysis of Metonymy in Text and Image', *Critical Discourse Studies*, 10(4), pp. 406–26.

Charteris-Black, J. (2004) *Corpus Approaches to Critical Metaphor Analysis*. Basingtoke: Palgrave.

Charteris-Black, J. (2005) *Politicians and Rhetoric: The Persuasive Power of Metaphor*. Basingtoke: Palgrave.

Charteris-Black, J. (2014) *Analysing Political Speeches: Rhetoric, Discourse and Metaphor*. Basingtoke: Palgrave.

Chilton, P., and Ilyin, M. (1993) 'Metaphor in Political Discourse: The Case of the "Common European House"', *Discourse & Society*, 4(1), pp. 7–31.

Chilton, P. (1996) *Security Metaphors: Cold War Discourse from Containment to Common House*. New York: Peter Lang.

Chilton, P. (1998) 'The Role of Language in Human Conflict: Prolegomena to the Investigation of Language as a Factor in Conflict Causation and Resolution', in S. Wright (ed.) *Language and Conflict: A Neglected Relationship*. Clevendon: Multilingual Matters, pp. 2–17.

Chilton, P. (2004) *Analysing Political Discourse. Theory and Practice*. London: Routledge.

Chilton, P. (2005a) 'Missing Links in Mainstream CDA: Modules, Blends and the Critical Instinct', in P. Chilton and R. Wodak (eds) *A New Agenda in (Critical) Discourse Analysis: Theory, Methodology and Interdisciplinarity*. Amsterdam: John Benjamins, pp. 19–52.

Chilton, P. (2005b) 'Vectors, Viewpoint and Viewpoint Shift: Toward a Discourse Space Theory', *Annual Review of Cognitive Linguistics*, 3, pp. 78–116.

Chilton, P. (2010) 'The Conceptual Structure of Deontic Meaning: A Model Based on Geometrical Principles', *Language and Cognition*, 2(2), pp. 191–220.

Chilton, P. (2014) *Language, Space and Mind. The Conceptual Geometry of Linguistic Meaning*. Cambridge: Cambridge University Press.

Chilton, P. (2017) 'Toward a Neuro-Cognitive Model of Socio-Political Discourse, and an Application to the Populist Discourse of Donald Trump', *Langage et Societe*, 160–1, pp. 237–49.

Chilton, P. A. (2003) 'Deixis and Distance: President Clinton's Justification of Intervention in Kosovo', in M. N. Dedaic and D. N. Nelson (eds) *At War with Words*. Berlin: De Gruyter, pp. 92–126.

Chilton, P., and Schäffner, C. (1997) 'Discourse and Politics', in T. A. Van Dijk (ed.) *Discourse as Social Interaction*. London: Sage, pp. 206–30.

Chilton, P., and Schäffner, C. (2002) 'Introduction. Themes and Principles in the Analysis of Political Discourse', in P. Chilton and C. Schäffner (eds) *Politics as Text and Talk. Analytic Approaches to Political Discourse*. Amsterdam: John Benjamins, pp. 1–41.

Chiluwa, I. (2021) 'Discourse, Conflict and Conflict Resolution', in I. Chiluwa (ed.) *Discourse and Conflict. Analysing Text and Talk of Conflict, Hate and Peace-building*. Basingtoke: Palgrave Macmillan, pp. 1–16.

Cienki, A. (1997) 'Some Properties and Groupings of Image Schemas', in M. H. Verspoor, K. D. Lee and E. Sweetser (eds) *Lexical and Syntactical Constructions and the Construction of Meaning*. Amsterdam: John Benjamins, pp. 3–16.

Cienki, A. (2004) 'Bush's and Gore's Language and Gestures in the 2000 US Presidential Debates. A Test Case for Two Models of Metaphors', *Journal of Language and Politics2*, 3(3), pp. 409–40.

Cienki, A. (2007) 'Frames, Idealised Cognitive Models and Domains', in D. Geeraerts and D. Cuyckens (eds) *The Oxford Handbook of Cognitive Linguistics*. Oxford: Oxford University Press, pp. 170–87.

Cienki, A. (2013) 'Bringing Concepts from Cognitive Linguistics into the Analysis of Policies and the Political', *Journal of International Relations and Development*, 16(2), pp. 294–310.

Cienki, A., and Yanow, D. (2013) 'Why Metaphor and Other Tropes? Linguistic Approaches to Analysing Policies and the Political', *Journal of International Relations and Development*, 16, pp. 167–76.

Clausner, T. C., and Croft, W. (1999) 'Domains and Image Schemas', *Cognitive Linguistics*, 10(1), pp. 1–31.

Coakley, J. (2012) *Nationalism, Ethnicity and the State. Making and Breaking Nations*. London: Sage.

Cochrane, F. (2021) *Northern Ireland. The Fragile Peace*. 2nd edn. New Haven, CT: Yales University Press.

Cohen, R. (2010) 'Language and Conflict Resolution: The Limits of English', *International Studies*, 3(1), pp. 25–51.

Colfer, B., and Diamond, P. (2022) 'Borders and Identities in NI after Brexit: Remaking Irish–UK Relations', *Comparative European Politics*, 20, pp. 544–S65.

Collins (2024) *Collins English Dictionary*. Available at: https://www.collinsdictionary.com/ (last accessed June 2025).

Considère-Charon, M. C. (2018) 'Brexit and the Irish Question', *European Issues*, 583 (February), pp. 1–4. Available at: https://www.robert-schuman.eu/en/european-issues/0583-brexit-and-the-irish-question (last accessed June 2025).

Croft, W., and Cruse, D. A. (2004) *Cognitive Linguistics*. Cambridge: Cambridge University Press.

Crowley, T. (2005) *Wars of Words. The Politics of Language in Ireland 1537–2004*. Oxford: Oxford University Press.

Crowley, T. (2022) *Murals of Northern Ireland, The Claremont Colleges Digital Library*. Available at: https://ccdl.claremont.edu/digital/collection/mni (last accessed June 2025).

Culpeper, J. (2011) *Impoliteness. Using Language to Cause Offence*. Cambridge: Cambridge University Press.

Dancygier, B. (2012) 'Negation, Stance Verbs, and Intersubjectivity', in B. Dancygier and E. Sweetser (eds) *Viewpoint in Language. A Multimodal Perspective*. Cambridge: Cambridge University Press, pp. 69–94.

Dancygier, B. (2017) 'Viewpoint Phenomena in Constructions and Discourse', *Glossa*, 2(1), pp. 1–22.

Dancygier, B. (2023) 'Multimodal Media: Framing Climate Change', *Discourse Studies*, 25(2), pp. 220–36.

Dancygier, B., and Sweetser, E. (2005) *Mental Spaces in Grammar*. Cambridge: Cambridge University Press.

Dancygier, B., and Sweetser, E. (2014) *Figurative Language*. Cambridge: Cambridge University Press.

Dancygier, B., and Vandelanotte, L. (2016) 'Discourse Viewpoint as Network', in B. Dancygier, B. Lu and A. Verhagen (eds) *Viewpoint and the Fabric of Meaning: Form and Use of Viewpoint Tools across Languages and Modalities*. Berlin: De Gruyter Mouton, pp. 13–40.

Darby, J. (1976) *Conflict in Northern Ireland: The Development of a Polarised Community*. Dublin: Gill & Macmillan.

Darby, J. (1983) 'The Historical Background', in J. Darby (ed.) *Northern Ireland. The Background to the Conflict*. Belfast: Appletree Press, pp. 13–31.

Darby, J. (1995) 'Conflict in Northern Ireland: A Background Essay', in S. Dunn (ed.) *Facets of the Conflict in Northern Ireland*. London: Macmillan, pp. 15–23.

Darby, J. (1997) *Scorpions in a Bottle. Conflicting Cultures in Northern Ireland*. London: Minority Rights Publications.

Darby, J. (2003) *Northern Ireland: The Background to the Peace Process., CAIN Archive. Conflict and Politics in Northern Ireland*. Available at: https://cain.ulster.ac.uk/events/peace/darby03.htm (last accessed June 2025).

de Chastelain, J. (2003) 'Statement by the Independent International Commission on Decommissioning (IICD)'. Belfast. Available at: https://cain.ulster.ac.uk/events/peace/decommission/iicd211003.htm (last accessed June 2025).

De Fina, A. (1995) 'Pronominal Choice, Identity, and Solidarity in Political Discourse', *Text*, 15(3), pp. 379–410.

De Mars, S., Murray, C., O'Donoghue, A. and Warwick, B (2018) *Bordering Two Unions. Northern Ireland and Brexit*. Bristol: Policy Press.

de Vreese, C. H. (2005) 'News Framing: Theory and Typology.', *Information Design Journal + Document Design*, 13(1), pp. 51–62.

Dédaic, M. N., and Nelson, D. N. (eds) (2003) *At War with Words*. Berlin: Mouton de Gruyter.

Divjak, D., Milin, P. and Medimorec, S. (2020) 'Construal in Language: A Visual-World Approach to the Effects of Linguistic Alternations on Event Perception and Conception', *Cognitive Linguistics*, 31(1), pp. 37–72.

Dixon, P. (2001) *Northern Ireland: The Politics of War and Peace*. Basingtoke: Palgrave.

Dixon, P. (2002) 'Political Skills or Lying and Manipulation? The Choreography of the Northern Ireland Peace Process', *Political Studies*, 50(4), pp. 725–41.

Dixon, P., and O'Kane, E. (2014) *Northern Ireland since 1969*. London: Routledge.

Du Bois, J. W. (2007) 'The Stance Triangle', in R. Englebreston (ed.) *Stancetaking in Discourse*. Amsterdam: John Benjamins, pp. 139–82.

Dunmire, P. L. (2012) 'Political Discourse Analysis: Exploring the Language of Politics and the Politics of Language', *Language and Linguistics Compass*, 6(11), pp. 735–51.

Dunn, S. (1995) 'The Conflict as a Set of Problems', in S. Dunn (ed.) *Facets of the Conflict in Northern Ireland*. London: Macmillan, pp. 3–14.

Dunn, S., and Dawson, H. (2000) *An Alphabetical Listing of Word, Name and Place in Northern Ireland and the Living Language of Conflict*. Lampeter: The Edwin Mellen Press.

Đurović, T., and Silaški, N. (2018) 'The End of a Long and Fraught Marriage', *Metaphor and the Social World*, 8(1), pp. 25–39.

Ecker, U. K. H., Lewandowsky, S., Cook, J., Schmid, P., Fazio, Lisa K., Brashier, N., Kendeou, P., Vraga, Emily K. and Amazeen, Michelle A. (2022) 'The Psychological Drivers of Misinformation Belief and its Resistance to Correction', *Nature Reviews Psychology*, 1(1), pp. 13–29.

Eckert, P. (2000) *Linguistic Variation as Social Practice*. Oxford, Blackwell.

Edwards, A., and McGrattan, C. (2010) *The Northern Ireland Conflict: A Beginner's Guide*. London: Bloomsbury.

Eliott, S., and Flackes, W. D. (1999) *Northern Ireland. A Political Directory. 1968–1999*. Belfast: Blackstaff.

Englebretson, R. (2007) 'Stancetaking in Discourse. An Introduction', in R. Engelbreston (ed.) *Stancetaking in Discourse*. Amsterdam: John Benjamins, pp. 1–25.

Entman, R. M. (1993) 'Framing: Toward Clarification of a Fractured Paradigm', *Journal of Communication*, 43(4), pp. 51–8.

Evans, M., Jeffreis, L. and O'Driscoll, J. (eds) (2019) *The Routledge Handbook of Language in Conflict*. London: Routledge.

Evans, V., and Green, M. (2006) *Cognitive Linguistics. An Introduction*. Edinburgh: Edinburgh University Press.

Fairclough, N. (1989) *Language and Power*. London: Longman.

Fairclough, N. (2003) *Analysing Discourse. Textual Analysis for Social Research*. London: Routledge.

Fairclough, N. (2008) 'The Language of Critical Discourse Analysis: Reply to Michael Billig', *Discourse and Society*, 19(6), pp. 811–19.

Fairclough, N. (2010) *Critical Discourse Analysis: The Critical Study of Language*. London: Longman.

Farquharson, D. (2005) 'The Language of Violence in Robert McLiam Wilson's "Eureka Street"', *New Hibernia Review / Iris Éireannach Nua*, 9(4), pp. 65–78.

Fauconnier, G. (1994) *Mental Spaces. Aspects of Meaning Construction in Natural Language*. Cambridge: Cambridge University Press.

Fauconnier, G., and Turner, M. (2002) *The Way We Think. Conceptual Blending and the Mind's Hidden Complexities*. New York: Basic Books.

Feeney, B. (2004) *Pocket History of the Troubles*. Dublin: O'Brien.

Feldman, A. (1991) *Formations of Violence. The Narrative of the Body and Political Terror in Northern Ireland*. Chicago: University of Chicago Press.

Fierke, K. M. (2013) *Political Self-Sacrifice: Agency, Body and Emotion in International Relations*. Cambridge: Cambridge University Press.

Filardo-Llamas, L. (2008a) 'A Comparative Study of the Discursive Legitimation of the Agreement by the Four Main Northern Irish Political Parties throughout Time', *Ethnopolitics*, 7(1), pp. 21–42.

Filardo-Llamas, L. (2008b) 'The Journey to Peace Metaphorical Representations of Post-Agreement Northern Ireland', in M. J. Carrera de la Red, Anunciación Carrera de la Red, Enrique Cámara Arenas and María Celsa Dapía Ferreiro (eds) *The Irish Knot: Essays on Imaginary / Real Ireland*. Valladolid: Universidad de Valladolid, pp. 243–52.

Filardo-Llamas, L. (2010) 'Discourse Worlds in Northern Ireland: The Legitimisation of the 1998 Agreement', in K. Hayward, and C. O'Donnell (eds) *Political Discourse and Conflict Resolution: Debating Peace in Northern Ireland*. London: Routledge, pp. 62–76.

Filardo-Llamas, L. (2012) 'To Live in the Heart (and Mind) of Others. The Construction of Memory in Northern Irish Commemorative Plaques', *CADAAD Journal*, 5(2), pp. 152–70.

Filardo-Llamas, L. (2013) 'Committed to the Ideals of 1916. The Language of Paramilitary Groups: The Case of the Irish Republican Army', *Critical Discourse Studies*, 10(1), pp. 1–17.

Filardo-Llamas, L. (2019) 'Cultural Responses to 9/11 and the Healing Power of Songs: A Text-World Theory Analysis of Bruce Springsteen's "The Rising"', in C. Hart (ed.) *Cognitive Linguistic Approaches to Text and Discourse. From Poetics to Politics*. Edinburgh: Edinburgh University Press, pp. 111–30.

Filardo-Llamas, L. (2021a) 'From the War on Covid-19 to Political Wars: Metaphor as a Mechanism of Polarization in the Early Stages of the 2020 Pandemic', in L. Filardo-Llamas, E. Morales-López and A. Floyd (eds) *Discursive Approaches to Sociopolitical Polarization and Conflict*. London: Routledge, pp. 192–212.

Filardo-Llamas, L. (2021b) 'To Brexit or not to Brexit? Media Re-contextualization of the Brexit Process in Spain. A Case Study', *CADAAD Journal*, 13(1), pp. 12–30.

Filardo-Llamas, L., and González-Cascos Jiménez, E. (2014) 'Memory and Identity in the Public Sphere: Northern Irish Murals', in M. Kopytowska and Y. Kalyango (eds) *Why Discourse Matters: Negotiating Identity in the Mediatized World*. New York: Peter Lang, pp. 57–72.

Filardo-Llamas, L. and Boyd, M. 2017. 'Critical Discourse Analysis and Politics', in John Flowerdew and John E. Richardson (eds) *The Routledge Handbook of Critical Discourse Studies*. London: Routledge, pp. 312–27.

Filardo-Llamas, L., Hart, C. and Kaal, B. (eds) (2016) *Space, Time and Evaluation in Ideological Discourse*. London: Routledge.

Filardo-Llamas, L., and Morales-López, E. (2021) 'Introduction', in L. Filardo-Llamas, E. Morales-López, and A. Floyd (eds) *Discursive Approaches to Sociopolitical Polarization and Conflict*. London: Routledge, pp. 1–22.

Filardo-Llamas, L., and Perales García, C. (2022) 'Widening the North/South Divide? Representations of the Role of the EU during the Covid-19 Crisis in Spanish Media: A Case Study', *Journal of Language and Politics*, 21(2), pp. 233–54.

Filardo-Llamas, L., and Roldán-García, A. (2024) 'From the Closet to the Stars. Metaphoric Construals of Gender Identity in Tumblr. A Case Study', in M. Romano (ed.) *Metaphor in Socio-Political Contexts: Current Crises*. Berlin: De Gruyter, pp. 51–80.

Fillmore, C. J. (1985) 'Frames and the Semantics of Understanding', *Quaderni di Semantica*, 6(2), pp. 222–54.

Fitzzduff, M., and O'Hagan, L. (2009) 'The Northern Ireland Troubles: INCORE Background Paper', *CAIN. Conflict Archive on the Internet*. Available at: https://cain.ulster.ac.uk/othelem/incorepaper09.htm (last accessed June 2025).

Flowerdew, J. and Richardson, J. E. (eds) (2017) *The Routledge Handbook of Critical Discourse Studies*. London: Routledge

Flusberg, S. J., Matlock, T. and Thibodeau, P. H. (2018) 'War Metaphors in Public Discourse', *Metaphor & Symbol*, 33(1), pp. 1–18.

Fowler, R., Hodge, B., Kress, G. and Trew, T. (1979) *Language and Control*. London: Routledge.

Fowler, R. (1991) *Language in the News*. London: Routledge.

Gadd, E. (2019) 'Brexit Glossary', *House of Commons Briefing Paper*, 7840 (December). Available at: https://researchbriefings.files.parliament.uk/documents/CBP-7840/CBP-7840.pdf (last accessed June 2025).

Gavins, J. (2007) *Text-World Theory. An Introduction*. Edinburgh: Edinburgh University Press.

Geeraerts, D., and Cuyckens, D. (2007) 'Introducing Cognitive Linguistics', in D. Geeraerts and H. Cuyckens (eds) *The Oxford Handbook of Cognitive Linguistics*. Oxford: Oxford University Press, pp. 3–21.

Gillespie, G. (2009) *The A to Z of the Northern Ireland Conflict*. Lanham, MD: The Scarecrow Press.

Goatly, A. (2007) *Washing the Brain. Metaphor and Hidden Ideology*. Amsterdam: John Benjamins.

Goodman, S., and Speer, S. A. (2007) 'Category Use in the Construction of Asylum Seekers', *Critical Discourse Studies*, 4(2), pp. 165–85.

Goulding, S. (2021) *From Militancy to New Media: The Discursive Construction of Irish Republicanism*. PhD Thesis. Ulster University. Available at: https://pure.ulster.ac.uk/ws/portalfiles/portal/102651278/2021GouldingSPhD.pdf (last accessed June 2025).

Goulding, S., and McCroy, A. (2021) 'Representing the (Un)finished Revolution in Belfast's Political Murals', *Critical Discourse Studies*, 18(5), pp. 538–64.

Grady, J. E. (1997) *Foundations of Meaning: Primary Metaphors and Primary Scenes*. University of California. PhD Thesis. Available at: https://escholarship.org/uc/item/3g9427m2 (last accessed June 2025).

Grice, H. P. (1989) *Studies in the Way of Words*. Cambridge, MA: Harvard University Press.

Grimshaw, A. D. (ed.) (1990) *Conflict Talk: Sociolinguistic Investigations in Conversations*. Cambridge: Cambridge University Press.

Gumperz, J. J. (1982) *Discourse Strategies*. Cambridge: Cambridge University Press.

Halliday, M. A. K., and Matthiessen, C. M. I. M. (2014) *Halliday's Introduction to Functional Grammar*. 4th edn. London: Routledge.

Hampe, B. (2008) 'Image Schemas in Cognitive Linguistics: Introduction', in B. Hampe (ed.) *From Perception to Meaning: Image Schemas in Cognitive Linguistics*. Berlin: De Gruyter, pp. 1–12.

Hampl, M. (2020) 'The Use of the Path and Force Image Schemas in Barack Obama's Counterterrorism Discourse against ISIL', *Critical Discourse Studies*, 19(3), pp. 274–89.

Hampl, M. (2021) 'The Container and Force Schemas in Political Discourse', *Metaphor and the Social World*, 11(1), pp. 23–45.

Hart, C. (2008) 'Critical Discourse Analysis and Metaphor: Toward a Theoretical Framework', *Critical Discourse Studies*, 5(2), pp. 91–106.

Hart, C. (2010) *Critical Discourse Analysis and Cognitive Science. New Perspectives on Immigration Discourse*. Basingtoke: Palgrave Macmillan.

Hart, C. (2011a) 'Force-Interactive Patterns in Immigration Discourse: A Cognitive Linguistic Approach to CDA', *Discourse & Society*, 22(3), pp. 269–86.

Hart, C. (2011b) 'Legitimizing Assertions and the Logico-Rhetorical Module: Evidence and Epistemic Vigilance in Media Discourse on Immigration', *Discourse Studies*, 13(6), pp. 751–69.

Hart, C. (2011c) 'Moving beyond Metaphor in the Cognitive Linguistic Approach to CDA: Construal Operations in Immigration Discourse', in C. Hart (ed.) *Critical Discourse Studies in Context and Cognition*. Amsterdam: John Benjamins, pp. 171–92.

Hart, C. (2014) *Discourse, Grammar and Ideology. Functional and Cognitive Perspectives*. London: Bloomsbury.
Hart, C. (2017) 'Cognitive Linguistic Critical Discourse Studies', in J. Flowerdew and J. E. Richardson (eds) *The Routledge Handbook of Critical Discourse Studies*. London: Routledge, pp. 77–105.
Hart, C. (2018) 'Event-Frames Affect Blame Assignment and Perception of Aggression in Discourse on Political Protests: An Experimental Case Study in Critical Discourse Analysis', *Applied Linguistics*, 39(3), pp. 400–21.
Hart, C. (2020) '"28 Palestinians Die": A Cognitive Grammar Analysis of Mystification in Press Coverage of State Violence on the Gaza Border', in M. Giovannelli, C. Harrison, and L. Nuttall (eds) *New Directions in Cognitive Grammar and Style*. London: Bloomsbury, pp. 93–116.
Hart, C. (2021) 'Animals vs. Armies. Resistance to Extreme Metaphors in Anti-Immigration Discourse', *Journal of Language and Politics*, 20(2), pp. 226–53.
Hart, C. (2023) 'Frames, Framing and Framing Effects in Cognitive CDA', *Discourse Studies*, 25(2), pp. 247–58.
Hart, C. (2025) *Language, Image, Gesture: The Cognitive Semiotics of Politics*. Cambridge: Cambridge University Press.
Hart, C., and Marmol Queralto, J. (2021) 'What can Cognitive Linguistics Tell us about Language-Image Relations? A Multidimensional Approach to Intersemiotic Convergence in Multimodal Texts', *Cognitive Linguistics*, 32(4), pp. 529–62.
Hayakawa, S. I. (1965) *Language in Thought and Action*. London: George Allen & Unwin.
Hayes, B. C., and McAllister, I. (2001) 'Who Voted for Peace? Public Support for the 1998 Northern Ireland Agreement', *Irish Political Studies*, 16, pp. 73–93.
Hayward, K. (2008) 'The Role of Political Discourse in Conflict Transformation: Lessons from Northern Ireland', *Peace and Conflict Studies*, 15(1), pp. 1–20.
Hayward, K. (2023) 'It's Time to Fix the Good Friday/Belfast Agreement', *The World Today*, 22 November. Available at: https://www.chathamhouse.org/publications/the-world-today/2023-04/its-time-fix-good-fridaybelfast-agreement (last accessed June 2025).
Hayward, K., McEwen, N. and Komarova, M. (2022) 'Managing Scotland's Borders after Independence and European Union Accession', *National Institute Economic Review*, 260, pp. 40–50.
Hedblom, M. M., Neuhaus, F. and Mossakowski, T. (2024) 'The Diagrammatic Image Schema Language (DISL)', *Spatial Cognition and Computation*, Online First, pp. 1–38.
Hennessey, T. (1997) *A History of Northern Ireland, 1920–1996*. Basingstoke: Palgrave Macmillan.
Heyvaert, L. (2003) *A Cognitive-Functional Approach to Nominalization in English*. Berlin: De Gruyter.
Heyvaert, L. (2008) 'On the Constructional Semantics of Gerundive Nominalizations', *Folia Linguistica*, 42(1–2), pp. 39–82.

Hidalgo-Downing, L., Pérez-Sobrino, P., Filardo-Llamas, L., Maíz-Arevalo, C., Núñez-Perucha, B., Sánchez-Moya, A. and Williams Camus, J. (2024) 'A Protocol for the Annotation of Evaluative Stance and Metaphor across Four Discourse Genres', *Revista Española de Lingüística Aplicada/Spanish Journal of Applied Linguistics*, 37(2), pp. 486–517.

Hutchby, I. (1996) *Confrontation Talk: Arguments, Asymmetries and Power on Talk Radio*. Hillsdale, NJ: Erlbaum.

ICPNI and Patten, C. (1999) *A New Beginning: Policing in Northern Ireland: The Report of the Independent Commission on Policing for Northern Ireland*. Available at: https://cain.ulster.ac.uk/issues/police/patten/patten99.pdf (last accessed June 2025).

Janicki, K. (2006) *Language Misconceived. Arguing for Applied Cognitive Sociolinguistics*. London: Lawrence Erlbaum.

Janicki, K. (2015) *Language and Conflict. Selected Issues*. Basingtoke: Palgrave.

Jeffries, L. (2010) *Critical Stylistics. The Power of English*. Basingtoke: Palgrave Macmillan.

Jeffries, L., and McIntyre, D. (2018) 'The Devil Has All the Best Tunes: An Investigation of the Lexical Phenomenon of Brexit', in R. Page, B. Busse and N. Nørgaard (eds) *Rethinking Language, Text and Context: Interdisciplinary Research in Stylistics in Honour of Michael Toolan*. London: Routledge, pp. 100–19.

Jeffries, L., and O'Driscoll, J. (2019) 'Introduction. Textual Choice and Communication in Conflict', in M. Evans, L. Jeffreis, and J. O'Driscoll (eds) *The Routledge Handbook of Language and Conflict*. London: Routledge, pp. 13–24.

Johnson, D. M. (1994) 'Who Is We? Constructing Communities in US-Mexico Border Discourse', *Discourse and Society*, 5(2), pp. 207–31.

Johnson, M. (1987) *The Body in the Mind: The Bodily Basis of Meaning, Imagination, and Reason*. Chicago: University of Chicago Press.

Johnson, M. (2008) 'The Philosophical Significance of Image Schemas', in B. Hampe (ed.) *From Perception to Meaning: Image Schemas in Cognitive Linguistics*. Berlin: Mouton de Gruyter, pp. 15–33.

Kaal, B. (2024) 'Language, Space and Politics', in P. Cap (ed.) *Handbook of Political Discourse*. Cheltenham: Edward Elgar, pp. 128–44.

Kahan, D., and Braman, D. (2006) 'Cultural Cognition and Public Policy', *Yale Law & Policy Review*, 24(1), pp. 149–72.

Kaufmann, E. P. (2007) *The Orange Order: A Contemporary Northern Irish History*. Oxford: Oxford University Press.

Keating, M. (2021) 'Brexit and the Irish Border', *RIPS: Revista de Investigaciones Políticas y Sociológicas*, 20(1), pp. 1–17.

Kelleher, W. F. (2003) *The Troubles in Ballybogoin: Memory and Identity in Northern Ireland*. Ann Arbor: University of Michigan Press.

Kelsey, D. (2017) *Media and Affective Mythologies. Discourse, Archetypes and Ideology in Contemporary Politics*. Basingtoke: Palgrave.

Klar, Y., Bar-Tal, D. and Kruglanski, A. W. (1988) 'Conflict as a Cognitive Schema: Toward a Social Cognitive Analysis of Conflict and Conflict Termination', in W.

Stroebe, A. W. Kruglanski, D. Bar-Tal and M. Hewstone (eds) *The Social Psychology of Intergroup Conflict*. Berlin: Springer, pp. 73–85.

Koller, V. (2004) *Metaphor and Gender in Business Media Discourse: A Critical Cognitive Study*. Basingtoke: Palgrave.

Koller, V. (2012) 'How to Analyse Collective Identity in Discourse – Textual and Contextual Parameters', *CADAAD Journal*, 5(2), pp. 19–38.

Koller, V. (2014) 'Cognitive Linguistics and Ideology', in J. Littlemore and J. R. Taylor (eds) *The Bloomsbury Companion to Cognitive Linguistics*. London: Bloomsbury, pp. 234–52.

Kopytowska, M. (2015) 'Ideology of "Here and Now": Mediating Distance in Television News', *Critical Discourse Studies*, 12(3), pp. 347–65.

Kövecses, Z. (2017) 'Levels of Metaphor', *Cognitive Linguistics*, 28(2), pp. 321–47.

Kövecses, Z. (2020) *Extended Conceptual Metaphor Theory*. Cambridge: Cambridge University Press.

Kowalski, G. (2022) 'Proximization and Dialogue in Internet News Texts and Comments', *Language and Dialogue*, 12, pp. 218–44.

Lakoff, G. (1987a) 'Cognitive Semantics', in U. Eco and M. Santambrogio (eds) *Meaning and Mental Representations*. Bloomington: Indiana University Press, pp. 119–54.

Lakoff, G. (1987b) *Women, Fire and Dangerous Things. What Categories Reveal about the Mind*. Chicago: University of Chicago Press.

Lakoff, G. (2002) *Moral Politics: How Liberals and Conservatives Think*. Chicago: University of Chicago Press.

Lakoff, G. (2018) *Ten Lectures on Cognitive Linguistics*. Leiden: Brill.

Lakoff, G. and Johnson, M. (1980) *Metaphors We Live By*. Chicago: University of Chicago Press.

Langacker, R. W. (1987) *Foundations of Cognitive Grammar. Volume I: Theoretical Prerequisites*. Stanford, CA: Stanford University Press.

Langacker, R. W. (2008) *Cognitive Grammar. A Basic Introduction*. Oxford: Oxford University Press.

Langacker, R. W. (2019) 'Construal', in E. Dąbrowska and D. Divjak (eds) *Cognitive Linguistics – Foundations of Language*. Berlin: De Gruyter, pp. 140–66.

Lavietes, M. (2023) 'Johns Hopkins Pulls "Lesbian" Definition after Uproar over Use of "Non-men" instead of "Women"', *NBC News*, 14 June. Available at: https://www.nbcnews.com/nbc-out/out-news/johns-hopkins-pulls-lesbian-definition-uproar-use-non-men-instead-wome-rcna89307 (last accessed June 2025).

Levinson, S. C. (1983) *Pragmatics*. Cambridge: Cambridge University Press.

Levinson, S. C. (2003) *Space in Language and Cognition: Explorations in Cognitive Diversity*. Cambridge: Cambridge University Press.

Lewin-Jones, J., and Webb, M. (2013) 'Ideology in Disguise: Place Name Metonyms and the Discourse of Newspaper Headlines', *Sociological Research Online*, 18(4), pp. 167–81.

Littlemore, J. (2015) *Metonymy: Hidden Shortcuts in Language, Thought and Communication*. Cambridge: Cambridge University Press.

Littlemore, J. (2017) 'Metonymy', in B. Dancygier (ed.) *The Cambridge Handbook of Cognitive Linguistics*. Cambridge: Cambridge University Press, pp. 407–22.

Mac Coinnigh, M., Ervine, L. and Deeds, P. (2019) 'The Irish Language in Belfast: The Role of a Language in Post-Conflict Resolution', in M. Evans, L. Jeffries, and J. O'Driscoll (eds) *The Routledge Handbook of Language in Conflict*. London: Routledge, pp. 556–73.

Mac Ginty, R., Muldoon, O. T. and Ferguson, N. (2007) 'No War, No Peace: Northern Ireland after the Agreement', *Political Psychology*, 28(1), pp. 1–11.

Mac Giolla Chríost, D. (2003) *Language, Identity and Conflict*. London: Routledge.

Mac Giolla Chríost, D. (2005) *The Irish Language in Ireland from Goídel to Globalisation*. London: Routledge.

Machin, D., and Mayr, A. (2012) *How to Do Critical Discourse Analysis: A Multimodal Introduction*. London: Sage.

Machin, D., and van Leeuwen, T. (2016) 'Multimodality, Politics and Ideology', *Journal of Language and Politics*, 15(3), pp. 243–58.

Marín-Arrese, J. I. (2011a) 'Effective vs. Epistemic Stance and Subjectivity in Political Discourse. Legitimising Strategies and Mystification of Responsibility', in C. Hart (ed.) *Critical Discourse Studies in Context and Cognition*. Amsterdam: John Benjamins, pp. 193–224.

Marín-Arrese, J. I. (2015) 'Epistemic Legitimisation and Inter/subjectivity in the Discourse of Parliamentary and Public Inquiries. A Contrastive Case Study', *Critical Discourse Studies*, 12(3), pp. 261–78.

Marín-Arrese, J. I. (2021a) 'Stance, Emotion and Persuasion: Terrorism and the Press', *Journal of Pragmatics*, 177, pp. 135–48.

Marín-Arrese, J. I. (2021b) 'Winds of War: Epistemic and Effective Control in Political Discourse', *Cultura, Lenguaje y Representacion*, 26, pp. 289–307.

Martín de La Rosa, V. (2023) 'Taking Back Control: The Role of Image Schemas in the Brexit Discourse', *Russian Journal of Linguistics*, 27(2), pp. 276–96.

Martin, J. R., and White, P. R. R. (2005) *The Language of Evaluation. Appraisal in English*. Basingstoke: Palgrave.

Masalha, N. (2012) *The Palestine Nakba: Decolonising History, Narrating the Subaltern, Reclaiming Memory*. London: Zed books.

Mateo, J., and Yus, F. (2013) 'Towards a Cross-cultural Pragmatic Taxonomy of Insults', *Journal of Language Aggression and Conflict*, 1(1): 87–114.

Mautner, G. (2016) 'Checks and Balances: How Corpus Linguistics can Contribute to CDA', in R. Wodak and M. Meyer (eds) *Methods of Critical Discourse Studies*. London: Sage, pp. 154–79.

McCall, C. (2021) *Border Ireland: From Partition to Brexit*. London: Routledge.

McCormick, J. (2023) *Mural Directory, CAIN. Conflict Archive on the Internet*. Available at: https://cain.ulster.ac.uk/mccormick/index.html (last accessed June 2025).

McEvoy, J. (2013) 'We Forbid! The Mutual Veto and Power-Sharing Democracy', in J. McEvoy and B. O'Leary (eds) *Power Sharing in Deeply Divided Places*. Philadelphia: University of Pennsylvania Press, pp. 253–77.

McGee, P. (2018) 'Vague Language as a Means of Avoiding Controversy', *Training, Language and Culture*, 2(2), pp. 40–54.

McKittrick, D., and McVea, D. (2000) *Making Sense of the Troubles*. Belfast: Blackstaff Press.

McLiam Wilson, R. (1996) *Eureka Street*. London: Random House.

McLoughlin, P. J. (2008) '"Humespeak": The SDLP, Political Discourse, and the Northern Ireland Peace Process', *Peace and Conflict Studies*, 15(1), pp. 95–114.

Meadows, B. (2007) 'Distancing and Showing Solidarity via Metaphor and Metonymy in Political Discourse: A Critical Study of American Statements on Iraq during the Years 2004–2005', *CADAAD Journal*, 1(2), pp. 1–17.

Melaugh, M. (2023) *CAIN Archive. Conflict and Politics in Northern Ireland, CAIN*. Available at: https://cain.ulster.ac.uk/index.html (last accessed June 2025).

Melaugh, M. (2024) 'Devolved Government in Northern Ireland', *CAIN. Conflict Archive on the Internet*. Available at: https://cain.ulster.ac.uk/issues/politics/government.htm (last accessed June 2025).

Melloni, C. (2011) *Event and Result Nominals. A Morpho-Semantic Approach*. Bern: Peter Lang.

Moltmann, B. (2017) *Northern Ireland: The End of the Story? The Peace Process and the Brexit*. Frankfurt: Peace Research Institute Frankfurt. Available at: https://www.prif.org/publikationen/publikationssuche/publikation/northern-ireland-the-end-of-the-story (last accessed June 2025).

Morrison, J. (2004) 'Shall We Dance? Movement Metaphors as Political Discourse', in B. Cliff and É. Walshe (eds) *Representing the Troubles. Texts and Images. 1970–2000*. Dublin: Four Court Pres, pp. 106–16.

Morrow, D. (1995) 'Church and Religion in the Ulster Crisis', in S. Dunn (ed.) *Facets of the Conflict in Northern Ireland*. London: Macmillan, pp. 151–67.

Morrow, D. (1996) 'Northern Ireland 1972–95', in A. Aughey and D. Morrow (eds) *Northern Ireland Politics*. New York: Longman, pp. 20–8.

Musolff, A. (2004) *Metaphor and Political Discourse. Analogical Reasoning in Debates about Europe*. Basingtoke: Palgrave.

Musolff, A. (2006) 'Metaphor Scenarios in Political Discourse in Britain and Germany', *Metaphor & Symbol*, 21(1), pp. 23–38.

Musolff, A. (2012) 'The Study of Metaphor as Part of Critical Discourse Analysis', *Critical Discourse Studies*, 9(3), pp. 301–10.

Musolff, A. (2017) 'Truths, Lies and Figurative Scenarios', *Journal of Language and Politics*, 16(5), pp. 641–57.

Nelson, D. N. (2003) 'Conclusion: Word Peace', in M. N. Dédaic and D. N. Nelson (eds) *At War with Words*. Berlin: Mouton de Gruyter, pp. 449–62.

Nic Craith, M. (2001) 'Politicised Linguistic Consciousness: The Case of Ulster-Scots', *Nations and Nationalism*, 7, pp. 21–37.

NIO, [Northern Ireland Office] (1998) *The Belfast Agreement: An Agreement Reached at the Multiparty Talks on Northern Ireland*. Available at: https://www.gov.uk/government/publications/the-belfast-agreement (last accessed June 2025).

Núñez-Perucha, B. (2011) 'Critical Discourse Analysis and Cognitive Linguistics as Tools for Ideological Research: A Diachronic Analysis of Feminism', in C. Hart (ed.) *Critical Discourse Studies in Context and Cognition*. Amsterdam: John Benjamins, pp. 97–118.

O'Connor, F. (1993) *In Search of a State. Catholics in Northern Ireland*. Belfast: Blackstaff.

O'Donnnel, C., and Hayward, K. (eds) (2010) *Political Discourse and Conflict Resolution. Debating Peace in Northern Ireland*. London: Routledge.

O'Driscoll, J. (2007) 'Brown and Levinson's Face: How It Can – and Can't – Help Us to Understand Interaction across Cultures', *Journal of Politeness Research*, 1(1), pp. 9–33.

O'Driscoll, J. (2013) 'Situational Transformations: The Offensive-izing of an Email Message and the Publicization of Offensiveness', *Pragmatics & Society*, 4(3), pp. 369–87.

O'Driscoll, J. (2019a) 'Introduction: Conflict as It Happens', in M. Evans, L. Jeffries and J. O'Driscoll (eds) *The Routledge Handbook of Language in Conflict*. London: Routledge, pp. 167–75.

O'Driscoll, J. (2019b) 'Introduction: Conflict with the Fabric of Language', in M. Evans, L. Jeffries and J. O'Driscoll (eds) *The Routledge Handbook of Language in Conflict*. London: Routledge, pp. 331–8.

O'Halloran, K. (2005) 'Mystification and Social Agent Absences: A Critical Discourse Analysis Using Evolutionary Psychology', *Journal of Pragmatics*, 37(12), pp. 1945–64.

O'Reilly, C. (1999) *The Irish Language in Northern Ireland: The Politics of Culture and Identity*. London: Macmillan.

Oakley, T. (2005) 'Force-Dynamic Dimensions of Rhetorical Effect', in B. Hampe (ed.) *From Perception to Meaning: Image Schemas in Cognitive Linguistics*. Berlin: De Gruyter, pp. 443–74.

Oakley, T. (2007) 'Image Schemas', in D. Geeraerts and D. Cuyckens (eds) *The Oxford Handbook of Cognitive Linguistics*. Oxford: Oxford University Press, pp. 214–35.

OED (2024) *Oxford English Dictionary*. Oxford: Oxford University Press. Available at: https://www.oed.com/?tl=true (last accessed June 2025).

Oswald, S. and Rihs, A. (2014) 'Metaphor as Argument: Rhetorical and Epistemic Advantages of Extended Metaphors', *Argumentation*, 28, pp. 133–59.

Panther, K. U., and Thornburg, L. L. (2007) 'Metonymy', in D. Geeraerts and H. Cuyckens (eds) *The Oxford Handbook of Cognitive Linguistics*. Oxford: Oxford University Press, pp. 236–63.

Park, C., and Park, B. (2017) 'Cognitive Grammar and English Nominalization: Event/Result Nominals and Gerundives', *Cognitive Linguistics*, 28(4), pp. 711–56.

Parnell, T. (2023) 'Humiliating and Dividing the Nation in the British Pro-Brexit Press: A Corpus-Assisted Analysis', *Critical Discourse Studies*, 20(1), pp. 53–69.

Patterson, H. (2002) *Northern Ireland since 1939*. Oxford: Oxford University Press.

Pavlenko, A., and Blackledge, A. (2004) *Negotiation of Identities in Multilingual Contexts.* Clevendon: Multilingual Matters.

Peterssen, S., and g da Silva, A. (2024) 'Polarising Metaphors in the Venezuelan Presidential Crisis', *Journal of Language and Politics*, 23(4), pp. 1–29.

Piaget, J. (1959). *The Language and Thought of the Child.* London: Routledge & Kegan Paul.

Polyzou, A. (2014) 'Presupposition in Discourse: Theoretical and Methodological Issues', *Critical Discourse Studies*, 12(2), pp. 123–38.

Porto, M. D. (2022) 'Water Metaphors and Evaluation of Syrian Migration: The Flow of Refugees in the Spanish Press', *Metaphor and Symbol*, 37(3), pp. 252–67.

Powell, T. E., Hajo G. Boomgaarden, Knut De Swert and Claes H. de Vreese (2015) 'A Clearer Picture: The Contribution of Visuals and Text to Framing Effects', *Journal of Communication*, 65(6), pp. 997–1017.

Pujante, D. (2016) 'Constructivist Rhetoric within the Tradition of Rhetorical Studies in Spain', *Res Rhetorica*, 3(1), pp. 30–49.

Radden, G., and Dirven, R. (2007) *Cognitive English Grammar.* Amsterdam: John Benjamins.

Ramsbotham, O. (2010) *Transforming Violent Conflict. Radical Disagreement, Dialogue and Survival.* London: Routledge.

Ramsbotham, O. (2017) *When Conflict Resolution Fails: An Alternative to Negotiation and Dialogue: Engaging Radical Disagreement in Intractable Conflicts.* Cambridge: Polity Press.

Ramsbotham, O. (2021) 'Taking Radical Disagreement Seriously: Filling the Discourse Analytic Gap in the Study of Intractable Asymmetric Conflicts', in I. Chiluwa (ed.) *Discourse and Conflict. Analysing Text and Talk of Conflict, Hate and Peace-building.* Basingtoke: Palgrave Macmillan, pp. 19–50.

Ramsbotham, O., Miall, H. and Woodhouse, T. (2011) *Contemporary Conflict Resolution.* 3rd edn. Cambridge: Polity.

Rapp, M., and Rhomberg, M. (2012) 'Seeking a Neutral Identity in Northern Ireland's Political Wall Paintings', *Peace Review*, 24(4), pp. 470–7.

Reisigl, M., and Wodak, R. (2001) *Discourse and Discrimination: Rhetorics of Racism and Antisemitism.* London: Routledge.

Reisigl, M., and Wodak, R. (2002) 'The Discourse Historical Approach (DHA)', in R. Wodak and M. Meyer (eds) *Methods of Critical Discourse Analysis.* London: Sage, pp. 87–121.

Reyes, A. (2011) 'Strategies of Legitimization in Political Discourse: From Words to Actions', *Discourse and Society*, 22(6), pp. 781–807.

Roe, M., Pegg, W., Hodges, K. and Trimm, R. A. (1999) 'Forgiving the Other Side: Social Identity and Ethnic Memories in Northern Ireland.', in J. P. Harrington and E. J. Mitchell (eds) *Politics and Performance in Contemporary Northern Ireland.* Amherst: University of Massachusetts Press, pp. 122–56.

Rolston, B. (2010) *Drawing Support. Murals in the North of Ireland.* 2nd edn. Belfast: Beyond the Pale.

Romano, M. (2019) '"Refugees are Streaming into Europe": An Image-Schema Analysis of the Syrian Refugee Crisis in the Spanish and British press', *Complutense Journal of English Studies*, 27, pp. 39–57.

Romano, M., and Porto, D. (2021) 'Framing Conflict in the Syrian Refugee Crisis: Multimodal Representations in the Spanish and British Press', in L. Filardo-Llamas, E. Morales-López and A. Floyd (eds) *Discursive Approaches to Sociopolitical Polarization and Conflict*. London: Routledge, pp. 153–73.

Ruiz de Mendoza Ibañez, F., and Díez Velasco, O. (2002) 'Patterns of Conceptual Interaction', in R. Dirven and R. Pörings (eds) *Metaphor and Metonymy in Comparison and Contrast*. Berlin: De Gruyter, pp. 489–532.

Saeed, J. I. (2015) *Semantics*. 4th edn. Oxford: Wiley-Blackwell.

Santibañez, F. (2002) 'The Object Image-Schema and other Dependent Schemas', *Atlantis*, 24(2), pp. 183–201.

Schäffner, C., and Wenden, A. (eds) (1995) *Language and Peace*. London: Routledge.

Schegloff, E. A. (2007) *Sequence Organization in Interaction a Primer in Conversation Analysis*. Cambridge: Cambridge University Press.

Schmitt-Beck, R. (1998) 'Of readers, Viewers, and Cat-Dogs', in J. W. van Deth (ed.) *Comparative Politics: The Problem of Equivalence*. London: Routledge, pp. 222–46.

Schröter, M. (2013) *Silence and Concealment in Political Discourse*. Amsterdam: John Benjamins.

Scott, S. (2002) 'Linguistic Feature Variation within Disagreements: An Empirical Investigation', *Text & Talk*, 22(2), pp. 301–28.

Semino, E. (2008) *Metaphor in Discourse*. Cambridge: Cambridge University Press.

Semino, E., Demjén, Z., Hardie, A., Payne, S. and Rayson, P. (2018) *Metaphor, Cancer and the End of Life: A Corpus-Based Study*. London: Routledge.

Semino, E., Demjén, Z. and Demmen, J. (2018) 'An Integrated Approach to Metaphor and Framing in Cognition, Discourse, and Practice, with an Application to Metaphors for Cancer', *Applied Linguistics*, 39(5), pp. 625–45.

Shirlow, P. (2004). 'Sinn Féin: Beyond and Within Containment', in J. Neuheiser and S. Wolff (eds) *Peace at Last? The Impact of the Good Friday Agreement in Northern Ireland*. New York: Berghahn Books, pp. 60–75.

Shirlow, P. and McGovern, M. (1998) 'Language, Discourse and Dialogue: Sinn Féin and the Irish Peace Process', *Political Geography* 17(2), pp. 171–186.

Shotter, J. (1993) *Cultural Politics of Everyday Life*. Buckingham: Open University Press.

Sifinanou, M. (2019) 'Conflict, Disagreement and (Im)politeness', in M. Evans, L. Jeffries and J. O'Driscoll (eds) *The Routledge Handbook of Language and Conflict*. London: Routledge, pp. 176–95.

Simone-Charteris, M. T. (2017) 'State Intervention in Re-Imaging Northern Ireland's Political Murals: Implications for Tourism and the Communities', in J. Skinner and J. Lee (eds) *Murals and Tourism: Heritage, Politics, and Identity*. London: Taylor & Francis, pp. 217–35.

Simpson, K. (2013) *Truth Recovery in Northern Ireland. Critically Interpreting the Past.* Manchester: Manchester University Press.

Simpson, M. (2021) 'NI 100: How was Northern Ireland's Centenary Year Marked?', *BBC News*, 30 December. Available at: https://www.bbc.com/news/uk-northern-ireland-59669635 (last accessed June 2025).

Slobin, D. I. (1991) 'Learning to Think for Speaking. Native Language, Cognition, and Rhetorical Style', *Pragmatics*, 1(1), pp. 7–25.

Smith, D. (1997) 'Language and Discourse in Conflict and Conflict Resolution', *Current Issues in Language and Society*, 4(3), pp. 190–214.

Spisak, A. (2022) 'Fixing the Northern Ireland Protocol: A Way Forward', *Tony Blair Institute for Global Change*. Available at: https://www.institute.global/insights/economic-prosperity/fixing-northern-ireland-protocol-way-forward (last accessed June 2025).

Stapleton, K., and Wilson, J. (2004) 'Ulster Scots Identity and Culture: The Missing Voices', *Identities* 11(4), pp. 563–91.

Stewart, A. T. Q. (1989) *The Narrow Ground. The Roots of Conflict in Ulster*. 2nd edn. London: Faber & Faber.

Stockwell, P. (2020) *Cognitive Poetics. An Introduction*. 2nd edn. London: Routledge.

Storey, D. (2001) *Territory: The Claiming of Space*. London: Routledge.

Suurmond, J. M. (2005) 'Our Talk and Walk. Discourse Analysis and Conflict Studies', *Working Paper* 35. The Hague: Clingendael – the Netherlands Institute of International Relations. Available at: https://www.clingendael.org/sites/default/files/pdfs/20051000_cru_working_paper_35.pdf (last accessed June 2025).

Tagg, C., Seargeant, P. and Brown, Amy A. (2017) *Taking Offence on Social Media: Conviviality and Communication on Facebook*. Pivot: Palgrave Macmillan.

Talmy, L. (2000a) *Toward a Cognitive Semantics. Vol II. Typology and Process in Cognitive Structuring*. Cambridge, MA: MIT Press.

Talmy, L. (2000b) *Towards a Cognitive Semantics. Volume I. Concept Structuring Systems*. Cambridge, MA: MIT.

Talmy, L. (2007) 'Attention Phenomena', in D. Geeraerts and D. Cuyckens (eds) *The Oxford Handbook of Cognitive Linguistics*. Oxford: Oxford University Press, pp. 295–324.

Tannen, D. (1993) 'What's in a Frame? Surface Evidence for Underlying Expectations', in D. Tannen (ed.) *Framing in Discourse*. Oxford: Oxford University Press, pp. 14–56.

Taylor, C. (2019) 'Conflict and Categorisation. A Corpus and Discourse Study of Naming Participants in Forced Migration', in L. Jeffries (ed.) *The Routledge Handbook of Language and Conflict*. London: Routledge, pp. 128–44.

Taylor, C. (2021) 'Metaphors of Migration over Time', *Discourse & Society*, 32(4), pp. 463–81.

Taylor, J. R. (1995) *Linguistic Categorization. Prototypes in Linguistic Theory*. 2nd edn. Oxford: Clarendon Press.

Tenbrink, T. (2020) *Cognitive Discourse Analysis. An Introduction*. Cambridge: Cambridge University Press.

Thibodeau, P. H. (2016) 'Extended Metaphors are the Home Runs of Persuasion: Don't Fumble the Phrase', *Metaphor and Symbol*, 31(2), pp. 53–72.

Thompson, G., and Alba-Juez, L. (eds) (2014) *Evaluation in Context*. Amsterdam: John Benjamins.

Thompson, G., and Hunston, S. (eds) (1999) *Evaluation in Text: Authorial Stance and the Construction of Discourse*. Oxford: Oxford University Press.

Tomlin, R. S., and Myachykov, A. (2019) 'Attention and Salience', in E. Dawroska and D. Divjak (eds) *Cognitive Linguistics – Foundations of Language*. Berlin, Boston: De Gruyter Mouton, pp. 36–60.

Tonge, J. (2014) 'Britishness, Identity, and Belonging', in J. Tonge, M. Braniff, T. Hennessey, J. W. McAuley and S. Whiting (eds) *The Democratic Unionist Party: From Protest to Power*. Oxford: Oxford Academic, pp. 110–32.

Trope, Y., Liberman, N. and Wakslak, C. (2007) 'Construal Levels and Psychological Distance: Effects on Representation, Prediction, Evaluation, and Behavior', *Journal of Consumer Psychology*, 17(2), pp. 83–95.

Vandelanotte, L. (2017) 'Viewpoint', in B. Dancygier (ed.) *The Cambridge Handbook of Cognitive Linguistics*. Cambridge: Cambridge University Press, pp. 157–71.

Vanderbiesen, J. (2016) 'Mixed Viewpoints and the Quotative-Reportive Cline in German: Reported Speech and Reportive Evidentiality', in B. Dancygier, W. Lu, and A. Verhagen (eds) *Viewpoint and the Fabric of Meaning: Form and Use of Viewpoint Tools across Languages and Modalities*. Berlin: Mouton de Gruyter, pp. 41–92.

Van Dijk, T. A. (1997) 'What is Political Discourse Analysis?', in J. Blommaert and C. Bulcaen (eds) *Political Linguistics*. Amsterdam: John Benjamins, pp. 11–52.

Van Dijk, T. A. (1998) *Ideology. A Multidisciplinary Approach*. London: Sage.

Van Dijk, T. A. (2005) 'Contextual Knowledge Management in Discourse Production: A CDA Perspective', in R. Wodak and P. A. Chilton (eds) *A New Agenda in (Critical) Discourse Analysis*. Amsterdam: John Benjamins, pp. 71–100.

Van Dijk, T. A. (2006) 'Discourse, Context and Cognition', *Discourse Studies*, 8(1), pp. 159–77.

Van Dijk, T. A. (2008a) 'Critical Discourse Analysis and Nominalization: Problem or Pseudo-problem?', *Discourse and Society*, 19(6), pp. 821–8.

Van Dijk, T. A. (2008b) *Discourse and Context: A Sociocognitive Approach*. Cambridge: Cambridge University Press.

Van Dijk, T. A. (2011) 'Discourse and Ideology', in T. A. Van Dijk (ed.) *Discourse Studies: A Multidisciplinary Introduction*. 2nd edn. London: Sage, pp. 379–407.

Van Dijk, T. A. (2014) *Discourse and Knowledge. A Sociocognitive Approach*. Cambridge: Cambridge University Press.

Van Leeuwen, T. (1996) 'The Representation of Social Actors', in C. R. Caldas-Coulthard and M. Coulthard (eds) *Text and Practices. Readings in Critical Discourse Analysis*. London: Routledge, pp. 32–70.

Van Leeuwen, T. (2007) 'Legitimation in Discourse and Communication', *Discourse & Communication*, 1(1), pp. 91–112.

Van Leeuwen, T. (2008) *Discourse and Practice: New Tools for Critical Discourse Analysis*. Oxford: Oxford University Press.

Van Leeuwen, T. (2012) 'The Critical Analysis of Musical Discourse', *Critical Discourse Studies*, 9(4), pp. 319–28.

Van Leeuwen, T. (2017) 'Moral Evaluation in Critical Discourse Analysis', *Critical Discourse Studies*, 15(2), pp. 140–53.

Van Leeuwen, T., and Wodak, R. (1999) 'Legitimizing Immigration Control: A Discourse Historical Analysis', *Discourse Studies*, 1(1), pp. 83–108.

Verhagen, A. (2007a) 'Construal and Perspectivization', in D. Geeraerts and D. Cuyckens (eds) *The Oxford Handbook of Cognitive Linguistics*. Oxford: Oxford University Press, pp. 48–81.

Verhagen, A. (2007b) *Constructions of Intersubjectivity: Discourse, Syntax, and Cognition*. Oxford: Oxford University Press.

Verschueren, J. (1999) *Understanding Pragmatics*. London: Edward Arnold.

Vygotsky, L. (1986). *Thought and Language*. Cambridge, MA: MIT Press.

Watts, R. J. (2003) *Politeness*. Cambridge: Cambridge University Press.

Werth, P. (1999) *Text Worlds: Representing Conceptual Space in Discourse*. Harlow: Pearson Education.

Whyte, J. H. (1990) *Interpreting Northern Ireland*. Oxford: Clarendon Press.

Wilson, J. (1990) *Politically Speaking. The Pragmatic Analysis of Political Language*. Oxford: Basil Blackwell.

Wilson, J., and Rose, J. (1997) 'The Language of Peace and Conflict: Relevance Theory and the Anglo-Irish Agreement', *The Journal of Conflict Studies*, 18(2). Available at: https://journals.lib.unb.ca/index.php/jcs/article/view/11751/12524 (last accessed June 2025).

Wodak, R. (2007) 'Discourses in European Union Organizations: Aspects of Access, Participation, and Exclusion', *Text and Talk*, 27(5–6), pp. 655–80.

Wodak, R., de Cillia, R., Reisigl, M. and Liebhart, K. (2009) *The Discursive Construction of National Identity*. Edinburgh: Edinburgh University Press.

Wodak, R., and Fairclough, N. (2010) 'Recontextualizing European Higher Education Policies: The Cases of Austria and Romania', *Critical Discourse Studies*, 7(1), pp. 19–40.

Wodak, R., and Meyer, M. (2016) *Methods of Critical Discourse Studies*. 3rd edn. London: Sage.

Wright, S. (ed.) (1998) *Language and Conflict: A Neglected Relationship*. Clevendon: Multilingual Matters.

Yu, N. (2022) *The Moral Metaphor System: A Conceptual Metaphor Approach*. Oxford: Oxford University Press.

Yule, G. (1996) *Pragmatics*. Oxford: Oxford University Press.

Zappettini, F., and Bennett, S. (2022) 'Reimagining Europe and Its (Dis)integration. (De) legitimising the EU's Project in Times of Crisis', *Journal of Language and Politics*, 21(2), pp. 191–207.

Zeman, S. (2017) 'Confronting Perspectives: Modeling Perspectival Complexity in Language and Cognition', *Glossa*, 2(1).

Zhao, J., Song, T., Song, X. and Bai, Y. (2022) 'Analysis on the Linguistic Features of Conflict Discourse in Mathematical Cooperation Problem Solving in China', *Frontiers in Psychology*, 13, 945909.

Zimbardo, P. (2007) *The Lucifer Effect: How Good People Turn Evil*. London: Rider.

Zinken, J. (2003) 'Ideological Imagination: Intertextual and Correlational Metaphors in Political Discourse', *Discourse and Society*, 14(4), pp. 507–23.

Index

www.ingramcontent.com/pod-product-compliance
Ingram Content Group UK Ltd.
Pitfield, Milton Keynes, MK11 3LW, UK
UKHW020248290926
15470UKWH00002B/816

9 781350 373761